LIGHTNING STRIKES

LIGHTNING STRIKES

Hugh Cannell

Book Guild Publishing
Sussex, England

First published in Great Britain in 2011 by
The Book Guild Ltd
Pavilion View
19 New Road
Brighton, BN1 1UF

Copyright © Hugh Cannell 2011

The right of Hugh Cannell to be identified as the author of
this work has been asserted by him in accordance with the
Copyright, Designs and Patents Act 1988.

All rights reserved. No part of this publication may be reproduced, transmitted, or stored in a
retrieval system, in any form or by any means, without permission in writing from the publisher,
nor be otherwise circulated in any form of binding or cover other than that in which it is published
and without a similar condition being imposed on the subsequent purchaser.

Typesetting in Garamond by
YHT Ltd, London

Printed in Great Britain by
CPI Antony Rowe

A catalogue record for this book is available from
The British Library.

ISBN 978 1 84624 520 6

*This book is dedicated to my late wife,
Judith Marjorie Cannell 1936-2005
who always encouraged me and whose memory
still does.*

Contents

Acknowledgments		ix
Introduction		xi
1	Thunderstorms, Lightning and Ships	1
2	Lightning Strikes on People	17
3	A Proposal for the Protection of Ships from Lightning Strikes	32
4	The Whigs: Reform or Bust	53
5	John Barrow: A Flawed Administrator	69
6	William Snow Harris	89
7	The Surveyor and His Opponents	103
8	1841: The Phoenix Rises	123
9	Exposure of Whig and Admiralty Manipulation of Facts	135
10	House of Lords Misinformed: The Whigs Again, 1846-52	147
11	Harris' Reward: 1852-70	161
12	Modern Times and Barrow's Epitaph	167
Index		197

Acknowledgements

It is a great pleasure to be able to thank the many people who have encouraged me and whose efforts have contributed to this book.

The National Maritime Museum (NMM) Greenwich, London and especially Dr R J B Knight who, when Deputy Director, kindly brought to my attention various artefacts concerning lightning conductors, which he discovered in the furthermost recesses of the storage areas, as did his colleague, Mr N Upham. The staff of the Caird Library were kind and helpful and always ready to produce original documents. Many happy hours of reading were made available to me by their efforts. Professor N A M Rodger most kindly advised me early on in my researches. His many excellent publications have been an inspiration to me.

I record my grateful thanks to Dr Roger Morriss of Exeter University for his advice concerning access to collections of papers.

Many archives and institutions were visited or were asked for information and for copies of primary material including: The National Library of Scotland, Edinburgh; Miss P Borron, Archivist to the Lampton Estate; Dr R H Smart, Keeper of MSS, University of St Andrews Library; Dr D M Owen, The Keeper, University Archives, The University Library, Cambridge.

The British Library's Department of Manuscripts was a most helpful and courteous ally in my work. The staff, although busy, always found time to assist me. Lenore Symons, Archivist, The Institution of Electrical Engineers, London, was diligent in producing obscure papers and MSS. Letters to Faraday from Harris were particularly helpful.

Various sources within the Ministry of Defence (N) were most generous with their time and efforts to produce original books and documents. Miss K Riley of the Naval History Library was happy to help find books and manuscripts, and Ms Polly Dawes, RN Engineering Library, HMS *Manadon*, Plymouth, introduced me to the volumes of the Navy Records Society. Mr A J Scott, Ship Department/D171, Ministry of Defence, obtained permission to release archived information and the most up-to-date advice for lightning protection to HM ships as provided by Mr R Ball of Y-ARD Ltd Consulting Engineers, Glasgow. The Royal Naval Museum, Portsmouth kindly searched their records on my behalf, and Commanding Officer Lt Cdr D J Whild RN kindly granted permission for use of an image from HMS *Victory*.

The staff of the National Archives, formerly the Public Record Office, Kew, always took an interest in my amateur researches into history and were constant and helpful with their advice. Only once during my many years of part-time research did I succeed in outpacing their accurate and speedy production of records.

Plymouth Central Library, Plymouth Art Gallery and Museum, The *Western Morning News* Ltd. and Devon Record Offices have each assisted me in this work. Westerly Marine Construction Ltd., Portsmouth and Lloyds Register of Shipping, London were kind enough to consider and to respond to my requests for information and advice as to modern standards for lightning protection for yachts and ships.

Original correspondence from Harris to the most prominent scientists of the mid-nineteenth century were produced with my thanks from AIM25 archives; Kings College Library, London; by Dr A Kuein, Archivist, Trinity College Library, University of Cambridge; by The Royal Commission on Historical Manuscripts, London, and much useful information and primary sources of material were obtained from The Scottish Record Office, now National Archives of Scotland, Edinburgh.

The Science Museum Library, London, assisted me and The University of London Historical Research Library allowed me to access their copies of Parliamentary Papers.

Professor Theodore Bernstein, Department of Electrical and Computer Engineering, University of Wisconsin-Madison, USA, who published an article on Harris, was kind enough to encourage me in my searches.

The compilers and publishers of the *Mariner's Mirror* on CD-ROM (Chatham Publishing) found new ways to allow cross referencing of subject matter which I used and for which I thank them.

An old school friend and historian, Roderick Braithwaite, kindly suggested the title of this book. My family and especially my son, Dollan, have at various times urged me to complete the work and have also very kindly helped me at the NRA with tracing papers and records.

Every effort has been made to trace copyright holders of material included in this book. The author and publishers apologise for any inadvertent omission and would be pleased to hear from any copyright holder they have been unable to trace.

Introduction

In 1967, my wife and I visited an auction house in Plymouth to buy some urgently needed second-hand furniture for our new home. The warehouse was badly lit and the furniture we could afford seemed to be in a loft reached by a near-vertical open staircase. In a dark corner were two dusty pictures of sailing ships being struck by lightning. Our bids were not successful, so we forgot about the pictures until about two months later when an advertisement caught my eye. This was for five paintings of the same subject. Could they be the same two, now part of a larger set? The seller's address was nearby at Chudleigh Knighton. Intrigued, we set off but with no great hope of success. Our meeting with the marine art agent, Morris Tucker, was lengthy and fascinating. Needless to record, we ended up buying the set of what indeed were original paintings. From this inauspicious beginning commenced a research trail which was to last over 30 years.

The paintings were by Nicholas Matthew Condy. They had been sponsored by a Plymouth apothecary, William Snow Harris. I wanted to know why. To my astonishment, it soon became apparent that Snow Harris had invented or developed a system of lightning protection which could withstand all that the weather at sea could throw at it. Moreover, his copper conductors were shown conclusively to be of adequate capacity to discharge the strokes of lightning so often encountered by the tall three-masted sailing ships.

It was surprising and perplexing then to find that between 1820 and 1860, details of his invention were denied, obstructed, lost and became for many years used as a game of football between opposing politicians. To add to this, I found increasing evidence of malfeasance by the senior official at the Admiralty.

How could this have happened? Why did the Victorians for so long ignore the deaths and mutilation from lightning strikes to their seamen whilst at work trimming the sails? What was the cost of repairs to the yards and masts of the ships? Were there any losses of ships after strikes by lightning?

Alas, once again it was politics that seems to have been responsible for much of the long, drawn-out struggle before official procurement of the invention. For it was to be 22 years before Harris' innovation was formally adopted and a further 18 years before he was adequately rewarded.

Much of the delay was due to a wearisome vendetta between arrogant Whigs and unbending Tories. The short-lived administrations at the Admiralty Board each failed to have robust reasons for any decision. Often, those decisions which were taken were short-term solutions of political expediency. There was a strong possibility, but a publicly unproven one, of corrupt practices. Plagiarism was proved. The senior staff of the naval ship constructors office stole Harris' ideas and hoped to benefit from their actions. Inadequate administration, particularly as to records and archives, led to chaos with respect to the production of packs of papers for the Board of the Admiralty. Those administrations which did serve a full term in office were Whigs and led by two indecisive and deceitful noblemen whose negative influence with respect to the system of lightning protection was profound.

The personalities involved at the time were to prove interesting and at times all too human. Letters, personal papers, diaries and notebooks were found. The development of the story was followed in detail and the result was the narrative in this book. Opinions as to the possible reasons for the various acts or omissions of the leading actors, are my own.

Who were the men responsible for the 40-year delay in procurement and reward? Apart from Snow Harris, the inventor, the most important influences for the eventual adoption of the system for protection of warships from lightning were a ferocious opponent, one Lt. Pringle Green, who although present at Trafalgar was virtually unemployable thereafter. Admirals Byam Martin and Cockburn were powerful men who eschewed being mainstream politicians and succeeded in maintaining their integrity as officers of the Royal Navy. Admiral Sir Charles Adam and his relatives largely failed to convince posterity of their worth. One relative, the Whig Civil Lord, Gilbert, Second Earl of Minto, was at all times acting beyond his abilities but dissembled very effectively for a while. The surveyor (Chief Naval

Constructor) and his staff were unable to compete in the broken seas of political diatribe but found their solace in deceit. The permanent civil servant, John Barrow, whilst finding time to cherry-pick the archives at the Admiralty for his own purposes, failed to administer the totality of his expanded department. Sir John Peel acted as a gentleman throughout but could do little to prevent petty squabbling between his party and the Whigs.

To achieve his ends and claim his rewards, Harris eventually used the British tradition of fair play to his advantage. By prodigious exertions he managed to gain alliances and friends amongst naval officers, officials at the Royal Dockyards, politicians of both Houses and from the leading scientists of his day. He remained bland, polite and friendly in his open letters and publications. His capacious lightning conductor, acting as a conduit to draw a stroke of lightning away from damaging men or ships, remains as good in scientific terms today as it was then. It was by his immense persistence and by his rigorous research that he was able to show the world that he was right and deserved his rewards. In other words, the goodie won for a change.

1

Thunderstorms, Lightning and Ships

Protection of a ship against the effects of strikes from lightning would seem to us now to be an obvious and routine matter. In the days of wooden sailing ships, serious injury and even loss of life with damage and fires on ships from lightning were accepted as a hazard of going to sea.

Complete loss of some ships during thunderstorms was suspected but for some time not known with certainty as many simply disappeared. A few were known to have blown up, for example HMS *Resistance* was in the East Indies in 1798 when lightning was seen to be playing around the warship. After a massive explosion only 13 men were left alive. Four of these men survived and one, a seaman named Scott, was eventually able to return to England. After his account had been given to the authorities, a link between a bolt of lightning striking his ship and the explosion of its powder magazine was suspected.

The subject of lightning protection was first considered in depth by a genius from Philadelphia, one Benjamin Franklin. He and others had long discussed the phenomenon of lightning in articles and pamphlets. Franklin had first published his invention of a lightning conductor in 1751. He concerned himself mainly with the protection of important buildings from damage by lightning and the first lightning conductors for use at sea were then adapted almost without modification from his iron-pointed lightning rod and its heavy bars of iron conductor. It was soon found that injuries and damage from lightning could occasionally happen even in the presence of Franklin's lightning conductor. The rigid iron bars as the conductors for ships were abandoned and iron chains were substituted for use in the British Royal Navy. The chains, which were suspended from high up on the mast, hung down to reach into the sea. They proved difficult to use when tacking or changing sail and hence tended only to be put in place when a thunderstorm threatened.

Lightning strikes to ships at sea, as well as killing or injuring many sailors, also often led to serious damage. In a total of 200 instances of lightning strikes to HM Ships, it was calculated that at least £70,000 of damage had occurred to their masts and spars. That is about £170 million today. What was to become unforgivable was that casualties among sailors and their ships continued to be accepted as inevitable for many years, even after the invention of a flexible but permanently fixed in place system of copper lightning conductors for the masts of ships. The fixed system was so effective that many Royal Navy ships' logs did not bother to record all the instances when they had been protected from damage by lightning. Even worse, after a decade of official trials of the fixed copper lightning conductors, the successful outcome was cynically ignored. The senior and permanent civil servant at the Admiralty, John Barrow, mysteriously could not produce the files of the trials on the 12 warships carrying the new form of lightning conductor. Intense political hostility, spite and ill will by successive Boards of the Admiralty then prevented adoption of the new system for a further ten years. It was due to such unfair opposition that the inventor of the successful permanently fixed copper lightning conductors for ships, William Snow Harris, was forced to battle for recognition of his invention, for nearly 40 years.

The risks of damage from lightning strikes to the wooden masts of ships was then, and remains now, a considerable one in some parts of the world. Some of the more distant areas (Fig.1a) in which the wooden sailing ships of the nineteenth-century British Navy were stationed were later found to be amongst those with the highest risk in the world from strikes during lightning storms. Many HM Ships thus damaged actually lost some of their masts and spars. The masts were particularly valuable items and had to be purchased from abroad, often a difficult matter in time of war. Even more difficult was finding an adequate replacement for a mast or a large spar whilst at distant foreign stations. Unfortunately, the wood of the mast of the sailing ships was such a poor conductor of any electric current that extensive damage to it and to the ship's hull could easily be caused by the massive flow of electricity from a strike of lightning. Sometimes the damage was obvious as fire, or as splintering of the wood, or even as an explosive destruction. Sometimes the damage was hidden inside the wood, only for the whole mast or spar to fail when next under serious stress, perhaps on a lee shore. There were even instances of a whole squadron of ships being damaged by lightning. Occasionally, as mentioned, a valuable warship and crew would sail into a thunderstorm and would become a total loss.

How did the injuries and loss of life happen? What could have been done to prevent them? How much damage did occur to our ships and how much were the consequent high costs for their repair?

To answer these questions we must consider exactly what the scientists of the era knew about thunder and lightning storms. Did the Admiralty attempt to prevent damage from lightning? Finally we must ask whether damage by lightning to men and their ships could still happen nowadays.

Thunder and Lightning

The noise so well known to each of us as a rolling rumble of vast amplitude heard from up to about nine miles (15km) away has its own adjective, 'thunderous'. Those deafening sounds are the result of a shockwave of air blasted into a colossal expansion of its constituent gases by the heat of the passage of a flash of lightning. There is also a less well known sound effect below the threshold of human hearing which occurs due to adjustments in the electrostatic field in the cloud after a lightning stroke.

As Golde[1] wrote in his excellent book on *Lightning Protection*, 'the exact mechanism by which a thunderstorm was generated was imperfectly understood'. That statement remains true today even though we do know much more about the conditions for the formation and maturation of a thunderstorm, these being the wind and its direction and force, the temperature gradient and the rapid formation of dark clouds with rain.

Ideal conditions[2] for thunderstorms were thought to occur about 50,000 times every day throughout the world. Recent observations have strongly suggested that many more storms than this happen, as judged by the almost constant flickering of lightning recorded by the crews of spaceships. Worldwide, it has now been calculated that there about there are 100 lightning strikes every second.[3] This gives a theoretical mean frequency of six strokes of lightning over each 0.386 square mile (or six per square kilometre). The true frequency over land is better calculated for each country in the world based on accurate observations rather than a theoretical calculation. This is because most lightning flashes are from one cloud to another cloud, whereas lightning strokes to the earth's surface tend to occur more often over land than over the oceans. Moreover, the true number of flashes over land varies widely and is at its highest in equatorial South America, Madagascar and in parts of the East Indian archipelago.[4]

Potential thunderstorms of cumulonimbus clouds occur as complexes with a radius of about 12½ miles (20-30km) and separated from the next complex by a further 31 miles to as much as 124 miles (50-200km). Such storms with the potential for lightning strokes to the earth have been found to tend to move in a straight line at about 25 mph, provided the ground over which they are moving is mostly flat. Mountains, or land to sea interfaces, may interfere with the straight line pattern of movement.[5] A single thunderstorm, more common in summer than in winter, lasts less than one hour in temperate latitudes such as around the British Isles, but can last up to three hours in the tropics and thus can move up to 75 miles (90km).[6]

Lightning strikes cause from 40-60 per cent of destructive forest fires,[7] such as those occurring in North America, thereby destroying valuable resources. Coniferous forests in America and Canada were of particular interest to the British as a very important source of ships' masts, trimmed only from their largest mature trees. Lightning strikes to trees in Australia cause vast fires there too, but then confer natural regeneration to some types of seeds.

A large amount of data as to lightning strikes was gathered from studies made on German forests. It was found that some types of tree of approximately the same height, when struck by lightning, suffered damage more often than some of the others, the explanation being that living trees of different types have large variations in their barks as well as some differences within their internal composition.[8] Water is contained in the tree trunk as free water in the natural channels for the nutrition of trees, as well as in the individual cells which make up the substance of the wood. Blast damage can be extensive after a lightning strike, which attempts to get to earth through the electrical resistance of the wood of the tree trunk together with its constituent water. The current passing into the water superheats it and causes an explosive formation of steam, perhaps deep within the trunk, with consequent extensive damage to the wood. By contrast, minimal damage may occur if a smooth-barked tree is hit by lightning, as rain pouring down the smooth trunk may allow the current a ready path over its surface to earth. This is possible as a large amount of electricity, such as that in a lightning stroke, will always take the path of least resistance towards earth. If that pathway can be provided by water, it will take it in preference to the higher electrical resistance from a depth of rough bark or from that of live but dryer wood of the branches or trunk.[9]

A dead tree, if struck by lightning, behaves quite differently from a live tree. If wet through and rotting, it may be blasted apart, partially or completely. If dry, it may catch fire and burn. Whole trunks of wood cut down and treated by gentle partial drying for use as poles or flagstaffs, or in the days of sail for masts, behave differently from a live tree in the event of a strike by lightning, the amount of residual water contained within the wood being crucial.[10] The less water, the more the trunk of wood itself has to act as the conductor, albeit one of high resistance, for the passage of the electrical current during a strike. The higher the electrical resistance, the higher the chance of fire and of the current leaping to a better conductor than the wood, for example to a man on the rigging of a sailing ship. If water is present through insufficient seasoning or through seepage into old dried out wood, then explosions from steam formation may occur in a mast exactly as in a live tree, with consequent loss of the entire mast or of parts of it. The effects of lightning on the wooden masts of warships made from a whole dead but seasoned fir tree trunk or on one 'made' up into a circular shape from several segments of interlocking slices of fir wood, will be considered in detail later.

Some idea of the current discharged by a lightning flash was given by Andrews *et al.*[11] The arc of electricity might be of a magnitude of 30,000 amperes generating a power of 12,000MW. It may strike unseasoned but dry wood but discharges only for a few tens of microseconds. Any residual water within the wood struck by the current helps maintain the arc. Steam formed at a very high pressure then splits the wood open and causes characteristic furrows on the damaged pole or mast. Not only masts and trees may be struck, but people, their farms, dwellings, power lines, cities and transport may be destroyed by lightning.

Tall structures actually encourage the formation of an upward (from earth to cloud), so-called 'leader' stroke of lightning.[12] This leader may then be followed by one or more downward strokes but of a complicated pattern rather than as one direct channel.

As has been explained, any calculation of the risk of a strike, perhaps to man-made structures on land or to a ship at sea, can only be made after an assessment of the number of lightning flashes over a given square area. That figure is impossible to assess for many areas of jungle or of ocean. Hence for an approximate guide as to risk, the number of thunderstorm days each year for several years in the general area is counted and a mean figure per year used to compare one area with another. Temperate zones have been found to have thunderstorms over a wide area consistent with their usual westerly advancing weather fronts, with cold air usually displacing a mass of warmer and moisture-rich air which is pushed upwards to form clouds of water vapour. The zones further towards the tropics were known to have their own patterns of thunder and lightning and these patterns were understandably much studied by sailors. The Byzantine Navy as long ago as AD 900 taught its young sailors that in the Byzantine region lightning mainly occurred between May and November.[13] A single flash of lightning and thunderous applause would be likely to signify a squall, at once followed by rough seas lasting a further 8 to 12 hours. In total contrast, a series of rapid flashes, whether by day or by night, indicated fair weather.

In tropical climates or, importantly for mountaineers,[14] in places with solitary high peaks or ranges of peaks, heat from convective storms is the main originator of thunderstorm conditions. The mechanism for a large potential difference in the cloud is the different charges of electricity on water droplets from those on any ice particles. The stabilisation of the electrical field only occurs due to a discharge of lightning.

Hot air in temperate areas cools quickly on rising up to high altitudes. The clouds formed at first as water droplets soon become ice. Ice crystals in an active cloud carry positive electrical charges. The main concentration of the positive charges in the thunderstorm cloud occurs at just less than 20,000 feet above sea level. The temperature at that altitude is likely to be about −8°C. Water droplets, by contrast, tend to carry a negative electrical charge and are concentrated at about 7,000 feet above sea level.[15]

For tropical areas and the longer lasting tropical thunderstorms, according to Golde's[16] research, the heights for positively charged ice particles reach 32,500 feet – that is the height of some commercial aeroplane flights. Negatively-charged water droplets are found at 16,250 feet.

The ground or the sea as an electrical earth, if under a thunderstorm cloud, carries a negative charge. A tall structure such as the 130-foot main mast of a wooden frigate of the Navy of the Napoleonic wars, may short circuit the electrostatic field between the charged cloud and the earth. If the short circuit does occur then a point discharge of ions moves upwards towards the cloud. St Elmo's fire, which sometimes can be seen as a glow from the pointed ends of the ears of mules or from sharp-ended grasses and ferns in high mountainous areas, or from the masts and yards of ships, then becomes visible. St Elmo's fire is prognostic of intense electrical activity and may presage a lightning flash.[17]

Lightning at sea could also strike other solitary tall objects such as lighthouses built on isolated rocks. The second Eddystone lighthouse, 14 miles off the coast of Devon, was destroyed by fire after lightning[18] struck in 1755.

A Lightning Stroke and a Flash

A stroke of lightning from cloud to cloud or from cloud to ground is the totality of the electrical discharge from a myriad of water droplets whose negative charges have coalesced into a single channel.[19] The multiple earth flash is the most common form of lightning and often begins as a so-called 'stepped leader'. Each step, as a downward stroke from the cloud, is about the length of a cricket pitch at 22 yards (20m). The current in the steps has been estimated to be about several hundred amperes. As soon as one of the steps of electrical current touches the earth with a faint glow, a return stroke of intense brightness travels upwards to the cloud. A further stroke may occur in the same small area but is not preceded by a step type build up and this type of stroke is known as a 'dart leader'. Single-stroke lightning is more common in temperate zones but multiple lightning strikes, termed 'flashes', are often seen in tropical areas.

Tall structures placed on mountains have enabled very detailed studies to be made of the initiation and decay of lightning discharges.[19] The importance of the findings for the further study of lightning strikes on sailing ships lies in the high probability that tall structures whose height is or exceeds about 130 feet (39.62m) actually reverse the initiation of an original pathway for lightning. Instead of a stepped leader of current extending down from a thundercloud towards the earth or sea in steps the length of a cricket pitch, the whole process is inverted. From the tip of a tall tower or mast, upward stepped leaders of current with multiple side channels may be generated. Once that has occurred the normal pattern of downward strokes may be seen.[19]

Examples of Lightning Strikes on Shipping

On 11 December 1806, a small 18-gun brig HMS *Surinam* (Fig.1b) was one of the lookouts for the fleet off the coast of France reporting to Rear Admiral Louis' blockading squadron.[21] There had been a storm all evening and at about eight o'clock the thunderstorm and lightning increased, together with high winds. At 11.30 a huge flash of lightning struck the ship at the mainmast and split it into pieces. The lightning flashed on from the mainmast into the hold and split open both iron pumps. The strike killed 23 seamen, wounded 4 more and did considerable damage to various parts of the ship. After great exertions, as the masts and riggings had to be cut through and thrown overboard, enough sail was set so as to allow the ship's head to be brought to the wind and this prevented her from drifting directly onto the rocks of the lee shore of Belle Isle. The captain of the ship made signals with rockets, blue lights and guns. However, due to the violence of the gale and the continual flashes of lightning, the rest of the fleet, wisely, were well offshore and could not see the signals of distress.

As has been explained, most storms which generate lightning occur in the tropics and in the southern hemisphere, adjacent to the larger land masses. If a map is made with the number of days marked on it when thunder has been heard in any given area, many of those areas will be found off the west and east coasts of Central and Southern Africa. Lines drawn on a map connecting areas with the same number of thunderstorm days per year are called 'isokeraunic lines' and the average number of thunderstorm days at any given place is called an 'isokeraunic level'. Some places, such as Java Head, have a level of as many as 120 thunderstorm days in any one year, whereas on the east coast of South America the isokeraunic level is about 50 days in any one year. It follows that any ship at sea off the southern continental coasts or islands is exposed to a high risk of one or more lightning strikes.

From historical records, we know that lightning has been known to strike any type and any size of ship at sea. According to Golde[22] the frequency of lightning strikes corresponds, quite closely but not invariably, with the square of the structure above the ground or above the sea.

Sailors of the ancient world were all too familiar with lightning strikes to their ships. E V Rieu's translation of Homer's *Odyssey*[23] reads:[24]

> The squall snapped both forestays together. As the mast fell aft, all the rigging tumbled into the bilge, and the mast itself, reaching the stern, struck the helmsman on the head and smashed in all the bones of his skull. He plunged like a diver from the poop, and his brave soul left his body. Then at one and the same moment Zeus thundered and struck the vessel by lightning. The whole ship reeled to the blow of his bolt and was filled with sulphur. My men were flung overboard and tossed round the black hull like sea-gulls on the waves. There was no homecoming for them: the god saw to that.

The Bible[25] also has allusions to lightning but none specific to strikes to ships at sea.

The earliest recorded strike on a ship that can be said to have been in the service of the British Crown was during the Crusades.[26] Richard I was on passage to Palestine in AD 1191. One of his galleys was over-wintering in Messina in Sicily when it was struck by lightning and sunk. The appearance of St Elmo's fire, which often appeared at the top of the mast of a ship during periods of atmospheric electrical activity, was thought by the Crusaders to be an apparition of the Virgin Mary. Pliny recorded that seamen used to believe that St Elmo's fire would vanish before the storm ended. Later, others thought that if the St Elmo's fire was on the shrouds of the ship rather than on top of the mast, it was a sign that the storm would continue.

Lightning and the patterns of weather was much studied, especially in the busy Mediterranean seas. According to a translation made from material written about AD 900–1000,[27] lightning 'may occur by day or by night between the months of May and November.

Other early accounts of the King's ships being affected by strikes from lightning are scarce but there was one in July 1418.[28] Henry V had ordered Huggkyns, the Dutch shipbuilder, to finish building the *Grace Dieu*. This ship was about 1,400 tons and had two masts. She was laid up in the mouth of the River Hamble at the bottom of Southampton Water. Unfortunately she leaked and lay there unused for some 30 years. In 1433, her mainmast was removed and she was warped upstream to a mud berth. In 1439, even without her mainmast but probably with perhaps one other mast standing, she was struck by lightning, caught fire and was burnt out and sunk. At the bottom of spring low tides her remains can be seen to this day.

On 26 June 1663, Samuel Pepys,[29] the famous diarist and Clerk of the Acts to the Navy Office, recorded in his diary that he had dined with Sir William Ridger and some others. During the evening, many stories were told of their personal knowledge of masts of ships being shivered by lightning from top to bottom. Sometimes the mast was only damaged on the inside and the outside of it remained whole. Sir William then told of a Genoese galley moored in Leghorn Roads that was struck by lightning. The mast of the galley was broken into pieces and the lightning stroke continued down to the shackle on the leg of a galley slave. The shackle was melted off whilst leaving his leg untouched. It is a sad end to the story that the poor slave was put back into fetters.

In Philosophical Transactions[30] of 1685, the effect of ball lightning on HMS *Coronation* was graphically described. Another ship struck during the same thunderstorm was *Royal James*, which was in dry dock. In 1741, HMS *Experiment*[31] was near Cuba when 'hard gales and cloudy weather with violent claps of thunder, much lightning and rain, at 5 pm. struck [down] yards and topmast, at 7 the ship broke loose'. Although on that occasion the ship was not struck by a flash of lightning, it was thought of by the captain and crew as an ever present threat.

In 1751, a letter from a certain Mr Benjamin Franklin of Philadelphia was printed in *Philosophical Transactions*.[32] It referred to a Captain Waddle's recent account of lightning after St Elmo's fire. Franklin noted that Captain Waddle had reported that St Elmo's fire had settled on the spindles of the topmast heads and they had burnt like very large torches before the lightning struck.

In his book, first published in 1752,[33] and in a new edition two years later, Franklin had suggested that a rod of sharp iron, gilded to prevent rusting, be placed at the top of a ship's mast. A gilded iron wire, or lead iron wire, should then be let down the shrouds of the ship to the sea in order to protect that ship from lightning. From this idea was to emerge the first lightning conductors for practical use on ships. It was accepted, albeit incorrectly, that Franklin's suggestion of a gilded wire would be of sufficient capacity to conduct a discharge of lightning away from the ship.

A Mr Collinson of Mill Hill, a village near London, had first communicated many of the methods and results of Franklin's experiments with electricity and with lightning protection to British scientists via the Royal Society. Collinson was an American botanist and merchant and became a co-founder of Kew Gardens. Interested in most aspects of natural philosophy, he lived at Ridgeway House, later the grammar school which then became Mill Hill School.

British shipping, Royal Naval and mercantile, formed the largest deep-sea force in the world and could be expected to have had many instances of damage from lightning. A Dr Watson recorded that the mainmast of HMS *Bellona*, a 74-gun ship, was split in pieces by lightning in January 1762.[34] Dr Watson acknowledged Benjamin Franklin's admirable discovery of conducting lightning from the clouds. By way of a practical improvement upon Franklin's work, he then suggested that if a wire of iron or any other metal were connected with the spindles and ironwork at the tops of masts on ships and then led down the sides of the masts and from thence into any convenient direction so as always to touch the sea water, the lightning discharge would be prevented and conducted silently away by the wire. He recommended, in particular, brass wire of the thickness of a 'large goose quill', as it would not rust. As an afterthought he added that the powder magazine being built at Purfleet should also be protected from lightning. Watson had also reported that HMS *Ramilles* whilst at Chatham, was struck by lightning and the mast was split and torn.[35] Watson later wrote to Admiral Lord Anson and recommended that HM Ships be issued with lightning conductors. Conductors as a simple small pointed rod with a long metal chain to reach the sea were ordered by Anson to be supplied to HM Ships and this order was carried out shortly after he died in 1762. Anson had directed that the flexible metallic chain lightning conductors should be set up whenever a thunderstorm threatened. A comment was soon made that they were hardly used at all.

The first Royal Navy ship to be supplied with this portable lightning conductor, was probably the frigate, *Alarm*.[36] Between 1761 and 1763, she was also the first Royal Navy ship to have her entire hull sheathed in copper as protection against barnacles and the *teredo navalis* worm, again on Admiral Anson's instructions.

In an open letter to Benjamin Franklin, published in the world famous scientific journal, *Philosophical Transactions*, an American sea captain named J.L. Winn[37] recorded his fears of his ship being struck by lightning. He commenced his letter by commenting that, 'It is a common, and, I am afraid, just complaint, that seamen are exceedingly backward in availing themselves of the discoveries which men of science have made, and the directions which they have given for their benefit and safety.' To his knowledge many ships were indeed damaged, or worse, by lightning. He stated that he had tried various types of marine lightning conductor but the one which he now used was of copper wire (an early form) made into a chain. Four drawings illustrated his letter. Winn described how in April 1769 his ship was approaching the coast of America when a storm blew up with great dark thunder clouds. There was a lot of lightning so he untangled his conductor and got it put up in place on the mast. When hauling up the mainsail, a sheet block struck violently against the back stays to which the chain had been fastened and he afterwards found out that the conductor had been broken. Near midnight he noticed a pale bluish light just a few feet above the quarter rail. The light appeared to go on and off. Sometimes there were sparks in the same area. On examining the lightning chain in the morning he found the chain had broken at one of the links and that the electrical current must have been arcing between two of the broken links. He hoped by his letter to persuade every mariner to use lightning conductors. The conductors which he used and to which he ascribed the preservation of his ship, he obtained from Nairn and Blunt, mathematical instrument makers, 20 Cornhill, London. Was that one of the first advertisements disguised within a scientific article?

On 17 May 1777, the powder magazine at Purfleet, which had been protected according to the standards of the time by a fixed pointed rod and metal conductor, was struck by lightning and damaged but not blown up. Public interest was based upon fear. The experimental electricians rushed to complete their work to answer the two questions posed by the public's interest. Did a blunt or a pointed lightning conductor have the greater efficacy? Should a lightning conductor be higher than the structure on which it was placed? It was unfortunate that the publication of the results of Dr Nairn's experiments[38] comparing blunt and pointed terminals for conductors in 1779 did nothing to reduce the prejudice already present in other scientists' minds. The excited public eagerly took sides. The King himself then took an interest. Under his auspices and in the hope that he could disprove the irritating upstarts in America and thereby perhaps destroy their credibility, George III himself paid for the great experiment. This was to be carried out by Mr Wilson at the Pantheon, London.

Wilson's limited set of experiments pointed to the superior efficacy of ball-ended compared with point-ended lightning conductors, as indeed his King had hoped. Unfortunately, for a definitive outcome, Wilson's experiments were objectively inconclusive. His results were attacked by Nairn in his paper. Nairn complained for example that the brass tubing which was the container for an artificial cloud was ineffectively insulated. Thus this very grand-scale demonstration with all the attendant publicity set the stage for further controversy, mostly based upon ill-informed opinion. That controversy was to continue for the next half century.

Benjamin Franklin, the inventor of the lightning rod, never varied from his original concept that a pointed terminal to the lightning rod was the most efficacious in preventing a strike to a building. If, however, a strike was inevitable, the presence of a pointed rod and a conductor would ensure the least possible damage to the structure on which they were mounted. It was inferred and accepted that a pointed lightning rod on a ship would confer the same degree of protection if fitted with a similar system for conducting the lightning to the sea.

The British thus had adopted Franklin's invention of the iron rod lightning conductor for buildings and benefited from his expertise during his time in London between 1757 and 1762; they regarded him as an honorary citizen of London. They had corresponded freely with him about lightning strikes to HM Ships[39] and had awarded him the Copley Medal from The Royal Society in 1753. In 1767, his iron conductors and pointed lightning rods were placed on St Paul's Cathedral. However, prejudice against Franklin and his ideas was to become widespread. After all, he was a Philadelphian and they, like many others in the British Colonies in America, were to assert their independence and ask for self-rule. It was also widely known to the British public that Franklin had raised a body of 10,000 volunteers for the defence and security around Philadelphia but against British interests. Franklin and his friends on the Committee on Lightning

Rods for powder magazines, of The Royal Society of 1772 did not offer confrontation with King George III's support for rounded ends for lightning rods but in 1772 a ditty was published:[40]

> While you, great George, for safety hunt,
> And sharp conductors change for blunt,
> The nation's out of joint:
> Franklin a wiser course pursues,
> And all your thunder useless views
> By keeping to the point.

George III then insisted that The Royal Society, which had opted for scientific evidence and thus for a pointed terminal for a lightning conductor, must reverse this decision. To his credit, the President of The Society, Sir John Pringle, who was also Physician to the King, at once objected saying that the laws of nature could not be reversed. Thereupon the King required Pringle to resign as his physician. The lively issue of whether lightning rod terminals should have sharp points rather than ball ends then spread to the Continent. Riots occurred in Italy, where lightning conductors were at first called 'heretical rods'. The controversy died down only very gradually. It was to be some years before Franklin's lightning conductors became a familiar sight on most of the public and on some of the larger private buildings across Europe.

Many continued to feel that any metallic object must attract strikes from lightning[41]. J. Bathoe in 1775 wrote that the wind vanes made of iron on masts would cause damage in this way. Ladies of the times felt it fashionable to wind wire round their hats as a most powerful personal lightning conductor. At the same time they wore stockings, shoes and gowns of silk, one of the most powerful insulators. Bathoe commented 'that they prepared their bodies in the same manner and according to the same principles as electricians prepared their conductors for attracting the fire and lightning'. His views, although correct, would have been unlikely to prevent the dictates of fashion but did expose the degree of ignorance of the public about the new science of electricity.

Benjamin Franklin and an Alliance with France

Franklin had many French friends and contacts. Those contacts were in themselves regarded as a threat to British interests and especially if concerned with technology or with warships. One of Franklin's friends was a French scientist appointed to the French Court, Jean Baptiste Le Roy, whose laboratories were at La Mouette, Passy.

In 1779, Franklin had officially been appointed American Ambassador to France. He was fêted by the French and soon was asked to advise them on proposed landings of their invasion force of troops to the British coast. The British were indeed right to suspect Franklin's loyalty to them. There was every reason for them to believe that he was an active ally of the French and therefore an enemy. America's intentions at first were far from clear to the British. They became threatening when they transferred one of their few frigates, the *Indien,* to the French war fleet.

Franklin was considered by the British not only to be a dangerous politician but also a religious heretic. They spied on him using two men to follow him in Paris.[42] It was found that Franklin had taken a mistress who lived nearby. She was a woman of small stature who Franklin termed his 'pocket wife'. She was none other than Madame Le Roy, the separated wife of Franklin's friend, Jean Baptiste Le Roy. The fact of his mistress was taken by the British to be yet more evidence of Franklin's unreliability. In 1784, and despite his liaison with Mme Le Roy, Franklin continued to cooperate closely with Le Roy and even sat on a committee with him. About this time Franklin met Le Roy's brother, Juliene-David, who was interested in maritime matters. It may have been his influence which persuaded J.B. Le Roy later to make his observations concerning lightning conductors for French men-of-war. Le Roy stated his advice to the Ministre de Marine very clearly, and based upon his own experiments was able to defend to the Academie des Sciences in Paris the use of points for the terminals of lightning rods. By 1784 there were a 'large number of ships of the French Navy' with lightning rods fixed in place.[43]

Some idea of the controversy amongst the scientists of the day concerning thunderstorms and lightning and how they occurred can be gained from an article by Professor John Lesley of the University of Edinburgh. Professor Lesley had apparently first read his paper before The Royal Society of Scotland in January and again in March 1792. He discussed the efficacy of the lightning rod, whilst admitting that a pointed end to it was superior to a blunt one. He did dispute that a lightning rod actually protected a building against a strike by lightning. Instead, he proposed that a lightning rod could hardly be expected to dissipate the immense electrical forces from thunder clouds. For reasons which are obscure, his article was not finally published until 1824. Titled 'Observations On Electrical Theories,' Lesley later published, in 1829, further articles on his views as to the lack of efficacy of lightning conductors.

2

Lightning Strikes on People

Even though there are a very large number of thunderstorms each day throughout the world, the risk of a person being struck by lightning is very small indeed, especially as most lightning discharges occur as flashes from cloud to cloud. In the UK, a mean of 12 lightning strikes to people occur each year and five of the people so struck are killed. Those injured undergo a transient loss of consciousness, become temporarily blind or deaf and burns to the skin may appear after several hours.[1] Those killed by the lightning strike are found to have had cardiac arrest after a fluttering rapid beat of the lower part of the heart or a complete suppression of the heartbeat.

In Germany, casualties from lightning over an eight-year period were studied. Lightning victims on land, or brought to land from lakes or from the sea, were found to have a 55 per cent chance of survival and the total number of lightning incidents to humans was found to be 93 cases per year by Taussig.[2]

By contrast, there are 300 injuries and 1,000 deaths each year in the USA.[3] The difference in the survival rate as compared to that of Europe is possibly attributable to the remoteness of vast areas of the North American continent. Lightning in fact causes more deaths each year in the USA than any other weather-related causes such as hurricanes, tornadoes, sudden spells of freezing conditions, or a prolonged hot summer.

African countries with a tradition of peasant farming still have a high rate of lightning strikes to people. The death rate from lightning-associated reasons is properly expressed as per million of the population. In South Africa alone the frequency is about 1.5 and in Singapore 1.7, whereas it is 0.4 in the USA and less then 0.1 in England and Wales. Eighty per cent of deaths are to males, but only 5.3 per cent occur when people are indoors. Eighty-five per cent of all deaths from lightning occur between midday and 4 p.m. It has been estimated[4] that only one ground stroke of lightning in every 6-8 x 10^5 flashes actually kills a person.[5]

Lightning strikes to people can happen in one or more of four ways.[6, 7]

1 The Direct Strike[3]

A person can be struck directly by a stroke of lightning, and sometimes, as happens in Africa, by a bolt from a blue sky. The channel down which lightning travels has been estimated to be about 18 feet in diameter but the channel usually branches out when in contact with the ground or sea. The lightning current may then be 'splashed' over an area of 100 feet or more. A stroke of lightning has been found to be a direct current of about 20–1000 million volts and 10,000 to 200,000 amperes but lasts only about one thousandth of a second. The composition of the forming channel may have as many as 40 successive peaks of current first and, mainly due to the stepped leaders of lightning, followed by the return stroke. The resistance offered by the human body to a large current from a direct strike is about 700 ohms. Momentarily, if struck by lightning, the current through the body transferred by the blood will reach about 1,300 amperes. This current continues for about 10 microseconds before it collapses to 5 amperes but is endured for several more milliseconds.

2 The Contact Type

This type of injury arises from touching a poorly-earthed person or object during a lightning flash sequence nearby. Hence the many reports of injuries amongst people crowded together under a tree struck by lightning. On the other hand, if the lightning is discharged to earth by a conductor of sufficiently large capacity, it should be possible to be in contact with it without any shock being transmitted to a poorly-earthed person. The current naturally follows the path of better conductivity. This fact of electricity was to be the basis of a much discussed remark by the inventor of the fixed system of lightning protection. It was possible, he said, safely to lean against a lightning conductor (of high capacity) fastened to the mast of a ship, without getting a shock, even when lightning struck.

The electrical current from lightning will route itself over external surfaces, especially if wet, rather than through the resistance of the whole body. Rubber-soled shoes or wellington boots are no protection against a stroke from lightning travelling to earth through the victim.

3 The Side Flash

Lightning can leap after striking a large metal structure unless that structure is adequately earthed. Hence metal fences, metal roofs, aerials or pipes can be responsible for conveying an electrical discharge of the lightning strike sideways to other nearby objects or living things. Alternatively, if lightning strikes the ground then an induction current may be caused and again a side flash may result. When people are crowded together and one is struck by lightning, part of the current may leap across any small air gaps from one person's body to another. Multiple casualties can result. This is why it is sound advice for people to avoid huddling together if caught out in the open during a thunderstorm. The side flash has been responsible for injuries to small groups in a field or players on a football pitch. Sailors on wooden warships, climbing in the rigging or standing together in any available shelter from the weather, frequently became multiple casualties in this way. As has been explained, people tend to shelter under large trees and especially under a solitary tree if caught in a sudden downpour of rain. In addition to the contact type of strike discussed above, injuries and death can occur after a side flash of the electrical current to the head level of the victim, sheltering under the branch of a tree.

The breakdown strength[4] for air or a pole of green wood occurs at about 30,000 volts across perhaps a mere 1 inch (2½ cm) gap. Once the channel is established, an electrical arc may be initiated and then maintained by a current of only 20 volts.

4 Step Voltage

A step voltage injury is caused by the potential difference during a flash of lightning between the two points earthed at the feet. If the resistance of the surface stood upon is naturally high, for example on a mountain track or on the wooden deck of a ship, then step voltage difference may result in a shock when lightning strikes nearby. People out in the open occasionally have been killed or injured from a step voltage effect. In electrical terms it is the potential difference leading to a current surge between two points each separately in contact with the earth – i.e. the feet. It follows that a person standing with both legs together is safer than one striding out. Four-legged animals with a long distance between fore and hind feet suffer injuries or death in this way.

Secondary Causes (Fig.4a)

There are many other causes of injury arising originally out of the effects of flashes of lightning. Falls from heights, or wounds from falling debris, for example. Climbers and hikers are particularly vulnerable. Importantly for the subject of this book, even more vulnerable were sailors on duty furling sails, attending to the rigging or trying to set up a portable lightning conductor. These men were at risk to the totality of the many effects of a lightning strike onto masts and spars. Their vulnerability would have been increased by the danger from falling debris, by flames from sails or ropes set afire or death or injury after a fall.

Nowadays the chances of being hurt from lightning are much reduced but not altogether eliminated, the change for most people from outdoor jobs such as agriculture or fishing, mainly to indoor occupations in urban centres, being responsible. Having said that, even people living or working in buildings can be affected by lightning storms. Surge currents, in power cables or even in telephone lines leading into a building, may result from nearby strikes of lightning to earth which causes a large rise in earth potential. Even cables buried underground may not be able to leak enough current to earth before a surge is delivered to a building due to a build up of large potential differences. Computers, televisions and telephones have all been implicated in damage and injuries to people using them due to current surges after lightning strikes to nearby feeder cables and lines.

More About Injuries from Lightning

The most common injuries from lightning have been studied in detail and reported by Andrews et al.[3] These are shown in an adapted Table 2.1.

Table 2.1 Relative frequency of various injuries from lightning

Injury	Frequency (%)
Loss of consciousness	72
Amnesia	86
Paralysis of legs	69
External burns – trunk	66
– legs	55
Ruptured ear drums	50
Overall mortality	30

Surprisingly, the heart and cardiovascular system is affected only in 30 per cent of cases but it is significant that this percentage is the same as the overall mortality. When a large current from lightning is conducted through the heart, the victim will invariably be placed in a state of cardiac arrest. Complete absence of a heartbeat may be followed by various types of dysrhythmias of the beat after resuscitation. Victims may continue with or develop irregularities of electrical conductivity within the heart which may require as long as three months to return to a normal rhythm.

The most common event after a strike by lightning is a loss of consciousness. This may last only a few minutes, or hours, but may even linger on for days. A state of suspended animation[9] – 'the only two-way street to heaven' – seems to be possible due to reduced demands of the brain for oxygen following a prolonged cessation of electrical activity due to the lightning. People struck by lightning appear brain dead. They are immobile, have flaccid limbs, fixed dilated pupils, an absent pulse and no respiratory movements. Prolonged resuscitation may result in recovery of consciousness.

Memory loss (amnesia) is usual for events before the person was struck by lightning as well as subsequently.

If a lightning stroke has affected a group of people, resuscitation of the apparently hopelessly dead should be carried out even though there may be other live, injured victims.

Falls after loss of consciousness and the blast effect of lightning may cause haemorrhage into parts of the brain. Even on resuscitation, a cerebrovascular accident (stroke) from other causes may be mimicked or may have also occurred due to the lightning strike.

Occasionally, neurological signs and symptoms of late onset[10] have been reported. These vary from tremors, to paralysis, to progressive disorders affecting nerves supplying the muscle and hence movement. Psychiatric problems have been found to affect victims of lightning strikes. Not only post-traumatic stress disorder (PTSD) but depression and emotional lability are common. So-called kerauno-paralysis has been described and consistently appears in both early and in more modern accounts of sailors who have suffered strikes from lightning. It is a temporary paralysis of movement of the legs with absence of the senses of feeling and of reaction to pain or to temperature. Some observers also strongly suggest that the circulation is impaired due to interference with the small nerve networks around the blood vessels. Recovery follows in 1-24 hours, with or without treatment. Recent research[11] has suggested that much of the selective damage to muscles from a stroke of lightning may occur due to the formation of free radicals.

Of extreme concern to any victim is damage to their eyes and this has been a consistent feature in accounts of sailors struck by lightning. Pain in the eye, pain on exposure to light, complete or partial loss of vision and more permanent visual field defects, along with, later, the development of cataracts have all been reported.

More commonly, in 50 per cent of cases, deafness occurs. This loss of hearing is often accompanied by a loss of balance and a facial paralysis. Some of the damage seems to occur as a result of blast-type injuries similar to those induced by explosions.

Burns occur in most victims.[12] The time during which the current[13] passes through the body is short and this makes it usual for burns from lightning, although spectacular to look at, also to be superficial. This should be compared and contrasted with accidents involving man-made electricity. In the latter case, although the current is lower than that of lightning, the time during which it may be in contact with or passing through the body almost always causes deep burns.

Burns from lightning have several other characteristics. There may be entry and exit burn marks as though from a gunshot wound. Feathery branching (so-called 'keraunic figures') on the skin surrounded by areas of intense redness due to surface burns are common. Where the skin is in contact with metal, for example from jewellery or buttons, deeper marks and burns may be visible as contact burns.

Sailors Struck by Lightning

In 1968, Taussig wrote that it was remarkable how few attempts were made to resuscitate apparently dead people after a lightning strike.[14] Statistically, within the European land mass, from 55 to 68 per cent of people involved have been found to have survived a lightning incident.[15] For those at sea, but only in larger vessels, a doctor with very limited facilities for resuscitation would have been available in British naval vessels. For those in smaller ships, there was only an under-trained 'loblolly boy' or 'sickbay man', with even less to assist him. For the sailors, lightning was just one more risk of their seagoing life likely to result in a work-associated injury or their death. Throughout history,[16] there have been many reports of strikes by lightning affecting the crew of a ship. The men most exposed were the agile young 'top men' or any other sailors working on the masts, yards and rigging of sailing ships. Nowadays it is accepted that it is the height an object rises above its surroundings that governs the risk of being struck in a thunderstorm. Where the height was that of a mast of a tall sailing ship, then it was also the height above the surface of the sea whereby an upward leader pathway for lightning may have been initiated.

Sailors[17] were in no different circumstances to others out in the open except that they tended to be wet through. As we have seen, the human body acts as a homogeneous gel, with a resistance to passage of the current of about 700 ohms. The skin has no insulating effect, the oilskins, rubber of boots or canvas of shoes, or bare feet of the sailors provided no protection against the effects of the lightning stroke. If the current from a strike happened to be low, then it flowed through their body. Increases in the current led to a surface discharge and burns occurred at places where there were metal objects on their clothes such as buttons or fastenings. Other places where burns might occur were the skin next to objects carried for use by sailors in their work, such as spikes or knives. An even higher current led to a flash over to anything nearby or through the air, in preference to passage through the sailor's body.

The effects of lightning on a sailor were very variable. For many, death was likely, due to a fall from the rigging. In sailing ships many men were needed to attend to the sails high up on the masts and yards. In the event of a lightning strike these were the men injured and often killed by the fall alone.

If the lightning strike had also affected those on deck then their appearance of dilated pupils, no visible breathing, no pulse but perhaps with burns or marks on the skin was presumptive of their death. These apparently dead men were likely to be left lying there while those seen to have been blinded or fallen or be bleeding were attended to. Many of the casualties knocked down on deck did recover later although some of the apparently dead may have been fortunate not to have been buried at sea. As mentioned above, an induced state of suspended animation would have been responsible for an apparent absence of the normal signs of life. The normal pace of the metabolism of the cells of the body was reduced by the short burst of intense current and hence the degenerative processes were also delayed.

Still others lying on the deck might have been seen to be breathing but to be unable to move their limbs or to speak or to hear for up to 24 hours (keraunoparalysis). Imagine the problem on board a sailing ship for those left able to help. The many stunned and shocked men lying in all attitudes on the deck. The man (or men) actually first struck by the lightning was probably dead, as indeed was likely if he had fallen from the rigging. After the colossal shock and flash of the lightning, it must have been difficult for those left untouched to see to the safety of the ship while trying to attend the unconscious – normally agile top men with limb muscles flabby and unusable. Many would look dead with their skin white or even blue in colour due to spasm of the blood vessels. A return to normal was possible within 48 hours and would show the paralysis was temporary and had affected the nerves of the limbs, rather than those of the spine or of the brain.

Partial or even complete blindness or deafness or both was

common. Sight tended to return but the disturbances of vision were more likely to remain. Deafness, if due to bursting of the eardrums, was usually permanent. Loss of parts of the hair occurred (alopecia) or the hair colour was turned white. The loss or injury to many men by one stroke of lightning must at times have contributed to placing the ship in danger. Certainly lightning at times caused so many injuries that the ship could not have been properly manned.

The late effects[18-22] on the body after a strike by lightning were known about by seagoing men.[16] These effects were feared but codified only as non-lightning related statistics by medical staff. In at least one case[23] a flogging for a miscreant was reduced and his rum ration withdrawn from him, as he had been mentally affected by lightning and could not hold his liquor. So it was accepted, by the majority of enlightened captains and ship's doctors, that lightning could affect judgement, memory and behaviour, even months after the original incident. Some modern medical authors have denied that long-term neurological illnesses could be attributable to a lightning strike. Whilst it was stressed that long-term complications and permanent disability were rare, most agreed that it could happen and many sailors were recorded as sick and hurt as a result of lightning.

Those previously affected by problems with their sight[24] later tended to develop cataracts, dry eyes and scarred eyelids. By contrast, those with burns, even apparently deep burns, soon healed and were left with little or no scar. Those who had suffered only burns, and a brief period of loss of consciousness, recovered fully.

Experienced sailors recounted that their hair standing on end warned them it was time to get down from the rigging due to the risk of a strike by lightning from an impending electrical storm. A firsthand account of an injury from lightning was recorded by the brother of the First Lord of the Admiralty. When Admiral G. Elliot[25] was a young trainee officer, he was helping to reef the sails for a squall when a flash of lightning passed between him and the next man. The pair of them were only ten yards from the top of the mast. All nearby were blinded for a while but he and the man next to him were blinded over some days. Elliot did not remember how he got down on deck. He was placed in a darkened cockpit with his eyes bandaged. His eyesight gradually came back but remained weak for months. He admitted he felt very nervous too. Elliot recorded that he was never a year in the Mediterranean without the ship being struck by lightning, but without 'serious' injury to the crew. He once saw every pig in a pen killed by a strike but not the sheep, due, he asserted, to their greasy wool.

Veicht[26] described 60 sailors simultaneously being hurt by lightning in about 1763: 'Some of these were stunned and fell down to the deck and they had a sort of paralysis which continued for some time but from which they later recovered'. The paralysis was mainly in their arms and may therefore have been a small amount of side flash from the mast to the group of men. Another possibility is that they were temporarily paralysed by step voltage.

Paradoxically, the use of electricity to restore the apparently dead was first recorded in 1809.[27] Resuscitation of the drowned was attempted by repeated shocks from galvanic batteries. The shocks were given to the mouth, the armpits and the feet whilst the subject was partially submerged in water. Their lungs were inflated, their bodies were massaged, buckets of water were thrown over them and tight clothing was stripped off them. If such methods of resuscitation (the kiss of life) of the apparently drowned were made by these means on land, it is highly likely that apart from the electric shocks, the rest of the techniques used were likely to have been applied to victims of lightning strikes in the British Navy.

William Snow Harris

A central collection of incidents when naval ships or men had been struck by lightning was not available at the Admiralty. The inventor of the permanent system for marine lightning conductors, William Snow Harris, had commenced his records in the 1820s. It seems possible that he got the idea of a proper index and record from reading a list of lightning incidents published by one of his most public and unfriendly opponents, Lt. William Pringle Green. Later, Harris collated reports from ships' logs and published the results in pamphlets and in scientific books. Before Harris made sure of a proper set of records dedicated to damage from lightning, the only other good reports were in private letters or in diaries of naval officers. Any formal accounts of strikes by lightning to HM Ships were sparse entries and remained hidden in masters' logs, which were not read unless a ship had been wrecked or stranded. For example, Harris published an account he had been sent of a lightning strike to HMS *Southampton*.[28] Lightning had struck the mizzen mast on 6 November 1832. It knocked down several men and filled the hold with smoke. A man called Simpson had his trousers set on fire and was paralysed and severely scorched, but eventually recovered. Murray[29] described the same incident and added that a 24 lb cannon ball was found to be fused by the lightning strike. The latter also gave the first account of a lightning strike to a paddle steamer, the *Dart*, whilst the ship was off Whitstable.

Harris' collection of statistics was undeniable as the overwhelming majority of his incidents had been obtained by him after he had searched the daily logs of many HM Ships at the end of a commission. In addition he made retrospective searches amongst piles of dusty ships' logs at Somerset House and also possibly in the damp attics at the Admiralty. If he found a case where a ship had been struck by lightning, he copied it carefully with exact detail. To complement it, he obtained further confirmation as to the effects of strokes of lightning on HM Ships in letters from officers who had served on those ships, his correspondence file being a tribute to the esteem in which his plan for protection from lightning was held by officers of the Navy. Accounts of the costs of any damage or of complete protection from lightning damage if the ship bore his fixed system began to fill his files. Sketches were made and illustrations sponsored. Harris amassed so much detail that his list became the best and most carefully recorded research in the world as to damage from lightning to ships. It remains an unassailable and factual record. Unassailable even by a cabal of those bent on manipulating the evidence.

The statistics Harris collected as to loss of life were appalling. They were published in full as a report printed for the House of Commons in 1854.[30] In 280 cases of ships exposed to lightning during thunderstorms, 97 men were known to have been killed. In addition, two complete ships' companies had disappeared after their ships had blown up, in all probably another 800 or more men.

Those injured amounted to at least 325 known and separately described cases with 'many, several, all on deck, and crew disabled', accounting for an unknown number but certainly very many more. In some cases, 20-40 men at a time were struck down by lightning. It was a horrific catalogue. A catastrophe. It displayed the deadly results of the mismanagement of a simple procurement matter by the Admiralty. It demonstrated a poverty of oversight of many departmental tasks by their senior civil servant, John Barrow. The bigoted views of Barrow the second (permanent secretary) were to delay adoption of the fixed lightning conductor for HM Ships for 22 years.

Partial Protection of the French Fleet from Lightning

The French fleet enjoyed the scheme invented by their American ally, Benjamin Franklin. This scheme was not altered for many years despite an obvious lack of capacity of the iron used as a conductor for the lightning. A simple conductor was made for the *Etoile* galley of 700 tons and this was fixed onto the vessel's mast on November 18th 1784. This was the first semi-fixed conductor ever placed on a French ship. Le Roy's lightning conductor system took the form of a point fixed to the mainmast with a metallic conductor attached to it a small distance below. The length of the conductor was a chain of copper rings continued on to part of the rigging itself employed to steady the main topmast. From there, thick metal plates formed the connection between the copper rings and the sea. This original type of lightning conductor often broke in use and had to be modified.

M Le Roy, in an article subsequently translated for the Naval Chronicle,[31] confirmed that some French ships had borne semi-fixed forms of lightning conductors for many years. Their American allies had a similar type of portable lightning conductor to those in use in a few ships of the British Navy.

M Le Roy of Paris, a friend of Franklin's, was one of the original members of a committee of the French Academie des Sciences. The Academie later published in 1808 the first of a long series of written pamphlets, *Instructions sur les Paratonnerres*. Le Roy had a brother who was interested in ships; together they visited French military installations and dockyards, one then became a member of the subcommittee of the Committee of Fortifications of France. As a result of their joint efforts they were able to make recommendations for lightning rods and conductors to be placed on French military installations and on warships.[32]

The Franklin lightning conductor system was demonstrated by a piece from the French battleship *L'Orient*. The *L'Orient* was blown up by Nelson's squadron at the Battle of the Nile in 1798. One of the British sailors recovered as a trophy the main topgallant masthead from the little that remained of that huge ship after the massive explosion. The masthead contained a fixed lightning rod. This was presented to Admiral Nelson. Nelson then had the end of it twisted into a convenient shape and used it as the hat-stand at his new house at Merton Place near London. (Fig. 6a).

Lightning Strikes on British Warships[33]

On 21 November 1790, HMS *Elephant*, whilst lying in Portsmouth Harbour was struck by lightning; the iron hoops round the mast were broken into a thousand pieces and the topmast was fractured. HMS *Russell* was struck by lightning on 1 October 1795. The 1st Lt. was killed standing near the wardroom table, the 2nd Lt., standing close to him, was knocked out but recovered. The ship was very nearly blown onto the French coast.

On Friday 23 February 1796, HMS *Terrible* was struck by lightning which shivered the fore topmast and the foremast, broke into the galley and singed two men's shorts. There were many other accounts, but found only in letters and in personal diaries, of the effects of a lightning discharge upon a warship. For example, the Duke of Clarence was 1st Lt., and later became Captain of HMS *Pegasus* in 1787. Whilst in Cork harbour his ship was struck by lightning on the mainmast. Some iron hoops were broken off but the lightning then passed off through the copper fastenings on the ship's bottom. This confirmed that the Duke of Clarence, later to become Lord High Admiral before his enthronement as William III, had personal experience and knowledge of the effects of lightning strikes on ships. The Duke was to support William Snow Harris' proposal for a trial of his system of lightning conductors in 1829.[34] Unfortunately for the success of the project, the reputation of the Lord High Admiral was later lost due to a series of poor decisions on naval affairs made without consultation. That then tended to taint, in his successor's mind, all other subjects which he had supported. Possibly that experience of unilateralism by the Duke was also to push later Admiralty Boards into opposition to the idea of fixed lightning conductors.

British ships[35] continued to be struck by lightning and most were unprotected as they had failed to put up their portable chain conductor. In addition they were disadvantaged by the conductor's low current-carrying capacity, when tested by a lightning strike. Some ships failed to use them at all. On at least one occasion this led to a catastrophe. HMS *Resistance* of 44 guns was anchored in the Straits of Banca on 23 July 1798 when the ship blew up after being struck by lightning. Only one man returned to England from the original 12 survivors of the explosion.

HMS *Sultan* was struck by lightning[33] when off Port Mahon in 1808. Nine men were killed and three wounded. The catalogue of British ships struck by lightning continued.

The *Naval Chronicle*[36] was influential in forming naval opinion, in educating and in conveying news and information. Its section on naval improvements had an article in 1811 which proposed hollow iron masts for ships. A model had been constructed. The cylinders of iron for the mast had to be thick enough to bear the weight of the same height and diameter as a wooden mast. It was pointed out that an iron mast would weigh only 12 tons and cost at the most £45 per ton. This would give a total of £540 for the entire mast. Its strength would be nearly 50 per cent greater than that of a wooden mast.

By contrast, a wooden mast weighed about 23 tons for a first-rate ship and cost in 1811 nearly £1,200. The patent iron mast had been made so as to strike nearly as low as the deck in order to ease the ship in a heavy sea. It was noted by the author that ships furnished with iron masts would not be exposed to the risk of receiving damage from lightning. The master, who is not named, suggested using an iron bolt from the bottom of the mast led through the keelson and the keel, and said that this would provide electrical continuity to the water so that lightning would not do any damage. The inventor also proposed that yards and bowsprits be made of wrought iron and that chain shrouds and stays of iron be used for the masts. He even daringly proposed that the whole hull be made of wrought iron. These suggestions forecasted what would eventually happen but were too far ahead of their time. The very first iron vessel in the Royal Navy did not appear until 31 years later.

Meanwhile, HM Ships continued to be struck by lightning and men and materiel lost at great expense to the nation. For example, ordinary seaman Stokes on board HMS *Ocean* in October 1813, recorded that 'the heavens were black with clouds and (another) dreadful storm burst over their heads and not a ship in the fleet was free of damage from lightning.'[37] His ship suffered most with the mainmast shattered and with the iron hoops that held the segments of wood together being melted like lead by the lightning. Not a man was killed in his ship on that occasion although it was very common for men to be killed during thunderstorms[38].

In the preface to his book on shipwrecks,[39] the author, a Canon Gilly, recorded that what motivated him to write it was that he was crossing the Bay of Biscay when the ship was struck by lightning and set on fire. Fortunately the fire was speedily put out and he survived. His collection of cases of lightning strikes included the information that flashes of lightning could be helpful, as the crew of HMS *Nautilus* found when a storm came up during darkness. A flash showed them that they were near land but despite avoiding action they struck rocks and were wrecked. Similarly the crew of the schooner HMS *Magpie* in 1826 found themselves in water after being wrecked and their only help was flashes of lightning which illuminated their plight.

Fire was an ever present hazard at sea in wooden ships and HMS *Amphion*, *Sceptre*, *Queen Charlotte*, *Hindostan* and *Ajax* were each lost by fire. It was not recorded whether lightning was implicated.

Of course, storms without thunder and lightning were the main reason for losses of masts and of ships. In a strong westerly wind the whole of the French Atlantic coast became a lee shore to the blockading fleet. Admiral Parker[40] noted that in the year 1809, 18 of the British fleet were wrecked and six foundered. In 1810 another 12 were wrecked and two foundered, each in the cause of blockading the French naval ports. An extraordinary sum of £3,675,750 was voted for this extreme 'wear and tear' to the fleet. But the unnecessary cost of damage from lightning was fully preventable by Harris' invention after 1830. Even before that time it could have been much reduced by use of the small-capacity portable chain conductors.

3

A Proposal for the Protection of Ships from Lightning Strikes

In 1820, William Snow Harris, an apothecary of Plymouth, began his experiments in the new science of electricity. His particular interest was to test the conducting capacities of various metals and their more common alloys. He found that, apart from gold, copper as pure as he could make it, was the least expensive but by far the best conductor of electricity. A coarsely refined form of this widely available metal was already used in his Devonport Yard as sheathing for the wooden hulls of ships.

After some practical tests Harris developed a permanent lightning rod and conductor system of copper metal whose innate flexibility, he suggested, allowed his invention to be used even in the extreme conditions found at sea. He also published his ideas and subsequent practical demonstrations in articles[1] in the *Philosophical Magazine*. He reminded the reader that the advantages of lightning conductors on land were well known but the effects of lightning at sea had been neglected, even though wooden sailing ships were highly inflammable and carried gunpowder and other stores. He went on to describe the only form of lightning conductor available to HM Ships as a portable one, which was triced up just before or even during a thunderstorm. The upper terminal of the conductor was a metal rod at the masthead. The length of it consisted of a chain or long links of wire, with the lower end of the chain passed over the ship's side and into the water. Its inconvenience during all but calm seas was acknowledged (Fig.4a).

Early in 1821, Harris had written to the Commissioners of the Navy Board.[2] This was a subsidiary board of the Admiralty but one which exhibited remarkable control over all aspects of the Royal Shipyards, technical work on ships, their building and supplies.

The local Royal Yard was at Devonport, where interested and practically minded Navy Board officials were invited to see the invention tested at a large practical demonstration. Harris knew he must make extensive preparations. He could not expect to be able to wait for a lightning strike to a building or ship protected by his invention. Instead he had to generate a large electrical current, show that the current could be transmitted along the copper conductor safely, and on reaching the terminal, demonstrate its continued presence by allowing it to set off a small controlled explosion. Friends amongst the officers and the Dockyard staff helped him set up the apparatus. He was allowed access to the moored flagship HMS *Caledonia*, to a small cutter and to a saluting gun but had to pay for any materials that were to be consumed.

Monday 16 September 1822, the day of the experimental demonstration, finally dawned. The audience of important persons on board *Caledonia* included Sir A. Cochrane, Commissioner Shield representing the Navy Board, several captains of the Navy and the Principal Officers of Devonport Yard.

HMS *Caledonia* was a first rate ship of the line of 120 guns. As a flagship moored at Plymouth and in full commission, she was often used as a convenient test bed for inventors to try out any new materials, methods or developments potentially of service to the Navy.

The primary purpose of the demonstration was to prove the ability of Harris' copper lightning conductor to transmit a large current of electricity with perfect safety. There was no better way could he have devised of demonstrating its very low resistance to the passage of electricity than by covering part of it with a small amount of gunpowder. If the gunpowder was set alight, the current must have jumped from the copper to the powder and the new lightning conductor system would have been a failure.

The electrical generating apparatus was mounted on the tiller head of *Caledonia*, and a wire from one terminal of it led to the masthead of the *Louisa* cutter which was moored astern. The cutter's temporary mast had been fitted with a lightning rod and conductor of copper tape let into the wood and leading down the mast in accordance with Snow Harris' design.

Some gunpowder was placed in contact with the copper at the bottom of the mast. If there was any sparking due to the large electrical current, then it would be visible as a small flare of fire. At the termination of the bolt for the mast at the keel of the *Louisa* a chain was attached, connected to an insulated pointed wire. This wire then led to a small boat, another 80 feet astern of the cutter. The small boat held a fully primed brass howitzer. The copper wire from the keel of the *Louisa* was placed in contact with the touch hole of the howitzer. The negative side of the electrical system led direct from the electrical generating machine on the *Caledonia* to the other side of the touch hole of the howitzer in the rowing boat. Everything was now ready.

Harris first created a large store of frictional (electrostatic) electricity using his electrical generator and a storage battery of Leyden jars. The terminals of the copper wires were then connected to the battery. The current passed first to the lightning rod on the masthead and then down the mast of the *Louisa*. For those who had feared the introduction of an electric current anywhere near to the loose gunpowder, this part of the experiment was to be an amazing but silent and invisible demonstration in itself. Even the powder grains scattered on the surface of the conductor were not touched off, as the electrical current preferred the efficient path of low resistance afforded by the copper. The electricity then passed out through the keel of the cutter, via the short length of chain and along the length of the wire to the small rowing boat. The very small air gap at the priming hole of the howitzer to the other side of the circuit allowed a spark of electricity to jump to the priming powder and to set off the charge in the small brass gun.

To show that sea water alone would be an efficient conductor for electricity and hence discharge a flash of lightning from a ship, Harris broke the continuous circuit by disconnecting the wire and chain from beneath the mast of the *Louisa*. Again he was able to discharge the brass howitzer, this time by means of leaving the end of the wire from the mast of the *Louisa* just trailing in the water near her keel.

The third part of the experiment was to show that Harris' copper tape on the mast of the *Louisa* was still able to conduct a current even though it had its continuity interrupted by a small saw cut. The apparatus passed this test too. The trials had been carried out in gusty, unfavourable weather and everybody present was fully convinced, and even more so by the weather conditions, of the decided advantages of Mr Harris' fixed form of lightning conductor for a ship's mast. The day had indeed been a great and well thought out demonstration. It had been a spectacular show as well as a scientifically credible experiment and was guaranteed to create favourable publicity. It was a spectacular which Harris would later repeat in front of the Admiralty Board itself, using ships moored on the Thames below Somerset House.

For the moment, the initial demonstration was so convincing that Sir T. Byam Martin, the Comptroller of the Navy Board, requested Harris to superintend the fitting of the lightning conductors of copper tape to the masts of two ships, HMS *Minden*, of 74 guns and HMS *Java*, a frigate.

Harris had difficulty in obtaining sufficiently pure copper to serve as conductors for electricity. Most of the mines from nearby Cornwall had their copper ore smelted in South Wales but this produced copper at a low standard of purity, used for sheathing for ships' hulls. His own research, carried out using his own furnace at his laboratory at George Street, Plymouth, had found that any impurities in the copper diminished its electrical conducting power by about half. The least impure copper had to be sourced and further refined, and hence cost more to buy. The manufacture of the new size of copper strip for the lightning conductor also had to be arranged. The Navy centralised any metalwork, and Portsmouth rather than Devonport Yard had to undertake the specialised work. The problem was to obtain copper as a strip or tape long enough to serve as a continuous lightning conductor for the 150ft height (or more) of a mainmast of a ship of the line. At the time it was easier to obtain commercial lengths of stout copper pipe about 1/16in thick and 1½-2in diameter. Whilst the copper pipe was proposed by Harris as satisfactory for the protection of buildings, he did not even try to use the pipes on ships at sea, as he knew from experiments that the constant flexing of masts in the wind would always threaten to break a long length of the soft, malleable, refined metal.

He eventually managed to overcome the problem of threat of breakage after repeated movements by substituting for copper tape or tube short plates of the metal which could overlap and slide over each other. The plates were inlaid into a special groove in the ship's mast using copper nails. Each plate was not less than 3½in wide and about 1/8in thickness. The invention used the overlap of the copper plates to maintain a sliding electrical connection even during the repeated bending and twisting movements of masts and spars when at sea. As Harris later acknowledged, his idea was similar to that first proposed but never developed by Henley[3] in 1774. In this way, a permanent fixed and effective lightning conductor was first brought to the notice of the Navy. It only remained for the Navy Board to advise their superior Board at the Admiralty of their findings; perhaps a large trial of the new apparatus under seagoing conditions could then be arranged. If successful, then the invention might be adopted for HM Ships and the inventor rewarded by a grateful nation for the Navy's permanent protection from damage by strikes of lightning. Unfortunately, these were but golden thoughts and optimistic dreams, for it was to be another two decades before the order was given to adopt the fixed form of protection from lightning for HM Ships.

Those two decades would try the patience of the inventor and of his supporters. The beliefs and prejudices of the detractors[4] would almost swamp Harris' scientific objectivity. The results of the practical trials of the invention would then be lost by maladministration. Harris' invention, which could have helped to preserve ships and men from lightning, would become a political shuttlecock. The issues would become submerged by spite and later by political chicanery, and by the arrogance of a sophist in the Civil Service.

At the suggestion of the cautious Comptroller of the Navy Board, Sir Byam Martin, Harris had brought his invention to the notice of The Royal Society in London.[5] Their minutes recorded that the Council met on 12 June to appoint a Committee. Harris had written from his then home and part-time dispensary in George Street and proposed that since the Navy Board had been kind enough to refer the matter of his plan for permanently fixed lightning conductors for HM Ships to their judgement, he would be pleased if he could make his position clear. He noted that the chain conductors in common use for ships were a nuisance, often broke and tended to be sent aloft too late, and that the transmission of electrical discharges was dependent upon the extent of the conducting surface and not upon the solidity of the conductor. He described his conductor system as now developed as a double layer of copper plates 4in wide, overlapping one another and screwed into a prepared groove of the mast. The lower mast would have on it about 9,600sq in of copper, the topmast 5,160sq in, and on the topgallant and royal pole about 2,000sq in each in a continuous line of copper nearly 1/8in thick from a pointed lightning rod to metallic fastenings in the hull. He enclosed a printed letter.

A Specialist Committee of The Royal Society sat on 26 June 1823 to consider his proposition. The President was in the chair, a Mr Combe, and a Captain Cater, and Drs Wollaston and Young were the other members. Probably Harris showed them his demonstration model of the conduction of an electrical current down a ship's mast. The Committee reported as follows:

> Resolve: that this committee do approve Mr. Harris' proposition of applying continuous conductors to ships but they are of opinion that a solid rod would be preferable to a thin plate of equal substance as less liable to oxidation or injury and they are likewise of opinion that if the conductor terminates in the keel it should be of copper united to a thicker plate than the usual covering of the ship.[6]

This was high praise indeed and it enhanced Harris' local scientific reputation to one known nationally. From that time on, he became the acknowledged expert on lightning protection for ships. Despite this endorsement, Harris' scheme was again to be attacked. He had already been accused of plagiarism by his near neighbour in Plymouth, a Lt. William Pringle Green. There may have been some shallow justification, but the criticisms as put were wild and lacked objectivity. Did Harris know of William Henley's accounts after 1771 of a similar system for lightning protection for ships?[7,8] Certainly as judged by his book, *On Thunderstorms*, published by Parker, London in 1843, Harris was familiar with the work of many of the early electricians. He quoted extensively from the works of Franklin and must have had access to libraries at The Royal Society and at Plymouth, containing copies of the main publications of science as the volumes of *Philosophical Transactions*. On balance, Harris must have read Henley's suggestion of a system of lightning conductors suitable for ships.

At least once, Harris referred to Henley's articles and apparently acknowledged the source of his own development of the ideas during his lectures. Henley's suggestion was not taken up by himself or by others at the time it was published, probably due to the difficulties of obtaining pure enough copper from the available techniques for smelting copper ore. Moreover, long strips of very pure copper or of copper wire would not have been available. Harris' later ingenuity was in overcoming the problem of a long length of the soft refined copper metal easily broken at sea, by means of using short overlapping plates of metal. Later, when copper manufacture was improved, a continuous thick copper tape became the acknowledged form of the lightning conductor. Harris continued to flirt with the idea of tubular conductors for those who did not wish to consider the expense of fixing a copper strip into a groove of the mast. Indeed, he suggested copper tubes might suffice for merchant ships (perhaps he had experience regarding the parsimony of the owners of such ships; he certainly was to have long experience of them at Plymouth in his capacity as quarantine officer for the port).

Further instances[9] of danger and of damage to ships were being brought to Harris' notice and old records searched. In July 1811, HMS *Kent* had been shattered by lightning and had several men killed on her masts. On another occasion in Port Mahon 15 men had been killed or severely injured. As Harris later pointed out, during a lightning strike the electric current may divide and thereby strike many men working in the rigging. On 14 September 1824, HMS *Phaeton* was hit by lightning and her new foremast set on fire. The list,[10] as persistently researched by Harris, went on and on. HM Ships continued to suffer damage, injuries and deaths from lightning but no one person or Board or Committee seemed to wish to consider the matter. What possible reasons could there have been for neglect of such a subject? Very probably the delay in the adoption of the solution to transmission of lightning safely to the sea was the residuum of a remarkable and widespread prejudice and also of religious hostility. Many, including the clergy, could not eliminate the fear that lightning conductors actually attracted a strike to a building or ship. Strangely, so also did many ordinary people, perhaps from feelings of guilt and disloyalty to the Crown, for George III had made clear his opposition to the pointed terminals.

Another delay in the adoption of Harris' plan was due to a large number of competitors as inventors and natural philosophers. Many publicised their ideas very well but omitted to mention that they had no objective or experimental basis for their assertions. One such man, already mentioned, was a rather sad figure but representative of the large number of previous sea service, then unemployed, naval officers on half pay. Lieutenant William Pringle Green, RN, had some good ideas, was well versed in his profession and above all other things was desperate to resume his career as an officer on an HM Ship.

Denied this, Green appeared to work out his frustration by

becoming one of the fiercest and most tenacious of Harris' critics. A near neighbour and living at George Street in Stonehouse, Devonport, his campaign was obsessive, overtly personal and hostile and was conducted simultaneously in the local press as well as via lengthy letters to the Boards, first at the Navy Office and then to the Admiralty.[11] It was to his shame that his campaign against Harris can only be described as vicious. By wrapping up his view as one which would save the fleet from Harris' proposals, he tried to conceal his real agenda. That was character assassination due to arrogance and his jealous nature.

Promoted lieutenant in 1806, Green had been present at Trafalgar as a master's mate on the *Conqueror*. He had written an account of the battle in which he had criticised the cowardly conduct of some of those present but without naming them. Unsurprisingly his naval career came to an abrupt end, not to be resumed after the end of the Napoleonic War in 1815. Like 83 per cent of officers of his rank he was placed ashore on half pay for many years.[12] He was fortunate to become an 'agent afloat' for the Transport Service in 1826 after 11 years on half pay. He continued afloat on packet service until his own command of the *Frolic* in 1829 but was paid off in 1832. He was again on half pay from 1832 to 1842 before joining *Victory*, the guard ship at Portsmouth under Captain Henderson. He was superseded after less than one year when aged 58 and was not again employed.[13]

In the 1820s, Green devoted much energy to finding employment, for he had eight (eventually ten) children and a wife to support. The youngest son he was to name Gilbert Elliott, presumably as a tribute to Lord Minto who was to grant Lt. Green an interview on at least two occasions in the 1830s. A most active writer of letters, Green demanded a lieutenant's posting from the Admiralty many times a year.[14] Every possible vacancy he applied for, but he was not successful.[15] What success he formerly had during the Napoleonic War was not only due to his own efforts but to the intercession of the Duke of Sussex, who was a powerful Whig patron willing to support him. Green did have a flair for new ideas and for inventions of practical use in sailing ships. He had published a manual for training men for active service which became used throughout the Navy.[16] He had been 1st Lt. of *Eurydice* in 1808 and then had a command, the *Resolute*, of 14 guns between 1812 and 1815. He had a wider understanding of nautical science than many of his peer group and suggested improvements in the steering, the running rigging and the staying of masts as well as for the fids of masts. In 1822 when aged 37 he had suggested[17] the use of iron masts and iron rigging.

Lt. Green was, however, unable to recognise that every invention arises out of small incremental developments by others, and also that most inventions are at least thought of by others, as well as by the men who actually patent them or claim ownership. For any and every improvement for use in ships that was made, Green claimed he had thought of it first. Some of his improvements he asserted had been tried for a time but fell into disuse at the end of a commission. His letters[18] to the Admiralty or to the Navy Board were often claims for a reward for his ideas, but he lacked supporting evidence from his seniors and his pleas remained on file without any action taken. Harris' lightning conductor, he wrote to the Admiralty, was 'an everyday experiment of surgeon's apprentices' and he could improve it.

Green published[19,20] several other monographs and pamphlets, the expense of which must have been considerable. To add to his expenditure, his house was wrecked in the hurricane that struck Plymouth in 1823. Green's letter to the Admiralty[21] had asked for their help which they could not give. In 1833 he had published a solemn portrait of himself in uniform (Fig.5b.), as a frontispiece for his book.[19] In the book he gave his views on many subjects, mostly about phenomena of nature. As if in competition with his neighbour, William Snow Harris, the irrepressible but sciolist Lt. Green then published another book,[20] Precautions To Avoid Accidents By Lightning in 1837. He continued to assert that ships were preserved from the effects of lightning by wet ropes and by men's wet clothes!

In one sense, he was correct to believe that wet ropes or clothes conducted an electric current better than dry ones. He could not know that the human frame, containing as it does so much water, behaves like a conducting gel when exposed to a large current such as that from lightning. His main problem was that he did not understand the qualities of and the differences between conducting and non-conducting substances. Green described metal objects including parts of the pumps and the spindles on masts as attracting the lightning to a ship. To complete his misunderstanding and to assist his readers to fall into the same state, he raised the old chestnut debate of pointed lightning rods also actually attracting lightning. In mitigation it should be remembered that originally Franklin too had thought that lightning could be attracted.

Green's proposed remedy was to substitute balls for points.

Amongst his efforts to publicise his pronounced views had been a very large illustrated memorial[22] probably first prepared in 1832 to illustrate his earlier book,[19] *Fragments etc*. Some time after 1840 he had sent it to Queen Victoria and Prince Albert. On this immense roll of paper he had drawn and coloured in illustrations of some of the ships he knew had been struck by lightning. This interesting and weighty relic of muddled ideas can still be seen by special arrangement with the National Maritime Museum Library. Green reduced the importance of the problem to his readers by revealing, without disclosing his source, that not more than five or six ships each year were struck by lightning. Despite this statement, which did not mention whether it was a parochial figure for HM Ships or worldwide for all ships, he ended by admitting that a lightning strike on HMS *Despatch* had injured 12 men before dissipating itself to sea via the chain cable. Possibly due to a lack of formal training in the art of debate, Green's attacks on Harris from their beginning were short on science and rich in prejudice. They were good material for the local newspaper, the *Plymouth Dock and Chronicle* as well as for the *Telegraph*. The collection of letters and papers was published by Green in 1824.[4] An example of his approach was to ask why the metalwork of the masts did not allow the lightning to enter them and destroy the mast. The vane spindles, about which he appeared to have an obsession, were screwed 6-8in into the truck of the mast. If, he wrote, as was inevitable, the spindle was to be struck by lightning, then the mast would be splintered. The hoops of iron that helped bind made-masts together and any other metal such as the chains that held the lower yards, were similarly attractive to the lightning. A man was killed on *Salvador* while climbing the rigging. HMS *Perseverance* was in Bengal Bay with both (chain) conductors up when lightning struck and split the foremast and killed one man. A reprint from the *Plymouth Telegraph*[23] recorded that a natural philosopher called Singer had first proposed fixed lightning conductors but they were connected at the junctions of the masts by a spiral wire and Lt. Green found that idea of no practical use.

In 1802, HMS *Cleopatra* was struck off Vera Cruz and the (chain) conductor was successful on the mizzen mast but the lightning darted down the rigging as well. HMS *Kent* in the Mediterranean was struck and three men were killed and the topgallant mast splintered. A brig was struck off Isle of Wight in December 1823; four men were knocked unconscious and one was killed as a result. Green went on to record that 20 ships without conductors up had been struck without injury from the lightning. He wrote that he was concerned as to 'side flashes' (lateral explosions) from strikes by lightning. He preferred chain conductors to be led outside the hull to the sea, but wet ropes would suffice as conductors. In any case, he opined, Harris' plan would cost £500 per ship and most importantly, he wrote, the bilge water in the hold would imperil the lives of the seamen if lightning were brought into the ship by Harris' system. Paradoxically, he then stated that he first had the idea of placement of conductors around a hull. His comments were inconsistent as to his position and without scientific validity. They were clearly based upon his experiences but were muddled and did little but expose his prejudices. Green then very fairly but without quite knowing why or apparently understanding their meaning, put Harris' points of refutation in full in his published collection of items about lightning. He also recorded correctly that Harris declined to comment further without Green's production of experimental evidence.

It was of interest that Lt. Green did not mention the terrible damage, fire, loss of life and injuries to 16 men which had occurred due to a lightning strike in 1802 to his former ship, *Topaze*. He had left the ship just one year before that incident, to join a frigate. It would have been unlikely if not impossible for him within the circles of the professional Navy not to have known about his former ship being struck by lightning. Another example of possibly retrospective knowledge could have been HMS *Decade*, struck by lightning around 1802-3.[24] Green was to become her senior lieutenant in 1807.[25]

Harris, meanwhile, gave many talks and demonstrations about his own special interest in atmospheric electricity. One such event was more formal and was a lecture with question time at the Plymouth Institution. Due to his constant interruptions, the audience of 130 people had to shout down the heckling from Lt. Green. The latter was to say ever afterwards that he did not get a chance to speak. He failed to mention that he was not the person invited to take the floor and had not waited until question time to speak.

At first, the information contained in Green's letters was taken seriously by the Admiralty.[26] One letter from him alerted the Admiralty that HMS *Java* by 1823:

'had strips of copper nailed to her masts passing over and touching iron hoops and other metal; If [sic] these conductors be so efficient as to carry the electric fluid down clear of the hoops and all metal attached to, or touching them, as it is asserted and supported in argument, if I had no other to adduce, bears me out in assuring your Lordships, that the electric fluid which may strike copper spindles, placed in each of the mastheads by screwing into them passing down six or eight inches into the solid wood, will not be led out of its course, down the bottom of the spindle, by the ring passing around it for that purpose; to this ring the small chain conductor is attached'.

In other words, he stated that in his view, because the copper spindle at the masthead was the greater mass of metal than the small lightning rod, lightning would pass down it into the mast and cause damage.

The Navy Board, as it was used to doing and was entitled to do, had initiated the experiment and invited Harris to demonstrate his invention in practice. The Admiralty, on being informed about it by Green, had their suspicions about the Navy Board triggered. Once again the latter had exceeded its remit and usurped Admiralty business, even potentially endangering a ship. The reaction was a kneejerk one, and the Admiralty ordered the copper strips be removed. There was no record available which showed that *Java* had a trial copper strip put on her mast, although Harris later agreed it had been done. Possibly it was a temporary expedient or a development of his original idea. Harris' original letter to the Navy Board of 1821[27] had suggested a ½in copper wire flush with the mast and attached below to a copper keel bolt, terminating at its upper end above the vane spindle.

Sometime during 1822, Harris must have been forced to improve his prototype wire conductor in favour of the copper strip.[28] There was, as has been explained, a technical difficulty in manufacturing long bands of highly refined copper. Harris also tried tubular-shaped conductors and was to return to this shape for HMS *Warrior*, many years later.

In further letters to the Navy Board,[29] Harris set out his new idea of using overlapping copper plates. This method was to answer the very reasonable objection of a lack of flexibility of a continuous tape, rod or tube. He had already responded to The Royal Society's suggestion of another but more minor improvement.

Green's letter of 5 December 1822 to the Admiralty[30] had also complained of the vast expense of Harris' plan. That was an allegation which Harris was forced to dispute until he had proved the opposite. Many years later he was able to show that all other systems proposed for lightning conductors were *more* expensive than his system because his system alone could be recycled.

Green had let the Admiralty know that his model ship, the *Resolute* of 1812, had his plan for a lightning conductor demonstrated on it but he could not afford to travel to London to show it to them and in any case he was convalescing. Green's 'plan' for a suitable lightning conductor was a modification of the ring ordinarily attached to the vane spindle and thereafter a copper chain leading into the sea on the leeward side. It was in fact a minor variation only. Green's vendetta against Harris then resumed when he published more of his odd views and misapprehensions. His lists of ships struck and damaged, despite chain-type conductors, was finally shown in public to be faulty when he gave evidence to an Admiralty Committee in 1839. The Committee found he did not know as a witness exactly what had happened in a series of incidents of lightning strikes to ships. Additionally, he did not have relevant knowledge about electricity. His criticisms of Harris' work were, it was concluded, unfounded and dubious.

It was to be 20 years after the initial publication of a series of insults from Green in the letter columns of the Plymouth newspapers before Harris finally lost patience with him. Harris wrote in 1840 that he did not wish to notice Lt. Green's ridiculous queries any further.[31] Before he carried out this promise, he despatched to oblivion each of the partially true and the plainly untrue statements made by Green over many years. Green should have felt chastened but his arrogance was exceeded only by his self-belief. Most men in his position would have offered to apologise after his evidence as to lightning strikes had been found to be grotesquely flawed at the Admiralty hearing in 1839. Others, but not Green, would have been silenced.

The long campaign by Green had continued to exert some effect on the non-scientifically educated members of the Admiralty throughout those years. The barrage of letters from him had suggested that any metal would attract lightning. How should the Admiralty have dealt with Green's view that metal vane spindles would invite destruction of the masts?

An initial and inevitable result[32] came on 5 August 1823. A letter from Barrow, the Permanent Secretary at the Admiralty, was sent to the Commissioners of the Navy Board. It ended:

> "I have received their Lordships command to acquaint you that on mature consideration of the subject, they do not think it expedient to introduce the proposed arrangement in His Majesty's Ships".

The Admiralty Board that had made this decision consisted of Lord Melville, his Private Secretary G. Baillie Hamilton, Sir W. Johnstone Hope (naval), Sir J. Osborn, Sir G. Cockburn (naval), Hon. Sir G. Hotham (naval) and Sir G. Clerk. Much later, Admiral Sir George Cockburn was to correct this decision and reinstate Harris' permanent conductors on trial.

Admiral Sir Byam Martin,[33] the Comptroller of the Navy Board, commented (on an unknown date but after 1835) in his diary that lightning could safely be dissipated away:

> on the principle so forcibly pointed out by Mr John [sic] Snow Harris of Plymouth. It is extraordinary that the Admiralty still resist the introduction of Mr Harris' fixed lightning conductors – although its efficacy has been demonstrated to the satisfaction of the Royal Society, it is rejected, as I verily believe, because Sir John Barrow, the most obstinate man living, has presumed to set his face against it. This comes of permitting subordinates in office to acquire a sort of sway and habit of dictation which belongs not to their station. Mr Barrow has, in his time, greatly and mischievously misled the First Lords of the Admiralty; no public servant has done more harm for so little good.

Admiral Martin must have felt slighted; despite his careful preparation and promotion of Harris' sound ideas for lightning protection, the plan had been rejected by the Admiralty. For him to publish, albeit after Barrow's death in 1848, such a criticism of the Permanent Secretary of the Admiralty seems to have been because there was more to go on than the merest hint as to the truth. Indeed, as will be seen, this exposure of Barrow's sophistry was deserved.

The list of ships struck by lightning and damaged whilst at sea continued. In the case of HM Ships, despite the fact that few were at sea in peacetime in comparison with times of war. Occasionally, a warship would experience atmospheric electricity but without lightning. On 15 August 1825, HMS *Blossom*[34] was 120 miles south of Rio de Janeiro. St Elmo's fire was noticed at the weather vane of the main topsail yardarm and was seen at the weather side of the fore and main topsail yardarms and at each of the three topgallant mastheads. It remained visible for 15 minutes and then the lower examples disappeared before the upper ones. It is not known whether the ship had any form of a temporary lightning conductor triced up, but probably it had not.

In 1827, the New York packet boat[35] was twice struck by lightning. On the first occasion she had no conductor up and much damage was done. By the time the second strike happened, soon after the first, the crew fortunately had time to put up an iron rod with a stayed chain and this metallic mass carried away sufficient of the lightning to avoid further damage. It is interesting to note that this American ship was carrying the portable iron lightning conductor of poor quality of the exact type recommended by Franklin 50 years previously. According to Anderson[36], Snow Harris had views on whether a lightning conductor should terminate in a ball or a point. In 1827, Harris maintained that a recipient area, for example a building or a mast, even a foot in diameter, could be considered as a point when compared with the extent of 1,000 acres of charged thundercloud. Anderson quoted him as saying he had not the courage to act on this opinion and invariably adopted the point in his own constructions.

Convoy protection was a continuing duty for the Navy. Merchant ships in South American waters were at risk from enemies, known and unknown, due to the long continuing political instability in those developing countries. *Thetis* was prevented from duty with the convoys off South America due to lightning damage, as was *Heron*. Robert Fitzroy,[37] later Captain of HMS *Beagle*, recorded the incidents on 8 and 9 April 1828 from HMS *Thetis* whilst at Rio de Janeiro: 'Our fore topmast and foremast were shivered last night by lightning – very fortunately no men were hurt, as they were all below at the time. This accident will detain us here for some weeks, etc'. A further letter on 23 April followed:

> She cannot sail from hence in less than a month because we are getting a new foremast made on shore. The old one was shivered by lighting [*sic*] in an extraordinary way. Part of [it] looked

like an immense bundle of Laths. No men were hurt all being below at the time. The noise was like all the guns in the fore part of the Ship going off together. The mast did not fall, but had it happened at sea, it must have tumbled over the side of the Ship. We had no conductor up and it was raining hard at the time.

Captain Parker[38] in 1828 accepted with sangfroid that lightning could, and sometimes would, do damage. On 2 March, his ship HMS *Warspite* was at anchor off Napoli de Romania. He had just managed to land his passengers including Capo d'Istria, the President of Greece and six secretaries and servants. The ship was 'struck by lightning on the mainmast but without much damage'. Later that year, on Friday 6 June, it was struck again when off Navarino: 'A heavy storm of thunder and lightning: the electric fluid struck the mainmast, but happily passed harmless along the [chain] conductor.' This information as to the partial protection of his ship from lightning was not widely known even though Parker supported the Whigs when ashore. Nor was Parker's experience of the partial efficacy of the portable conductor on *Warspite* later used by the Whig cabal formed of Minto, the First Lord at the Admiralty, Symonds, the unpopular choice as Surveyor to the Navy and John Edye, his assistant. Harris, too, was to miss this important piece of information in his extensive researches.[39] In fact the Whigs were to make stubborn attempts during 1839-41 and thereafter to adopt for general use in HM Ships an almost identical version of the lightning conductor pilfered from its original inventor and developer, William Snow Harris.

Interest in the phenomenon of lightning continued amongst many scientists. Michael Faraday,[40] the reclusive but brilliant genius of experimental methods in science, had made The Royal Institution in London his chosen place for exchange of scientific knowledge. Benjamin Smith, an American, visited Faraday there. On learning of Smith's imminent return voyage across the Atlantic in March 1829, Faraday advised him concerning the earthing of kites carrying lightning conductors as Smith intended to fly them experimentally from the ship. There is no doubt that Faraday knew and approved of Harris' work and of the robust strength of his experimental evidence. At the time, Faraday was about to be asked to give official advice to the Admiralty about lightning. Even so, it was surprising that Faraday actively encouraged Smith when he also must have at least suspected that the packet ship only carried a thin chain conductor. It was also surprising that the captain of the New York packet[41] even contemplated allowing Smith to set up the experiment after the packet had been struck twice by lightning in 1827.

In 1827, the Duke of Clarence had taken office at the Admiralty. His tenure was to last for nearly a year as the First Lord High Admiral since Prince George in 1709. He was advised by a cabinet led by Admiral Cockburn, three MPs and by Barrow in his capacity as Second Secretary. The Tory government was headed by Canning and, after his early death, by Wellington. The Duke of Clarence was said to have been always kindly disposed to numerous petitions he received, including the concept of the permanent system of lightning conductors put forward by Harris. The Duke was familiar with the types of lightning conductor and he had experience of lightning when captain of the *Pegasus*. He was shown the elements of the new system by Harris at a demonstration lecture at the Plymouth Athenaeum in 1827, when visiting Plymouth to inspect the ships and the Yard and was accompanied by Barrow. It is not known whether Barrow was also present at Harris' lecture but it is certain that he knew about it and its purpose.

Harris' idea for a fixed and permanent system for lightning protection had begun to gain momentum, and after 1827 momentum with royal support. Admiral Brooking[42] wrote to the Duke of Clarence and alluded to objections to the old type of chain conductor for HM Ships. He also mentioned the problems of the proposed form (Harris') with its connections throughout the hull to the keel. He suggested a trial of the two types of conductor, chain and Harris' fixed type. He also went on to suggest a trial of his own plan for a new version of a rudder.

Eventually, a trial of the lightning conductor proposed by Harris was planned to commence by 1830 in ten ships. Before it could be set up, other energetic publicists and those with projects were also busy sending in their plans. A Mr Denyer[43] wrote that the iron conductor or iron chain was seldom made use of at sea. Therefore he suggested that a non-conductor or cylinder could be placed on top of every mast. Clothing of naval personnel should be free of metal buttons and the ships' guns insulated with, for example, glass. He received a reply to the effect, 'Their Lordships will give him no further trouble'.

Sir Byam Martin,[44] the Comptroller of the Navy Board, explained in a letter to the Duke that whilst at Plymouth he had seen Harris' experiments with fixed lightning conductors for ships. He re-explained the plan and its flexibility, whether the upper masts were in place or struck below. He referred to a private letter from Dr Wollaston in which Wollaston, a scientific adviser to the Admiralty, conveyed general approbation of Harris' proposals. The subject, Martin wrote, 'reduces itself to whether any conductor whatever is good and if so as Mr Harris' embraces so many conveniences let us introduce [it] into the Navy in preference to those now in use'.

Barrow, in his sanitised autobiography,[45] mentioned that the time up to the reforms of 1832 was 'a period of inactivity beset with projectors of all descriptions'. According to Barrow, 'projectors' were:

> a class of persons who are never satisfied, if each of their individual projects be so practically put to the test, however obvious it may be to a disinterested person capable of giving a second opinion, that the invention, as it is called, is bad in principal [sic] and worthless in design. To avoid the enormous expense that would be incurred by submitting these projects to the test of experiment, the inventors were now given to understand that facilities would be afforded in dockyards for preparing and trying their crotchets, but only at their expense, and that a limited time would be allowed, when they must be removed at their own cost; which had the good effect of reducing the number of useless projects. The dry rot doctors, with their numerous nostrums were the most pertinacious of all, and their various projects to expel the disease innumerable.

It was this agreement of 'trying their crotchets, but only at their expense' that Barrow was to use against the continuation of Harris' plan for lightning protection even in the face of its obvious success.

To adjust the balance it must also be recorded that there was immense pressure upon those at the Navy and Admiralty Boards to listen to pleading inventors, to arrange trials and to discuss any reward. Some idea of the pressures can be gleaned from Admiral Sir George Cockburn's records.[46] Lord Melville had resumed as First Lord in 1828 and Sir George became the senior naval lord. This was indeed an onerous job for Cockburn[47] who later was to complain of 'the fag of the Admiralty'. However, as senior naval member, it did give him a chance to use his own judgement as to the innovations put before him.

For example, Cockburn recorded[48] that he asked a Mr Morgan to attend the Admiralty to inspect a model of his invention. To a Mr R. Hindmarsh of Shadwell he wrote on 24 September 1829:

> and with response to pecuniary remuneration from the Public for the ingenuity of the continuation of your capstan I am sure the Treasury would not listen to it for an instant. The Admiralty have done all they can for you in allowing you to fit two of your capstans in two of His Majesty's Ships where any person may inspect them, and if they are deemed to have (as you suppose) a decided superiority over all others, you will soon have remuneration (as is the case with other valuable inventions), but I can neither force them (f)or the Public or into the Navy for you, their own merits must effect it.

Cockburn, when senior Naval Lord, was receptive of scientific ideas and was himself a Fellow of The Royal Society. According to Anderson,[49] Cockburn first met Harris at The Royal Society. Cockburn became a supporter and his patron as he was impressed with Harris' energy and his elegant plans for lightning protection for HM Ships.

A sine curve would, then, best describe subsequent events, the incline being the agreement to trial the conductors at sea; the apogee being their acceptance by the professional seamen after experience of them; and the decline immediately following being the neglect of those results. Further rises and falls in fortune for Harris were exactly to parallel Cockburn's appointments and reappointments as senior Naval Lord. Cockburn's ultimate success in achieving the universal adoption of the fixed conductors by the Navy and the recognition of the services of his protégé, was to progress only in step with the intermittent election of short-lived Tory-led administrations.

Harris had been asked to attend at the Admiralty on 11 November 1829 and was interviewed regarding his fixed lightning conductors for HM Ships. Cockburn, as we have seen, felt well disposed towards the invention. He knew that the Comptroller of the Navy Board, his co-MP Admiral Martin, also felt strongly that the plan ought to be tried out. He would have remembered that The Royal Society had approved the electrical system proposed by Harris and that calculations for the capacity of the copper conductors had shown they would be adequate to discharge a current of lightning. Now he had to persuade his Board. This took time but his efforts were assisted by Harris' timely publications. One particularly important one, published in 1830, was a pamphlet on the utility of fixing lightning conductors in ships.[50] Twenty-three pages long, the pamphlet gave an authenticated list of seven ships which had been struck by lightning and damaged. The author had learnt from Lt. Green's idea of making a list but unlike him had avoided hearsay evidence. Would the Admiralty reconsider their views as to the new idea for lightning protection? Would they accept the new science which could dare to lead the huge electrical current from lightning down the mast and through the ship?

The Admiralty and, before its abolition, the Navy Board, did have a good record of trying out new ideas. Melville, and later Minto, as First Lords of the Admiralty, did much to encourage the development and use of the new technology of steam power for the navy. As Hore[51] points out, Britain led the world in the technology of steam and in propulsion. The steam vessel *Congo* had been laid down for building at Deptford as long ago as 1815. There were steam vessels in the Solent from that year onwards. The Liverpool to Belfast packet service began to use steamers in 1819. The paddle-wheel steamer *Lightning* ferried George IV to Ireland in 1822. In 1823, Lord Melville ordered Byam Martin at the Navy Board to provide six steamers for naval use. In 1829, Vice Admiral Malcolm wrote from HMS *Asia* and suggested steam ships for the mail route for the Mediterranean station. Melville then continued to support steam for packet services provided the various governments of the day were in agreement. Minto,[52] the First Lord in 1835, himself studied steam engines in 1823 and thus encouraged their development.

However, most merchant and warships continued to rely upon wind power on their sails and sailing ships continued to be especially at risk from lightning in thunderstorm areas. The Admiralty then developed dual-powered steam and sail ships and began to experiment with the use of wire rigging. These developments also delayed the universal use of the fixed system of lightning protection. During these changes and developments, more of HM Ships were rendered unfit for duty after lightning damage. *Melville* and *Gloucester* were forced to remain in port at Malta for repairs in August 1830 after lightning had caused them extensive damage to their mainmasts. Neither ship was reported as having a conductor in use and both 74-gun ships had been on the point of sailing to join the admiral as part of the fleet. The matter was a serious one, for these were two first-rate battleships, now disabled. The Admiralty[53] was advised as to the damage. The entry read:

> WELLESLEY sails today from Spithead calling at Gibraltar if she can do so without attracting too much attention. Off Malta 3 AUG. left harbour on the 31 JUL. now proceeding to Corfu, Santi and Napoli at which latter place he is to meet his colleagues the French and Russian Admirals about the 25th AUG. He should then continue in the Archipelago for two or three months or longer if necessary and Napoli will be his Port of rendezvous. Whilst standing off yesterday, within a few miles of Valetta, waiting for ALLIGATOR from England, she having been seen in the preceding evening, a violent thunderstorm pushed near them towards the Island, GLOUCESTER's mainmast is splintered and almost destroyed and the MELVILLE's mainmast is also damaged.

HMS *Aetna*[54] was then struck and her people injured when at Corfu in 1830. Her copper chain from the mainmast had not been touching the sea.

Admiral Cockburn and his Board must have been hopeful that the new system under trial for protection from lightning would save HM Ships from such huge amounts of damage and the strategic loss of their ability to take up their station or, sometimes, even to remain on station. Cockburn's Order[55] was for a trial of the system for ten ships, liners or frigates, preparing for service, to be fitted with Harris' conductors. The Order had been sent to the Navy Board just seven months before the damage to the two battleships, *Melville* and *Gloucester*, in January 1830 and could have protected them. It was a great loss to the Navy that the original proposal had not been taken up as recommended in 1823.

In the economical way of the Admiralty, Harris' letter of January 1830 to Cockburn[56] had been overwritten on the last page, by Cockburn himself, in giving the Order: 'The Navy Board to fit the masts of any line of battle ship or frigate preparing for service with Mr Harris' lightning conductors, not exceeding ten, when it is to be suspended till reports as to its utility are received.'

4

The Whigs: Reform or Bust

Sir James Graham was first elected an MP in the Whig interests in 1818 at the age of 26. By 1826, he had made his name and secured a seat at Carlisle near his home at Netherby Hall. He began to play a leading part in Whig politics, especially in support of the Reform Act. His views and manner were analysed by his Tory opponents as irritable but clever. Their verdict, which was soon to be proved correct, was that he was a rash and inconsiderate politician. Many thought him stiff and pompous and others believed him to be 'a cold fish'. His fellow Whig, Captain Charles Napier,[1] later MP for Marylebone, thought very little of him: 'cloaking official incapacity under specious arguments, [he] displayed all the dexterity that might be expected from him'. Napier was right, especially if compared to his own bluff, overt, candid manner, for Graham had a politician's endless ability to amalgamate the truth to suit the moment.

Following the King's death in June 1830, Parliament was dissolved. The effect on the expectations of the country of the election of the reform-led Whig administration was profound. Young, thrusting politicians, at least in their own eyes suitable for high office, were ready to take on the worst that the Tory old guard could throw at them. The general election that ensued strengthened Graham's hold on his seat in Cumbria as no opponent stood. Later that year the new Prime Minister, Lord Grey, appointed Graham, a novice to office in government, to the Cabinet-level post of First Lord of the Admiralty, a post he held until 1834. He was instructed by Grey to reduce the expenditure on naval defence forces and their infrastructure. 'Retrenchment' became Graham's catchword, his catechism and finally his political epitaph.

He began his reforms at the Admiralty by conforming with his Whig predecessor (Earl St Vincent) and his current leader's intention of retrenchment of its budget.[2] He signalled an end to dispersed management by abolishing two Commissioners of the Navy Board and two from the Victualling Board, by sacking the Treasurer of the Navy and the Paymaster of Marines. He also made reductions in the pay of some clerical staff in the Yards. In all, this represented an immediate saving of £27,2438 p.a. His most telling, long-lasting and efficient administrative change was to appoint a clerk (Mr W.G. Anderson)[3] under Briggs at the Admiralty in the accounts department, to supervise the spending of the budget and to insist upon double entry bookkeeping for all departments. Nobody of that name was employed at the time in the Admiralty[4] and possibly the biographer made a mistake.

Graham advised the House that since 1798 the Appropriation Act[5] had been extended to include the Navy but that the House had never been fully informed as to naval costs because of virement between departments. This had taken place without either notice to the House or their permission. Indeed, whole projects had been undertaken without the House being made aware of them. As though that broadside were not enough, after 1831, Graham[6] steadily and inexorably put forward reduced demands to the Committee for Supply. Briggs[7] commented that Graham was adroit, skilled in drawing up a minute and clever. He often triumphed over colleagues by asking for a position paper about a subject by the next day but first agreeing its content privately.

Graham's economies[8] whilst First Lord at the Admiralty were legion. Beer allowance for seamen, the bookkeeping and costs of the Victualling Board, the packet service out of Falmouth, salaries, numbers of clerks borne, and meat rations, were each investigated and cut. The demands on the much-reduced peacetime fleet[9] however continued to increase and by the end of 1832, Graham was forced to employ 3,000 more seamen than allowed for by the vote of supply.[10] He persisted with strict economies and with severe retrenchment. By 1834 he was able to show a naval budget saving of £328,330 or about 6.5 per cent less than two years before. Graham had been two years preparing the ground at the Admiralty for his party's forecasted and long-awaited administrative reforms. He managed to avoid becoming a poodle reacting to the facts as supplied by his civil servants, chiefly those Barrow might have wished him to see.[11]

In February 1832, the Navy and Victualling Boards' administrative headquarters at Somerset House was replaced by a new streamlined model which had centralised authority and was directed entirely from the Admiralty at Whitehall. The most important aspect of Graham's administrative reform was that of control over accountancy for each major department and a set of procedures which allowed others to understand how the monies voted by Parliament for the upkeep of the Navy had in fact been spent. Graham's ideas were tested out, by his own candid admission, upon Lord Spencer and his son, a particular friend, Lord Althorpe. The Spencers had seen long service at the Admiralty and were to give sound advice to Graham. In return, he helped Lord Althorpe and even spoke on his behalf in the House.

Barrow, the Permanent Secretary, implied that the new scheme was completely successful: 'the proof of it is that no fault was found'.[12] Despite this unilateral view from him, it was not a convincing one. Pool[13] demonstrated that after the 1832 reforms, each Principal Officer placed his own contracts on a separate system without correspondence with the other departments. There was nothing to replace those day-to-day records from the former Navy Office. Pool also wrote that correspondence to the Admiralty increased and the volume of government business made it impossible to retain anything beyond the bare minimum of permanent records. An overview of Graham's centralising and clean-sweep management changes would nowadays be a matter of passing interest and a common experience for those working in large or multinational firms or institutions. Then, in 1832, it was a massive change principally brought about by historic Whig views, rather than by Graham's ideas *de novo*. The long-held Whig concerns were the prevalence and the risk of corrupt practices found so often amongst contractors dealing with state-funded and bureaucratic institutions. The siren mantras of power by central control and with reduced costs were alluring. Later in the century, centralisation was to become a source of tension between politicians who thought that it was always an improvement as against those who felt responsibility and governance should be locally led.

The abolition of the Navy Board and the Victualling Board in favour of departmentally led management at the Admiralty had other unwanted outcomes. Their demise as institutions was also to lead to the loss of much profound and detailed knowledge vested in the specialist and expert technical staff employed by the two Boards. Within a few years this pool of knowledge had to be replaced and the consequent costs of administration were increased. According to

Murray,[14] responsibility for the Board's acts rested entirely with the First Lord, who supported himself in most cases with the advice of his 'advising' or 'managing' naval Lord. Other members of Board had no specific duties. In practice, they were largely occupied with their political and parliamentary interests, or were often away holding fleet appointments. Thus the Board was a council where opinions might be expressed but the First Lord with the aid of his chosen adviser made the decisions. Later, each Lord was given specific duties and Sir James Graham facilitated this policy: 'It was a period of great scientific developments'.[15] Murray went on to write that it happened that all, except Sir Thomas Hardy, were men of conservative temperament, who viewed revolutions in the character of naval material with suspicion and dislike.

As will become apparent, another and even greater vacuum caused by the reform of senior management was the gradual loss, dispersal and wastage of irreplaceable records, mostly those of the Navy Board. Graham and his senior administrator, Barrow, did nothing to preserve them. Only a little later, during Minto's tenure as First Lord, Graham was to be roundly criticised. The records, Minto felt, were important as to detail, as to the legally agreed contracts with suppliers, as to the fall-back positions when supply did not match demand and as to the derivation of a sensibly sized strategic reserve of materiel.

Almost immediately following the reforms, the ponderous and uncertain pathway for correspondence between the Royal Dockyards and the Admiralty Board began to show signs of strain. The points of tensions being, at the Yards, their willingess to respond in full to instructions they did not like and at the Admiralty, the creation of a follow-up system for a subject yet to be decided, as well as archiving of material relevant to it. An example of the latter, and integral to Graham's methods of checking up on technical information, was an instruction which went out in August 1833:[16] 'Names of Ships fitted with Harris' lightning conductors to be sent to Hon. George Elliot CBE Secretary to First Lord.' Was this request the first attempt to collect evidence of the trials of the fixed system for protection against lightning? The Hon. George Elliott was the second son of the First Earl of Minto and brother to Gilbert, who was to become the First Lord in 1835. Sir James Graham had employed George[17] as his confidential secretary since 1830. As was the practice for his political master, he was obtaining hard information in addition to that given to him by civil servants. The reply from Portsmouth Yard signed by F. Maitland was that *'Asia, Spartiate, Sapphire, Acteon* had been so fitted'. The letter had not mentioned that *Spartiate* had her lower masts taken out and replaced a year later in 1833, presumably without reaffixing the conductors. The information from Plymouth Yard was that six ships had been fitted: *St Vincent, Druid, Blanche, Revenge, Forte* and *Beagle.* This reply[18] had omitted *Dryad*. Other ships experimentally fitted for the former Navy Board, *Minden* and *Java*, as well as *Caledonia*, also were missed out. Nil returns had been sent by the other Yards. Presumably these returns from the Yards were then archived.

At about the same time as Hon. G. Elliott was obtaining the data for Graham, Captain William Symonds, the newly appointed Surveyor to the Navy was required, for the use of the Board, to report which ships had been fitted with Harris' conductor. In keeping with the Whig obsession of retrenchment, the expense of fitting it in HMS *Forte* and in other ships was also to be reported. The Surveyor may have opted to store the letters and reports at Somerset House but later he appeared to have mislaid the data or was selective with the information he did disclose. Alternatively, it is very possible that the relevant files were lost or disposed of as not required. A considerable excuse for their non-production was that the Navy Office, once a model of precision as to its records, had by then been abolished. Its functions and those of the Surveyor's, Victualling and Storekeepers departments were now centrally controlled by the Admiralty but apparently with no dedicated clerks, space or databases for their records at either site. Certainly there had been no provision to retain an archive to store the former records of the Navy Board. This omission was to lead to many difficulties and much criticism. Admiral Sir Thomas Byam Martin,[19] for example, had been asked in 1841 to assist in tracking down some papers and precedent upon the supply and use of timber. In fact, the request was a loaded pistol at his head. This was because the assumption by opposing political forces was that some timber belonging to the crown, but contracted for by the Navy Board, had been illegally used to repair York Minster. Martin replied to Barrow, the Permanent Secretary, that as far as he knew the release of the timber was authorised. He then went on to write that the official records would bear him out. But 'Whether those records may have been swallowed up in the reform tempest which extinguished the Navy Office – I know not.'

Correspondence to and from the Admiralty had increased and the volume of government business made it impossible to retain anything beyond the bare minimum of permanent records. If tenders[20] were for items such as chain cable or for items where the safety of men or the ship was involved, the Admiralty would usually consult as to the reliability of the supplier. For most items the lowest price was always chosen in an unimaginative way, although contracts for hemp and canvas were made annually.

It is not certain how choices were made as to which documents were archived and which were not. Presumably, storage for current tenders and contracts took precedence over other papers for the available space. The business heaped upon a failing administration at the Admiralty increased as did the strategic demands upon the fleet. The requirements for yet more ships had served to put pressure upon Graham to keep a suitably sized fleet in being. The Whigs, even Graham and Minto, were in broad agreement with the Tories as to the 'two power standard'[21] for the size of the battle fleet. That notwithstanding, their professed and by then very public view of an exemplary reduction of the infrastructure of the Navy was to be carried out at all costs.

For example, the number of clerks and private secretaries available for administrative duties and borne on the Admiralty establishment altered very little, even after its consumption of the Navy Board in 1832. An altruistic act of Graham's upon taking up office at the Admiralty was to order a ten per cent drop in his own salary. On his retirement from that office, he would not accept the customary pension of £2,000 p.a. Graham argued that as he had private means, the Exchequer could find better uses for the salary saved. By contrast Auckland, Graham's successor, albeit with a very short term of office, had to renegotiate with the Treasury for reinstallation of the most generous pension rights before he would agree to take up the post as First Lord.

Byam Martin, a Tory and the superannuated Controller of the abolished Navy Board, was very critical of Graham and of his administration. Martin felt that the supposed savings made by Graham were only achieved by running down strategically important stores at the Royal Dockyards. This, he felt, was storing up trouble for the future and was a short-term specious gain for public appeasement.

The new First Lord at the Admiralty in the Whig administration of

September 1835 was Gilbert Elliot-Murray-Kynynmound, the second Earl of Minto. Educated for the customary time at Edinburgh University but without taking a degree, he had been trained for the diplomatic service. Previously a Whig MP for Ashburton, then Roxburgh, in 1814, on the death of his father, he took his seat in the House of Lords. He became Privy Councillor and Ambassador to Berlin 1832-4. He served for six years to 1841 at the Admiralty and was to become a loyal supporter of the new-style Surveyor to the Navy. His administration was, even at the time, much criticised as being overtly political and inefficient, with much evidence of unsuitable patronage and nepotism. 'The Scots Greys' being one description of his adherents and those of Grey the then Prime Minister, albeit with a ring of truth. He was to become father-in-law to Lord John Russell, later Prime Minister. Minto drafted several speeches in defence of his patronage when he was First Lord:[22]

> My Brother Admiral Elliot and Sir Chas. Adam, my brother in law, exchanged seats on the Board when posted to Foreign Commands. Of 12 Elliots [variously spelt] on the Navy list, only five were relatives and two had the benefit of patronage. My Son is Captain. Chas. Elliot, nephew Capt. George Eliot. Capt. Chas. Bethune, a second cousin, is on HMS *Conway*.

This draft was one of several in his papers.

In 1837, Byam Martin dined with Lord Minto at the Admiralty and sat next to him at dinner.[23] Minto said the system of the civil branch of the service for the Yards and for shipbuilders was impracticable in war and only superficially useful in peace. He said that Sir Charles Adam, the senior naval Lord, stated that he could not undertake the business of Somerset House (formerly the Naval Board) as well as that of the Admiralty. The consequence was that the civil branch was left to irresponsible persons and that sums of up to £50,000 were paid out without due supervision. Why did Minto not alter it, Martin asked? Parliament would agree and it would not cost more than £20,000 per year. Minto replied that if he were sure of staying on for five years in office he would do it but it was not worthwhile at that time. Martin said that the breaking out of a war would be a worse time to remodel the civil branch. Martin also correctly forecast the dismay and trouble that would ensue due to the reduction in numbers of shipwrights and the abolition of the Naval School of

Architecture. The trainees had paid for their education, had given an undertaking to serve in the Yards for a number of years after qualification and had been promised a position for life. After Graham's reforms, each of these promises had been broken, including that of a fast track for promotion for an educated elite. This elite group became disaffected and was to supply years of invective against those who supplanted their right to master shipwright or even higher status, as they saw it. They went on to provide destructive criticism of all ships built by the Whig-appointed Surveyor, Captain William Symonds, and to indulge themselves in their jealousy of him and of his deputy, Edye.

Graham had continued the previous administration's failure to cherish those who worked in the Royal Yards. He pruned 300 more shipwrights and blacksmiths, many of which found work in French and even Russian shipyards, to the loss of their own country's future war efforts. According to Dillon[24] (a Tory), Graham's retrenchments also downsized the Marine Artillery and abolished the Coast Guard (as well as the Naval School of Architecture and the Transport Board) and he halved the number of royal yachts. These reductions proved to be false economies over time. Graham attempted later to redeem his reputation by emphasising that he had carried these cuts out in times of peace and of budget deficits. This explanation did not convince his political opponents or posterity.

It was not until 1852, under Lord Aberdeen, that Graham's full circle of fate came around. He again became First Lord at the Admiralty but this time when conflict and the Crimean war were a reality. He was faced with a barrage of criticism[25] as to his overzealous economising and retrenchment decisions during his previous occupancy of the post. He was accused of being responsible for the fact that instead of a central pool of knowledge, archives and expertise, he had created only a diaspora. Many of the criticisms of his centralising reforms of 1832 at the Admiralty, admittedly so easy for his critics to make with hindsight, proved to be deserved when the path to a war footing was real. A blame culture was apparent even then.

Sir James Graham's first tenure of the post of First Lord at the Admiralty had ended in 1834. He was succeeded by George Eden, the Earl of Auckland, in early June. During the next seven months there were three changes of memberships of the Whig Boards and Auckland was out of office for four months and replaced by one short-lived Tory Board. The effect of constant change at the Admiralty was to destabilise policy whereas previously, subject-specific briefings might have led to a decision.

Thus, our inventor of the permanent form of lightning protection, William Snow Harris, must have been as discouraged by loss of continuity as were all other inventors and 'projectors'. Dry rot in the wood of ships, for example, was a huge problem and cost. It had continued to be studied and yet no cure or preventive found. Over 300 compositions and materials as cures for dry rot had been sent to the Admiralty which, in turn, felt besieged. Since a cure might be a chemical one, all new ideas of scientific merit were classified and held as records by the clerk in charge. Both in the *Admiralty Digest* and the synoptical table, the single universal number, '59.9 Dry Rot etc.' was to become a dustbin category for all projects and ideas and the pejorative term 'Dry Rot Doctors' became current at the Admiralty. This disdain for technology and for science, as well as the lack of will to sieve out the useful idea from the cranky, was to prove a cancer of the credibility of the permanent administrators from which they found it impossible to recover.

Activity in connection with existing trials of new inventions or ideas was stultified during the short-lived Tory administration of 1834–5. One ship, a crack frigate HMS *Acteon*,[26] had been included in the original trials of the fixed lightning conductor in 1832. Since that date no results of the trials had been published and the masts and yards bearing the copper conductors were stripped out on orders before the ship's recommissioning at Portsmouth Yard and then replaced.[27] The destruction of the costly and capacious conductor was a seemingly effortless act of stupidity by the Yard foremen or possibly an act inspired by jealousy of its evident success.

The inventor had meanwhile checked his calculations and the famous academic, Whewell of Cambridge,[28] had agreed the formula for estimating the electrical capacity of a conductor. Those who later challenged Harris on this aspect were shown to be incorrect. The Admiralty had been lulled into a belief that by some mysterious process the trial of the conductors commenced as far back as 1830–2, would be assessed and a report compiled. When another ship's captain requested the fixed and permanent conductors for the 50-gun HMS *Dublin* fitting out at Plymouth, his request was not allowed 'until those already fitted have been fully tried'.[29]

The tiresome Lt. William Pringle Green published his remarkably self-congratulatory pamphlet *Fragments etc.* in 1833[30] and this may accidentally have helped to bring to the notice of the Admiralty Board once again the matter of lightning conductors. Green described the old-style chain conductor used for the bulk of the fleet. It was attached to a copper spindle screwed to the head of the mast, just where a fixed lightning conductor would be placed. Fig. 2 of the publication showed Harris' plan for a fixed conductor on the mizzen of *Java*, passed through the powder magazine. The conductor was in contact with iron chains and slings of yards, with iron hoops and with copper at the shrieve holes. Fig. 3 gave Singer's plan of 1812. This was a spiral conductor on top of an iron mast leading to bolts on the keel.

In April 1835, Lord Auckland returned as First Lord and finally had five months of office uninterrupted by elections and Board changes. Each new Board had to be reconstituted by patent and it was not until this had been done that legally it existed to administer. Auckland, as Graham had been, was new to naval affairs. He was a kind and considerate man who realised his lack of experience and wrote at once to Admiral Hardy, the senior naval Lord, saying that he 'shall have to ask them [the Board] to bear with me in the novelty of my situation – advice of which I shall in the outset stand greatly in need'.[31] Auckland took a detailed interest in all naval matters and was an excellent administrator who might have achieved much. It was the Admiralty's loss that after a few months of office he was appointed Viceroy of India. In his private handover to his successor, Lord Minto, he wrote: 'The First Lord of the Admiralty, promotion occupies a very large portion of his time, he is overwhelmed with applications from every part of the country, backed by the strongest influences and to a very small proportion of which he can give a satisfactory answer.'[32]

On the state of dockyards in 1835, he wrote that there were 140 ships in the Navy and 350 smaller ships in ordinary. The latter had been examined and condemned as rendered utterly useless by constant exposure: 'It is received opinion that 14 years after a launch the ship will require refit and cost about ¼ of a new build – thus for a liner the cost would be about £20,000.'

Meanwhile, Harris was still attempting to obtain information about the success or otherwise of his lightning conductors as fitted on about 11 HM Ships on trial. Others, too, were becoming interested in the subject due to the publicity generated by Harris. In May 1835, a reply to an enquiry from a Mr Carter[33] to the Admiralty was 'conductors for HM Ships have long been in use'. Perhaps Harris had persuaded a member of the well-known Whig family of Portsmouth to make the enquiry. Certainly several ships carrying his original conductors on trial were employed on sea duties, including *Forte*[34] (Commodore Pell) in 1835 and in 1833 HMS *Blanche*,[35] both on the West Indies station under Admiral George Cockburn's command.

Was Harris exaggerating the risk of lightning to HM Ships? How many losses from weather-related causes were there? Did the Admiralty regard any losses from lightning as unimportant? Of course the risk to a sailing ship at sea was one of being wrecked by adverse winds and tides. The Royal Navy was exceptionally skilled at sea-keeping whatever the weather but even these sea-keeping skills were tested in winter as ships sometimes had to run into Torbay from their blockade positions off the French coast. Admiral Sir Byam Martin recorded in his memoirs that 'there were 524 shipwrecks during 1835 and in 1833 there were 595!'[36] This was an enormous number of wrecks which almost certainly alluded to all merchant ships, including foreign ones. By contrast, in 1835 there were six such losses from the Navy[37] and in 1833 there had been only four. Nevertheless, any loss from a preventable cause, such as protection from lightning, was important for HM Ships on station for their country. Harris therefore had the difficult task of convincing others in peacetime when absolute losses were about 7 per cent of HM Ships in full commission. He did so by exposing in his publications that, although losses of ships were recorded, neither the vast amount of damage to them by weather (lightning in particular) or the list of injuries and deaths were centrally collated at the Admiralty. The opinions of those at the Board he had to convince were dichotomous, the naval professional interests often being subjugated by political expediency. Harris approached each politically appointed First Lord at every change of administration and made sure that his views were personally delivered to them.

Gilbert Elliott, 2nd Earl of Minto, became the First Lord during 1835–41, and succeeded Lord Auckland on 19 September. Minto[38] had some scientific credibility in that he had researched changes in barometric pressure due to height whilst on climbing and walking holidays. He had also been up in a hot air balloon. He was interested in meteorology and used an accurate hygrometer invented by Professor Daniell.[39] His interests may have led him to suppose that his scientific abilities were enough to understand the new science of electricity. He was to show later that he entirely misled himself.

In February 1840, Minto wrote to Admiral Sir Edward Codrington, 'We are all a little nervous about the fire ship combustibles intended for China.'[40] This letter showed that Minto was aware of the extreme risks of a fire in a ship whilst at sea. It also meant that he was likely to have considered the possibility of a strike by lightning setting a ship on fire. Minto did consider, albeit too slowly for the effervescent inventor Lord Dundonald, the mass of new technology received at the Admiralty. Barrow, the Permanent Secretary at the Admiralty, revealed that he thought Lord Minto 'had first rate abilities, competent knowledge of mechanical powers, he was sure to be beset by a host of speculative inventors, not easy to satisfy or get rid of, especially if a Naval Officer of high rank who may fancy themselves'.[41] It would be unfair to describe the Whig-appointed Admiralty Boards of the 1830s and 1840s as so economy-minded that new technology was never considered. Their problem was the reverse: there was *too much* to consider, too many developments, ideas and inventions covering too many fields. The combined experience of the naval Lords was not enough. None of them had a proper staff, either civil or naval, to assist them. The rush of ideas about steam and propulsion was such that, for example, as early as 1836 the Admiralty prepared official circulars and memoranda about ventilation and about circulation of air in steamers.[42] Steamers were there to stay and the Admiralty was to be in the forefront of improving the overheated working conditions for the engine room staff, so as to make the steamer a potential war vessel without equal. Those who thought the Admiralty dragged its feet over technological change should read the many reports and memoranda about the problems. Minto himself studied the various types of Perkins engines and was generally supportive of steam power for the fleet.[43]

Peel, the recent Prime Minister, was himself a sound expert in mathematics and a supporter of scientific progress. He had been trying, before losing office to the Whigs, to obtain a pension from a grateful country for the famous scientist Michael Faraday.[44] The latter had proved altruistic but also shy if not reclusive, to the point of being a slave to his employer, The Royal Institution. At the change of government, the Whigs took office and the papers setting out the many recommendations for Faraday's pension were put aside and only reviewed months later. By December 1835, even the 'ecomaniacal' Whigs under Lord Melbourne felt that they could withstand no longer the lobbying on Faraday's behalf by supporters of both political parties, and granted him a pension for life of £300 p.a. The amount awarded was in keeping with the pronounced parsimony of the Whigs. Faraday was well known for eschewing all politics and it was this stance of being apolitical which allowed a piece of unfinished business from a previous and hated administration to be concluded in his favour. Compare that with what was to happen to Harris, who seemed to be, without any public evidence, a supporter of the Tory Party. Instead of months, he waited years for adequate recognition, although a pension for a similar amount was awarded sooner. To make things more difficult still for Harris, far away in Plymouth, supporters of the two political parties who were part of the social scene in London or those who contributed by artistic endeavours, were more often rewarded from the public purse than were scientists.

Minto was in a position to recognise and to adopt Harris' achievement and to reward him. Yet his stance seemed to be one of obfuscation and denial and later of officially-led theft of Harris' invention. To answer a number of critics, he was to attempt to use statistical analysis to calculate the risk benefit of lightning protection for ships. In his drafts for a speech to defend the Whig position of doing nothing about damage, deaths and injuries from lightning, he used the phrases, 'only a 1 in 5,714 chance of a loss of life or excluding the catastrophe of the *Resistance* [this ship blew up] a 1 in 40,000 chance. There was a 1 in 4,000 chance of injury from lightning'.[45] Minto was comparing deaths and sickness rates overall, which in 1813 were quoted as deaths of 1 in 143 serving seamen and the chance of sickness to them as 1 in 13.3.[46] An appalling statistic, although much improved from an earlier assessment in 1790 where the risk of death was 1 in 42. By 1836, the mortality figures in the Navy were given by one authority as 1 in 72 from all causes.[47] If a measure such as proper protection from lightning could prevent death, then that was a valuable development and a figure that Minto ought to have tried to estimate.

Table 4.1 Deaths and discharges

	1835	1836	1837	1838
Manpower	26,401	30,195	31,289	32,028
Died onboard	334	158	154	243
Died hospital	64	81	82	89
Total died	398 (1.5%)	239 (0.8%)	236 (0.8%)	332 (1.0%)
Means	1.03% cf. mean of 1.4%[48]			
Pensioned as invalided	116	242	191	160

The figures in Table 4.1 were taken from Charles Wood's memorandum book when he was Minto's political secretary. The table shows that deaths and injuries from all causes were low but significant in the Royal Navy, bearing in mind the workforce was a mean of 29,893 men and boys during that period. The figures do not agree with those quoted by Lloyd and Blane,[49] being 0.37 per cent less than theirs. If his political secretary's figures were correct, then Minto's attempt to dissemble them by risk aversion estimates seems even more curious.

Minto himself felt he had been treated with scant respect and less courtesy when he found he could not access papers which had been in use during his former Whig (now Tory) colleague, Sir James Graham's tenure as First Lord.[50] The tone of the correspondence between them about the lost papers from 1832 can only be described as glacial. Minto had complained that 'there were serious difficulties in tracing papers'. Perhaps the loss of the data was also responsible for his statistical difficulties. The lost papers mentioned by Minto were not identified but one subject would have spanned the period and had been extant prior to 1832, in fact since 1820. That subject was that of lightning conductors. Despite later public denials, both Minto and his Whig political aides must have had a great deal of information about them, mainly from Charles Wood, also from Barrow, the Admiralty's administrator and, most tellingly, from members of his own family.

Captain Hon. George Elliot,[51] the second son of the First Lord Minto and brother of Gilbert, Second Earl of Minto, was political secretary to a succession of First Lords including Melville, Graham and Auckland during 1830-4. His administrative experience was minimal and he was not an MP on appointment. He was also Third Naval Lord from 25 April 1835 to 22 July 1837. George Elliott had originally collected information about the lightning conductor trials on behalf of the then First Lords, Melville followed by Sir James Graham. Access to records would have been swift as other members of the Elliott clan had been appointed clerks to the Admiralty: G.J. Elliott, during 1836-7, and A.P. Elliott. for two months' temporary duty in 1841.[52]

Acteon, the ship bearing Lord Minto's own son, as well as his nephew, was one of the original ten or so ships on trial fitted with Harris' conductors. Captain G. Hamond[53] was in command in South American waters. On 3 June he wrote to Lord Minto: 'your note arrived on the *Goldfinch* packet on the 22nd of last month bringing at the same time your son to join the *Acteon*. He was fortunate in doing so for she sailed to Valparaiso'. In his papers, Hamond recorded that on 24th May 1836 'a very fine lad, son of Lord Minto, came out in the packet to join *Acteon*. Mr C. Eliot, Lt Elliot and eight to dinner.'

One of the topics of conversation might well have been how the ship was protected from lightning before their arrival: 'When tremendous rain and lightning all the first part of the night' of 20 March. Before that, according to Captain William Grey,[54] 'whilst in the Mediterranean between the spring of 1831 until September 1834 – the ship was several times exposed to severe thunderstorms but in our case [due to the fixed lightning conductors] not even a rope yarn cut'. Other ships without such good protection from lightning were being damaged and had to be sent for extensive repairs. HMS *Russell*, of 74 guns, a third-rate ship of the line, was at Ferrol in January 1836. Captain C. Key[55] heard a tremendous noise. He saw several sparks of fire on the mast about six feet above the deck; the noise brought every officer and man onto the deck, and a great many sang out, 'the ship is on fire!'. The next morning the only thing they could see was a little black mark on the mast. The carpenters examined the mast but found to be no other damage. In fact, only a 4in piece had been knocked out of it – seemingly insignificant damage. Later the mast was found to be quite ruined and had to be taken out at Plymouth the following August.

The senior naval Lord at the time was Admiral Sir Charles Adam, MP. He served the Admiralty Board for six years, was a loyal Whig and had represented the Admiralty in 1839 at the Committee of Enquiry into Protection Against Lightning. He had said that Harris' fixed system was not secure.[56] Later, he tried to manipulate the evidence[57] about lightning strikes in 1844 on *Scylla* and on *Electra*[58] in 1845, for his father-in-law, Lord Minto. In the former ship, Adam wrote, the lightning discharge had not been completely carried off and thus damage had been caused. In fact, damage to *Scylla* was to a very few small copper nails and butts and was minimal and damage to *Electra* exceedingly slight. The correct situation was later described and printed by Harris and proved beyond doubt by accompanying letters from the captains of the two ships at the time of the lightning strikes.[59] *Acteon* was completely protected during thunderstorms on several occasions between 1831–4 whilst in the Mediterranean. Her captain, William Grey, was most supportive of the permanent system of copper plates on the masts and wrote an encouraging letter to Harris.[60]

Adam had served as a young officer on HMS *Sybille*, a fifth-rate ship which had been captured from the French in 1794. In 1796, two years before he was commissioned lieutenant, he would probably have been told that the ship had suffered a man killed and another hurt due to lightning striking the ship's inadequate French version of the chain-type conductor. His evidence and opinion concerning Harris' permanent conductor was therefore surprising but of course in support of his father-in-law's interests. Thus it appears that the Elliot clan, as well as their wider family by marriage, were ready to be economical with and even suppress the truth, when it suited them to do so for allegedly 'political reasons'.

5

John Barrow: A Flawed Administrator

Throughout the entire period of 22 years before the Admiralty finally adopted William Snow Harris' plan for effective lightning conductors for warships, John Barrow was the Permanent Secretary (sometimes termed the Second Secretary) to the Admiralty Board. It was Barrow's responsibility to service the administration on behalf of the Lords Commissioners, to provide the material to answer any parliamentary questions and to compile the statistics in preparation for the Naval Vote. According to Lloyd's excellent biography of Barrow,[1] John Croker, who preceded Barrow as Second Secretary, had always insisted upon opening every letter received at the Admiralty himself. Barrow was to continue this self-imposed task which gave him unrivalled knowledge of every aspect of Admiralty business. The many changes in the membership of the 24 Admiralty Boards appointed between 1820 and 1850 revealed a lack of experience of administration in both the civil and naval Lords. The Political or First Secretary, of whom there were but nine during that 30-year period, was a particularly important appointment. A gifted young politician marked for higher office was usually chosen, but a tradition of patronage also resulted in at least one appointment of an inexperienced relative of a First Lord.

The First Secretary's importance to the Board was that whilst not a full member of it, he was always the official conduit for communication with Parliament. He was always available at his office in the Admiralty. That availability seems to have resulted in his opinion usually being sought by the civil servants. Since Barrow himself opened all letters,[2] it was usually he who brought the letter to the attention of the First Secretary or to the Duty Naval Lord. Where executive action or a reply was required, then a rapid consultation between the Second and First Secretaries ended with a draft summary written on the turned-up obverse of the left corner of the letter.

Letters were not always marked in this way and some were left unmarked as to file or digest numbers, initials, a draft summary or an action minute. Should the correspondence be ongoing and already allocated a file number and digest of the subject, then it seems that it was more than likely that complete replies would be drafted by Barrow. The draft might then be brought to the First Secretary for his initials or signature if of political interest but was usually sent out signed only by Barrow 'on behalf of the Lords Commissioners'.

Matters of naval interest or of naval technology would have been brought to the attention of the senior naval Lord. Sometimes he delegated a subject to one of the other naval Lords but according to Briggs,[3] the Reader to many of the Boards, due to the pressure of business there were times when discussion of the subject before the whole Board was replaced by dialogues in private rooms.

The difficulty faced both by the permanent staff and by the Board members together with its First Secretary, under successive administrations from 1830 onwards, was that of proper allocation of responsibility for certain matters of business. Decisions were needed, yet useful debates at the Board were becoming fewer. Many decisions were taken by an individual naval or political member in the mistaken belief that he had the sole overall knowledge about the subject. If a decision was taken in isolation then later collective ratification became less certain and overlapping areas of interest between departments would not be found.

The debates in Parliament about naval matters were widely discussed by the press and are considered elsewhere in this book. John Barrow, from his position as Second and Permanent Secretary to the Admiralty, had been foremost in suggesting that much financial and practical economy could be obtained by reductions in the personnel and remit of the Yards. He gave detailed evidence to Parliament and in his autobiography suggested that much of the credit for the subsequent administrative reforms to the Navy and the Yards was due to his evidence. In fact, this was an inflated view of his abilities, characteristic of its author. For example, there had long been disquiet as to the apparent autonomy of action of the Navy Board. Also, their dockyards were well known to be rife with nepotism and corruption. Political chicanery also occurred at every level. This included the naval bases and the Yards. Patronage was a most important credit and was also influential in the handing out of jobs in the Yards. Corruption in the matter of contracts granted by the Navy Board was a large and persistent problem leading to misappropriations of public monies. The Whigs, as far back as 1806, 'were not content with the white washing of the activities of the Board of Revision'.[4] A complete reorganisation was encouraged by Lord St Vincent but wartime conditions meant it was postponed.

One obvious and admitted flaw in an outwardly distinguished career in administration, both pre- and post-Reform, was John Barrow's almost total failure to admit that records and archives were amongst his prime responsibilities. He had not appointed a clerk whose task it should have been to provide a service as a librarian and archivist. The 'Record Office' at the Admiralty up to about 1841 seems to have been what the fighting Navy would term 'a ready use locker', as only very recent documents were filed by the seven attending clerks who occupied but two rooms. Total reliance for recovery of a pack (file) or an individual letter, was placed in the synoptical table originated by Finlaison and later extended. The digest occupied four immense volumes. Two were subject indices with a one- or two-line summary. The other two were indices of names. The whole digest provided a unique and ideal source for reference and retrieval which was much copied by other administrations. Yet although the digest was readily available, there seem to have been severe problems of disclosure of the full versions of previous papers, letters and collections of papers (packs).

Lord Minto complained during his administration as First Lord that many documents and past records were simply not made available to him. Possibly this was due to the limitations imposed by the available space in the two rooms which were by then used only for the recent administrative activities of the entire consolidated department. Those papers originally filed for the Navy Board before 1832 remained at Somerset House and had been inspected but not archived or consolidated by Graham during his tenure as First Lord. Visits by the Naval Lord overseeing the former functions of the Navy Board to the old offices in Somerset House gradually became fewer and it is likely that papers of interest to later administrations were indeed lost.

Charles Wood also admitted that he could not obtain the papers which gave the views of previous Boards.[5] Papers had indeed been lost or more probably thrown away, especially from the former Navy Board files at Somerset House. Barrow acknowledged that he blushed with shame when his son John, a clerk, found unique manuscripts and records of the Navy, decaying and lying abandoned to the damp in an attic at the Admiralty.[6] Some documents had even been purloined by Somerville, a messenger, many years before.[7]

Barrow had been in charge of administration at the Admiralty for 34 years, much of it in peacetime. His salary of £2,000 p.a. as the senior civil servant was equal to the First Lord's. It was clearly Barrow's responsibility to have supervised the keeping of all the records, including the archives, and he failed in this area of his remit. The consequences were that some subjects not to Barrow's liking were neglected. He had been made aware by 1830 that there remained a problem in the safe-keeping of records. Sir Nicholas Nicolas's pamphlet of that year had roundly criticised the absence of action as to archiving following the Commission into Public Records originally set up in 1800.

Yet Barrow must have busied himself amongst those same naval archives that later he was to blush about in front of his son. His researches were to find material for his books, *The Life of Admiral Lord Howe*, published in 1837 and *Life of Admiral Lord Anson* (1838). For his book on HMS *Bounty* (1831), which he edited, Barrow was to deny any new researched material except that given to him by the Heywood family. According to Bonner Smith,[8] Barrow was 'very hurried in his compilation and made mistakes and was economical with his account and with the truth. His editing came to be whole pieces lifted into his compilation'.

Perhaps he regarded the Admiralty archives as his personal treasure house from which to cherry-pick. Yet he had not troubled to arrange cataloguing, ensure the safety of the archives or to preserve the priceless records, whose totality was British naval history.

Barrow's son, also called John, was made Head of the Records Office in 1844. By order of the then First Naval Lord, Cockburn, he at once began to repair the long-standing and gross defect in his father's administration of the records and of the archives. No wonder Barrow senior had blushed. His son had found out about his imperious father's negligence and lies.

Barrow's Power Base

The power base of John Barrow has been much discussed.[9] Barrow himself took care to play down the abundance of power and influence he undoubtedly had. Whilst perhaps not quite a Uriah Heep, he behaved to his political masters in a seemingly subservient way. To his peers, he seemed to have wanted them to believe he was a calm, incorruptible, omniscient and balanced civil servant who remained polite and bland when others were not. Some facts demonstrated otherwise. Naval officers who crossed him, knowingly or unknowingly, were never again employed at a time when the large majority of officers were on half pay. That degree of malign influence was but a form of power, albeit concealed.

That apart, his real power was that given to him alone by the benefit of his continuity in office as a permanent civil servant. In June 1832, the Bill which reorganised the administration of the Navy became law. One detail which led to a further concentration of knowledge, and therefore power, was that all correspondence had to be addressed to the Secretary of the Admiralty - i.e. Barrow. His detailed knowledge of past decisions was also unrivalled, especially if the supporting papers could not be produced. Later, during Barrow's labours before the administrative reforms, his colleagues said 'Bless me, Barrow, how ill you look! These Whigs will be the death of you.'[10]

Further instances of his influence and power, but in his private capacity, were his 195 articles written for the *Quarterly Review*. Also his leadership of the Royal Geographical Society whose executive committee he chaired imperiously. There, when acting as a private citizen, he showed his intolerant nature, rather than bothering to act out his official bland one. The combination of the power bases emanating from his naval administrative as well as from his expedition planning roles, was recognised by the wide support he had already made certain to ensure from the Court and from some contemporaries.

Understanding how and why certain events delayed the adoption of improvements in warships for so long makes it necessary also to consider administrative factors. How was it possible for a senior civil servant such as Barrow to affect the progress of executive decisions made in his department and given to him as an instruction? One of the conflicting factors which affected the speed of progress of a decision was that Admiralty Boards were composed more often than not of men of very mixed abilities. 'A school for sucking statesmen' was a insult current in 1830 as a description of the ranks of aspirants to the sinecures the Navy and Admiralty Boards were thought to be.[11]

In fact, the reforms of 1832 ensured that no Board member was anything but oppressed by the workload expected of him, consequent on the subsumption of the Navy Board into that of the Admiralty. The number of new entrants to public office at the Admiralty produced a situation whereby the permanent staff had to be their mentors. In turn, this led to an indiscernible but very real power shift away from the appointed Commissioners and towards the permanent officials.

Was it possible, as was asserted by Admiral Byam Martin,[12] that the whole subject of the relatively important but small advance in technological achievement, as first proposed by William Snow Harris in 1820, was almost led to oblivion by the undue influence of a civil servant? Why, apparently in support of their effective pigeon-holing of Harris' plan during 1835–41, were the Whigs later to resort to such obfuscation and chicanery?

As we have seen, Barrow had been portrayed, most often in his autobiography, as a conscientious, very hard-working, efficient, placid and wise civil servant. Many believe he was the forerunner of the modern-day mandarin, with a facility for obsequious wit, for words and the paraphrase, all based upon his matchless experience and detailed knowledge.

Others, more prescient, did express misgivings that the perfect public servant was not all that he seemed to be. According to Murray,[13] Sir John Barrow, 'the patriarchal Second Secretary in his prime, sometimes showed himself to be remarkably obtuse'. The same man was also manipulative at least to the degree that many become in office life. Minto was an indecisive First Lord more interested in local feuds in Scotland than other matters. Barrow pandered to the pretence of his authority while making sure he and others actually made the decisions. For example, in response to a request (whose nature we do not know as the paper is missing) he wrote:[14]

> It is for your Lordships consideration whether the indulgence sought in the accompanying paper should be granted to this gentleman because the same has been conceded not long ago to two others. Lord Dalmeny thinks grant it and Sir Wm. Parker and Capt. Berkeley think with me, not. 'The sooner a bad precedent is got rid of the better' – refers to swarms of scribblers who have every access to newspaper and pamphlet writers, by which a vast portion of the public is guided – avoid giving them

the least morsel even so trifling one as to learn his trade at one of HM Yards. Your Lordship will not consider me as stepping beyond my line, in what I have done. I have always felt it my duty etc. JB.

The letter was interesting from another viewpoint. Barrow's use of the power of publication. It also exemplified his intransigence towards scientific progress. Yet the Admiralty, as Andrew Lambert[15] has commented, had become a past master at laying hold of technological breakthroughs after some of their financial risks had been taken up by private interests.

Whilst his official style never varied from the formal salutation such as 'I am commanded by my Lords Commissioners of the Admiralty,' followed by a polite and accurate letter, his private correspondence could show a sharp turn of phrase.

A letter to Professor Macvey Napier, for example,[16] showed that the normally careful civil servant could be far from civil when he felt that his omnipotence as an author and originator of expeditions of discovery was being challenged: 'to say that Belcher's book is so loose, unconnected and ill-written that I would only make it a peg to hang on some remarks on the proceedings of the French and the Americans against the poor people of the Pacific islands'.

Admiral Sir Byam Martin was formerly Comptroller to the Navy Board but was prematurely retired in 1832 due to Graham's downsizing policy. Barrow had published a biography of Admiral Lord Anson. It fell to Martin to review it[17]. He used the opportunity to rely upon an unspoken agreement to accept all criticism without resorting to the courts for libel and wrote: 'a ready constructor of a book, however deficient he may be in his notions of the construction of the naval service'. He went on to say that the volume should be reduced by 129 pages of extraneous matter to the size of a pamphlet and that it was 'a mere catch guinea book'. Martin concluded by asking how an under Secretary of the Admiralty could find leisure to read and to contribute to the *Quarterly Review.*[18]

In 1821, Barrow had been granted an LLD from Edinburgh University for advancing science and for his literary talents.[19] His lack of university tutelage at last had been made good, although strangely he did not use the honorary degree in the title page of his autobiography. Barrow's many anonymous contributions to the *Quarterly Review* sometimes used phrases and language which some felt could be ignored as from an opinionated antediluvian. In fact, the self-taught man became a literary critic and his reviews were compatible with a first-class brain and with his capability in running an entire branch of the Civil Service. His friendship with John Murray, the publisher, meant that each of his books was published under Murray's banner.

Barrow evidently had a complex character, and was said by some to be a wise and friendly administrator[20] and by others to be overvalued. As a young man, he had shown kindness to children whom he tutored and he had good teaching abilities. He had interests in mathematics and in travel. The latter interest was later to lead to him planning expeditions to Africa and the Arctic.[21] The planning was always done with the help of Sir Joseph Banks, the great and gouty naturalist. Barrow himself had travelled extensively. As a teenager, he had enjoyed one summer in the whaling industry and as a member of the Ambassador's household he had travelled in 1794 to the unknown and undiscovered land of China.

During his return voyage via the Cape of Good Hope on board HMS *Glatton*,[22] one night the ship was struck by lightning. The mizzen mast was much damaged as were other parts of the ship, including a porthole blown out of the surgeon's cabin. Two carpenters were sent on board from the accompanying *Lion* to help. The *Lion* also had her mizzen mast damaged. Barrow seems to have been fatalistic about his own life as well as those of others. He described how, when a boy, he attempted to repeat Benjamin Franklin's experiments. When he flew his kite during an impending thunderstorm, he obtained sparks and subjected an incautious old woman to an electrical shock. For this he was condemned by his fellow villagers and made to put away his kite by his mother. Perhaps the incident might help explain Barrow's later reluctance to promote Harris' work on protection from lightning, as he himself was likely to have felt guilty about the subject.

Perhaps a partial explanation for Barrow's lack of interest or of knowledge in scientific affairs was his experience of Dr Dinwiddie.[23] This 'Scotch philosopher, but of what school I know not' was to demonstrate to the Chinese Court various machines and instruments in the hope of impressing them with the power and technology of Great Britain. He had globes, a diving bell, barometers and a balloon. To demonstrate knowledge of the stars and of the planetary system, he had working model planetariums and orreries. The Chinese

Emperor was not interested and wrote in his dismissal of the expedition that he did not value such manufactured goods or ingenious devices. A further expedition, which Barrow had encouraged, set off in 1816. This second attempt at diplomatic and trading relations was similarly rebuffed by the conservative Chinese, but with less ceremony.

Barrow's formal education was between the ages of 8 and 13 at Towns Bank grammar school in Cumbria. Thereafter he was self-taught but with some additional tuition in mathematics under a recluse called Gibson. Of importance in understanding his actions in later life, Barrow had no opportunity to go to university. Thus traditional debate of ideas and discursive philosophy and the elements of science were denied to him as he had to earn a living.

After one tour as Second Secretary at the Admiralty from 1804–6, Barrow returned to that office in 1807 and continued in unbroken service until 1845. He learned his craft on the job and soon gained a reputation for a bland manner and for careful administrative work. Meanwhile his books on his travels to China and to Africa gained him acceptance to The Royal Society in 1806, but he must have found the scientific content of the meetings dull.

The long times of peace after the end of the Napoleonic War enabled the Admiralty to concentrate its minimal resources in ships for surveying work, hydrography and, due to Barrow's persistent optimism in promoting the virtues of British achievements, also to voyages of discovery.

Even critics of Barrow's overeager despatch of numerous expeditions between 1816 and 1845 have stated that he was to be applauded for his ideas to explore the world and to identify distant countries and cultures. Most would agree that he was in a unique position to foster voyages intended to discover new trade routes. He even managed to obtain full or partial Admiralty sponsorship for some voyages and overland expeditions.

On the other hand, Barrow could not countenance anyone but himself being the instigator of an Arctic expedition. He must have felt personal ownership of the project of the North West Passage and jealousy if others such as the Ross family in any sense supplanted him.[24] Later, Barrow was again to display his real self. He omitted all but slight mention of the Ross's partial success after four over-winterings in the high Arctic and actively belittled their achievements. This included the account of their travels and difficulties in their book, for which Ross received great acclaim and social esteem. For this caustic review, Barrow was termed harsh and cruel.[25] Barrow had, on the word of a purser's steward whose opinion he otherwise eschewed, suggested that Ross had left behind an injured man to perish.

An impartial assessment of the actual achievements of Barrow's expeditionary protégés suggests that the outcome was more often another book by Barrow than trade with new partners in distant places. Still fewer were the discoveries actually made. Early expeditions to Africa led to many deaths and little return except debts.[26] Barrow's reasons for a proposed route for an expedition were often plain wrong if not naive to the point of being absurd. Trying to find the source of the Niger by crossing the Sahara Desert, commencing from the Mediterranean littoral, was one such unrealistic expedition. Other expeditions to Africa were also fruitless. The legend of Barrow's expertise as a practical geographer is best identified correctly as but a series of disasters. Attempts to open up the north coast of Australia to settlement and trade, typically for Barrow's expeditionary planning, were unsuccessful and were always unrealistic.

Most of Barrow's efforts in sending out expeditionary forces were associated with Admiralty-sponsored attempts (a few privately funded ones were also unsuccessful) to find and then to force the North West Passage. There seems to be no doubt that those who gallantly took part were pushed into defeat and death by his stringent prescripts and not least by his curious ideas as to the geography of the Canadian Arctic. More disturbing was another criticism that Barrow's highly focused plans for fame by his chairmanship and influence in expeditionary work also unhinged the judgement of the normally temperate civil servant and savant manqué.

Fleming wrote that on the surface Barrow was a dull, humble Admiralty clerk,[27] used to plain food and an occasional glass of port. A man who never fell ill. He appeared to distance himself from decision-making but behind this exterior was a man of ambition, intellect and remorseless application. Barrow, according to Fleming's excellent biography, chose exploration as a way of making his name.

Jealousy of any similar work to one's own is after all a very real and dark side of human nature. Barrow had a surfeit of this proclivity. Throughout his career he seems to have done his best to discredit by his authorship those with whom he did not agree. When matters concerned his leisure and hobbies, and especially the hope of discoveries on the far side of the world, then self-interest interfered with his judgement. Could these traits of arrogance in his planning and a false sense of belief in the innate soundness of his judgement of risk also have affected him in his duties at the Admiralty? Some did think so – the former Comptroller of the Navy Board for example.[28] Others were envious of his ability. Barrow's use of his office time was questioned in a debate in the House of Lords in 1839. The House[29] was assured that his latest book on Admiral Anson and its supplemental chapter had not been written under Admiralty auspices. There was no mention of the sources and the means by which he had obtained the records, logs and papers from dusty attics at the Admiralty, which later he was to attempt to deny he knew existed. Barrow's industry was incredible but he had unrivalled, almost sole and private access to naval records.

Barrow At the Admiralty After 1832

Administratively, Barrow's first Whig political master, Sir James Graham, at first enjoyed a good reputation. Some of this was deserved because he helped bring about the desirable Reform Acts. His nemesis, although not suspected for some time, was to be his naive but conceited actions to consolidate the traditional and at the same time contain the considerable administrative burdens of the Naval Services.

Centralisation of authority under one Board had obvious advantages for dissemination of information and for the making of corporate decisions based upon interpretation of that information. What was not provided for was the burden of an increasing amount of administration. Although it enlarged the direct authority of the cohort of Members of the Board of the Admiralty, the responsibility for many aspects of an outcome decision became submerged in dark waters. The centralising reforms of the administration of the Navy were to be continued but with insufficient provision of an alternative infrastructure to support the former purposes. In 1835, the office of the former Treasurer of the Navy was relinquished and was passed under Board control to a specific Paymaster General.

The High Court of the Admiralty, with the First Lord at its head, had 31 independent jurisdictions headed by Vice Admirals on foreign stations. By 1833, the process of appeals against decisions by

Admiralty Courts was dramatically shortened by granting the legal members of the Privy Council[30] (the First Lord also sat as a member of that Council) jurisdiction over the subordinate Admiralty Court's decisions. The Royal Navy, as well as the mercantile marine, each was placed under the jurisdiction of Admiralty courts, and court martial procedures began to be codified. These arrangements added to the administrative burden at the Board and the clerks became busier. Another burden of office work requiring immediate management was the change after an effective nationalisation of trade and commercial interests from private hands to an Admiralty department. By 1834, the Royal Navy on behalf of the Crown took over the powers, sphere of influence and duties of the East India Company and the latter's monopoly upon trade with China was abolished.[31] The Far East, and in particular China, then became a growing and more important naval station, requiring ships and their consequent administration.[32]

The bringing together of the Navy Office and that of the Admiralty should have resulted in an enhanced flow of decisions and in speedy resolution of any administrative tensions and conflicts. It was surprising therefore to find that the First Lord, The Earl of Minto,[33] was at a loss for the recovery from the Record Office of previous papers. The continuity of the consolidated businesses at the Admiralty was not to be achieved at a satisfactory level for many years.

Barrow's workload had increased greatly since the abolition of the Navy Board. Even after the reorganisation of 1832 and the consequent increased volume of business, Barrow continued to open and read every 'in letter' addressed to the Admiralty. The fact that he did this of course gave him knowledge of the content of the correspondence sent to the department. It also gave him power. That power was so great it had to be hidden. Just occasionally, the real agenda of the man was visible. In 1838, according to Admiral Sir W. Parker,[34] the rapid development of the Russian Fleet had already caused astonishment, not unmixed with anxiety. A pamphlet by a naval officer and a letter to the Duke of Wellington from an unnamed flag officer were published. The Secretary to the Admiralty published a pamphlet in reply, in order to lessen the effect. The reply,[35] which 'expressed the hope that the Flag Officer will never be employed' can be found at the end of Barrow's book on the *Life of Anson*.

This was a good example of how Barrow the civil servant felt it was his duty to interfere with affairs even though he professed to be independent and apolitical. What may have encouraged him was a resignation letter, addressed to him, from Captain the Hon. M.F.F. Berkeley as the latter's response to the under-manning of warships sent on duties likely to become conflicts. Barrow should have been sacked for usurping political functions. That he was ready to publish in his own name demonstrated his confidence in the power of his pen. That the pamphlet was also an addendum to his book on Anson was specious, especially if 'the flag officer' had turned out to be a Whig and Barrow had acted on the Tory, Croker's, advice. Meanwhile Barrow, the administrator, had been made aware as early as 1832 that even important documents such as Admiralty Orders[36] were misfiled or missing from the records: 'The Admiralty Order for the previous ten years cannot be found'.

Another example of political expediency combined with administrative malfeasance was that of Admiral Sir Edward's Codrington's written request for recognition for winning so convincingly the Battle of Navarino in 1827. Codrington, also an MP, then spoke in the House of Commons: 'a general petition, by Sir James Gore, who by order of the Lord High Admiral, presented it to the Admiralty, and strange to say it was not to be found'. It was very likely that Barrow had been ordered to misplace the file.[37]

In his autobiography, Barrow[38] wrote that 'in 1827 there were 25,428 letters received and 25,402 despatched. By 1833, that is one year after consolidation of the Navy and Admiralty Boards, 31,330 had been received and 47,886 despatched'. This meant Barrow read about 86 original letters every day. He signed himself, or had knowledge of, 131 outgoing letters per day. The abolition of the Navy Board thus increased the administrative workload of himself and his Admiralty clerks by 20 per cent for in letters and by 47 per cent for out letters.

Recovery of previous correspondence was a matter first of proper recording and then of allocation of digest numbers for main subjects contained in each letter. Every letter was marked, usually at the top left-hand of the first page with the subject number allocated. In the case of 'Chemistry and Dry Rot', as has been explained, that digest number was 59.9. In addition, each letter was carefully given an alphabetical code letter or combinations of letters for source and finally a file number within that calendar year. For example, a letter raising a new point from Harris, or replying to one the Admiralty had made, would be marked in the top right-hand front page as 'Pro H

156' and filed for the month and year. 'Pro' (promiscuous) 'H' (Harris, in his case, but any correspondent's surname beginning with H) and the number of the letters from correspondents whose surnames began with H received that month, say, 156.

Letters from naval personnel were denoted by rank first and then by first letter of surname and a number as before. Thus 'Lts G 78' could be the alphabet code and file number for a letter received from Harris' opponent, Lt. Pringle Green. The number of letters received per day was a mean of 86. Thus it was not surprising that a rigorous system of record-keeping had to be in place. Thus one letter, although by itself unique, if a case study was to be made up into a brief in a pack for a Board member, had to be merged with a pile of other loose letters on the same subject or from the same correspondent. Thus it was not surprising when occasionally a pack containing a case study or an individual letter became misplaced or even lost. There was a system for marking the pack for temporary transfer to a reader but this proved insufficient for its accurate localisation and certainly not adequate to find an individual letter within it.

The constant turnover in Board members attempting to read up a subject must have created the conditions for a paper to be lost or misfiled. Moreover, there has not been an account published of how the Admiralty assumed responsibility and secured structured access to the records of the former Navy Board. Given the already chaotic state of the Admiralty's own archives, it seems that Navy Board records were simply kept at Somerset House and accessed (or more probably not) when desired. The relative difficulty of searching for relevant papers in two places, Somerset House and Whitehall, probably acted so as to reduce the chance of a complete pack being available to a naval Lord after 1832.

This problem of document recovery was especially likely to occur on a matter which already had been actioned in part by the two departments before the reorganisation. On 11 September 1832, Barrow[39] wrote of the ease of communication between the Admiralty at Charing Cross and Somerset House, but added 'there was no room at either venue for receipt of models, books and papers that are indispensable to business'. To his lasting shame, Barrow was to do nothing to improve that situation.

The manpower for administration at the Admiralty was increased by only seven extra clerks (Barrow's autobiography suggested the number was only three or four, but his memory was faulty), after the abolition of the Navy Board in 1832. This shortage of civil servants in naval administration goes some way to explain why Minto and indeed Barrow found difficulty in recovering from records a complete case file from which to brief the Board. A private secretary who might have acted as a Master Records Officer to the Second (Permanent) Secretary was not re-established until after Barrow's retirement as his sole attempt to employ one had not worked out satisfactorily.

It was this outcome of hitherto insufficient resource put into archiving that was to lead to repetitious and unnecessary extra work in establishing simple facts. The glaring example of this was the constant apparent absence of information at the Admiralty as to which ships had been fitted on trial with Harris' permanent system of lightning conductors, and also when they were fitted and what the outcome was. The search had to be carried out anew by many of the Admiralty Boards between 1832 and 1842.

Briggs,[40] in an assessment of the Admiralty Secretariat, wrote that in his view it was more efficient under Mr Romaine than under Barrow or Captain Baillie Hamilton. Perhaps this view, as recorded in his book, previously criticised as 'racy', was in fact a cooler look at the era of Barrow's administration.

The assumption of responsibility for an area of naval business by an individual naval Lord was hailed as a great advance at the time of Graham's administrative reforms. Minto's brother, Hon. Captain George Elliot, a Board member during 1835, must have been thus specifically tasked. He signed a series of requests to the Yards for information about the fixed lightning conductors. Later, the administrators at the Admiralty seemed to have 'forgotten' that this information had been so carefully gathered for it was not available to Boards succeeding those of 1835. Admiral Cockburn had already formed his opinion as to their efficacy and had asked, without success, for them to be fitted to his flagship for the West Indies station.[41]

By 1837, even the more reactionary Whig Board members conceded to the massive evidence of rapid scientific and technological changes in steam power. They reacted by appointing Captain Parry in a new permanent post as Controller of Steam with Ewart, an engineer, to assist him. Ewart had originally been appointed Inspector of Machinery as early as 1835. Other appointments to technical departments soon followed. In this way, the older and well tried system of the former Navy Board's departments, each staffed with experts with a wealth of technical knowledge, was reintroduced in all but name by political sleight of hand. Croker had previously admitted to the House that the vote for Sea Service costs allocated to 'wear and tear' was loosely defined. In turn, this gave an opportunity for rival politicians to comment upon all naval matters, rather than the broader aspects of the country's interests. Technical subjects were allowed to escape from a relatively informed environment within the Admiralty, only to become trivial sport for politicians of both parties. Whigs and Tories gloried in the commonly inept speeches from their naval officer MPs. Other place-men used the subjective debates to further their careers at the cost of informed opinion. This public rather than departmental debate was very much to the diminution of the authority of the Admiralty Boards. Into the cockpit of political infighting fell such matters as naval architecture, manning, stocks of material in the dockyards and the subject of this book, lightning protection for HM Ships.

By 1848, the area of responsibility for each naval Lord had become much more clearly defined. Within that structure, the Junior Naval Lord (Captain Milne)[42] tended to volunteer or to be allocated new 'blue-sky type' position papers. Thus Milne wrote, 'I rather like each Lord working in his own department, but when in doubt he can go before the Board'. Rodger,[43] in his penetrating articles about the administration at the Admiralty, wrote: 'The Naval Lords were engulfed (after 1832) in questions of detail which left them little time to run their departments efficiently, let alone attend to matters of policy for which, as a Board, they were supposed to be responsible.' This view was confirmed by Hamilton[44] who opined that after 1832, 'the First Lord, was the only member [of the Board] with the leisure to consider general questions, and the one who most commonly took decisions on them.'

As we have seen, Barrow managed to ensure that his relatives had posts within his department. Apart from his son, also John, G. Barrow became a third-class clerk in February 1824 but resigned on his appointment to the Colonial Office in 1825. P. Barrow was a third class-clerk from January 1833 but resigned in October 1834. Barrow's close friend, Croker, had a family member, T.C. Croker, entered as a third-class clerk in 1819 and retired as a first-class clerk in 1850. Thus, Barrow had his son and his closest friend's son as allies and assistants throughout much of his career as the chief executive at the Admiralty.

Barrow's youngest son[45] was fortunate to be appointed Vice-Consul for Caen by Lord Aberdeen in 1845. His behaviour just before his appointment had been 'thoughtless and extravagant' and 'severe correction' was administered by his father. Sir John Barrow then wrote in his letter of thanks to Aberdeen that 'he was vain enough to suppose that the appointment of his son was mindful of the long service of his father'. When Lord Haddington became First Lord in 1841, it was recorded that, 'he was not slow to investigate possible cases of ill-usage, but inevitably had to rely upon permanent civil servants to produce the relevant documents'.[46]

If the quality and depth of the material supplied to the Board was poor, then discussion would have been muted and any outcome decision possibly flawed. It is impossible to know exactly which papers were recovered and how complete a pack was before being placed before a Board for discussion. Continuity of the policy of a previous Board upon the succession of a new one remained a constant problem. Wood[47] attempted to make the handover easier in 1839 when he wrote 'the present Board of Admiralty having experienced the inconvenience, which naturally arose from their ignorance of the views of preceding Boards on matters which they had to carry on, have thought it right to leave to their successors the following memoranda on various points'.

One of the matters which must have led to his strong views was that of loss of files which showed the history of a subject during the recent few years of the current administration as well as the views of previous Boards. For example, the scheme of work of the carpenters in the Yards was creating difficulties for Minto's Board yet, 'The papers on which any system might have been framed were removed when the present Surveyor came into office, if they existed before and no attempt was made to supply the deficiency till 1837. The Surveyor's office was too weak to do so.'[48]

The problems of record-keeping seem to have been recognised, at least to a degree, when Brunel[49] was instructed to direct all correspondence about the researches and arrangements for the new screw propeller to Mr Waller Clifton, an Admiralty clerk and private secretary to Charles Wood, and to Moore O'Ferrall. Clifton had received much praise for his industry and fairness in the presentation of records of the minutes of the Committee on Shipwrecks by Lightning, which had sat in 1839. Was Clifton directed to prepare a case study for propellers? Was it possible that previous case studies or packs about a single subject had been lost or misfiled intentionally? It was certain that the 1839 Committee report on lightning had been filed under 'Admirals Unemployed' (AU). So that case study, as a separate identity, was not easily apparent to an incoming new Board.

To address 'in' letters to Clifton would result in an accumulation of power to him. Barrow did not care for that. It could to an extent also bypass the official system for cataloguing in letters. Barrow always opened all letters and all letters had to be addressed or directed to him, the permanent head of the Secretariat. Here, then, was a clear statement of recognition of the potential for problems if Clifton was to receive letters addressed solely to him. The instruction had been given in August 1842. By the following year, Brunel was corresponding directly with Barrow.[50] Perhaps Barrow had to point out the legal status of his job description which he had slid in on the back of Graham's reforms. From 1832, all letters on Admiralty Board business were to be addressed to the Secretary. What the Secretary or his deficient record system did with some of the letters about Harris' lightning protection scheme for ships remains a mystery.

The weakness in management has been well explained by Rodger[51] in his book, *The Command of the Ocean*. He emphasised the former well-tried direct communications by the staff of the Yards with the Navy Board, rather than with the Admiralty. Old habits did not die and most senior men in the Yards appeared to have been encouraged to cock a snook at the new regime which had dared to appoint a non-graduate of the Naval School of Architecture as Surveyor. Instead of communicating with him, they may have ignored both him and the Admiralty. There would have been much prioritisation of business for the succession of First Lords, by Barrow the Permanent Secretary. Thus Barrow could and did influence the matters discussed. This influence was biased against projectors (boffins). It was probably in this way that the case for fixed copper lightning conductors for the fleet became for so many years a decision postponed or only partially taken.

Barrow's views[52] as to new ideas other than his own were unhelpful. He wrote: 'every administration of the Admiralty has had to grapple with a host of charlatans with their absurd and useless projects, which they call inventions. Lord Melville was not disposed to encourage such', or, 'a dangerous set of projectors have supplied a whole fleet of useless iron steamers'. Barrow revealed a great deal of himself with these lines. Certainly he took a conservative if not an ostrich-like view of the expansion of uses for steamers in the Navy. He also felt very warmly concerning the time it took to deal with those clamouring to have invented something of use to the Navy. It was different when *he* proposed an idea: 'In 1817 I proposed a plan for two voyages for Lord Melville's consideration, which, after consultation with his colleagues, supported by the recommendation of The Royal Society, was adopted.'

A further example of Barrow's mandarin mask slipping was given by Sir James Graham's account[53] of a memorandum from Barrow. This had more or less ordered the new First Lord to send help to search for Captain Ross' Arctic expedition. Graham recorded that he 'refused to act upon the recommendation'.

Thus, Barrow used The Royal Society and later his status at The Royal Geographical Society to obtain credibility for his plans. He cannot have liked it when Harris later used the same device of institutional support from The Royal Society, followed by both Houses of Parliament, to fight back at the delays to his plans by the administration at the Admiralty.

As we have seen, Sir Byam Martin, in his edited autobiography published long after Barrow's death, wrote that the supposedly impeccable civil servant was indeed guilty of manipulation of Admiralty business.[54] In addition he did not demonstrate proper impartiality:

> Sir John Barrow, the most obstinate man living, has presumed to set his [will] against it [Harris' fixed lightning conductors]. This comes of permitting subordinates in office to acquire a sort of sway and habit of dictation which belongs not to their station. Mr Barrow has, in his time, greatly and mischievously misled the First Lords of the Admiralty: no public servant has done more harm for so little good.

Byam Martin was well known as a Tory MP. He must have known Barrow was also a covert Tory and that he and his family shared a house in West Molesley with the ultra right-wing Croker. It was therefore surprising but seemingly necessary that the honest and fair-minded Martin should publish this attack on Barrow.

Other public evidence sent as a letter to the Committee on Shipwreck by Lightning in 1839 by Martin had been more restrained.[55]

He had written more as a political opponent of the then current Whig administration and was point-scoring as to their record: 'I hear with concern that an objection has been raised against the fixed conductors on the grounds of expense; and we know that ill judged notions of economy are too apt to have an undue influence in matters regarding the Navy.'

6

William Snow Harris

The inventor of the permanent lightning conductor for ships was William Snow Harris. It took him 22 years, from 1820-42, to get his plan for lightning conductors for warships adopted by the Admiralty. Apart from political influences, were there other factors that delayed their acceptance and what were they? After all, it was a time when the second and rapid phase of the Industrial Revolution was taking place. The effect of the industrialisation was that the manual labouring sections of the workforce were being replaced by machinery, both on land and at sea. Production of metals was increased and many new inventions led to the flowering of the Victorian age.

The decades were also years of enormous strain at the Treasury, due mainly to the burden of debts from successive wars. The defence industry, as we now term it, was viewed by politicians as passé and as an improvident consumer of scarce resources. Progress meant that some ships were to use man-hauled sails only as auxiliary propulsion. Still fewer men were needed for ships powered solely by steam. On land, the increasingly mechanised production of coal, of iron, and above all of steel, replaced the older industries including agriculture, weaving and sewing. Mechanisation even began to encroach upon manpower needs in the supply of services.

People displaced by these massive changes were forced into action to prevent their starvation. The conditions and high prices for bread[1] led to unrest amongst the population in 1826, from 1829 to 1835, again between 1838 and 1844 and between 1846 and 1848. Poverty was reflected in high death rates. In towns such as Manchester the death rate for children under five was an appalling 57 per cent in 1843-4. According to Hilton[2] and to Lambert,[3] the Corn Laws were in place so as to keep marginal land in food production in case of a long war. Other foodstuffs, strategically important metals and machinery, were subsidised and prices ring-fenced.

The decade 1830–40 in particular was a period of profound discontent leading to political instability. The poor were not being paid enough. The opinion-forming groups[4] amongst the population wanted universal suffrage and an end to preferment by privilege. Equally important for those in institutions or in government-funded posts was the end of patronage. Patronage was particularly evident in the downsized Navy[5] and the majority of officers, including the few employed, wanted it to be substituted by promotion solely on merit.

William Snow Harris was born on 1 April 1791, as the only son of Thomas Harris and Mary, née Snow, of Plymouth. His upbringing in the great naval port and the conditioning produced by the long struggles against the French were to influence his life. Like many others, he was to find that he could not forgive the French their enmity, although later he was to flirt with the idea of helping them and was asked to assist another unreliable ex-enemy, the Russians.

Harris had attended Plymouth Grammar School and his record showed he was good at the arts subjects as well as at science (natural philosophy). There is no record of how he spent some gap years after leaving school and before going to Edinburgh University in 1811 at the age of 20. Probably he helped his father in the office and for his leisure honed his skills as a yachtsman and as a trout fisherman.

The Scottish universities[6] were a good choice for those unwilling to pay the high fees for tuition and for lodgings in the colleges and universities of the South. The age of matriculation was lower than at Oxford and at Cambridge and the standard of entry and of later examination tests not very high. More than a third of students were under 17 years and classes were large. The students were drawn from a wide field and included boys from poorer families. The reputation of the faculties and of teachers such as Dr Hope of the Department of Chemistry at Edinburgh, was deservedly high.

Harris matriculated in 1812, aged 21, in 'Materia Medica', 'Chemistry' and the 'Practise of Medicine' after one year's study.[7] He was to become by experience an accomplished, caring, scientifically alert local general practitioner and public officer of health, but his medical career can only be described as sporadic. When the Napoleonic War was at its height, the militia (army reserves) was expanded and Harris joined the Royal Cheshires as a military surgeon[8] on 5 September 1812.

The request for his commission as an Ensign had been made on 17th August to Viscount Sidmouth. Harris also apprenticed himself to a local doctor in or near Chester. Duties with the militia (an early form of the Territorial Army) were a daily parade, an annual camp of two weeks and many voluntary extra opportunities such as recruiting. One of the areas used as a recruiting ground for his regiment was Harris' native Plymouth. At the time, even after Waterloo had been won, military aid to civil power was very rare. Armed units of soldiers were often jeered at by urban mobs, thus it was unlikely that Harris' unit had many public duties during his time with the militia. He served six years in total and, when combined with the experience he gained in his mentor's practice in Cheshire, it expunged any possible call for a retrospective requirement for a full apprenticeship as an apothecary.

Sometime after his return to Plymouth in 1818, he met with another militiaman, Lt. Nicholas Condy, an artist. Condy had served in the 43rd Foot, later the Oxford and Buckinghamshire Light Infantry, in the Peninsular War. His son, Nicholas Matthew Condy, had just been born. Harris kept up this friendship and must have been delighted when the young Condy showed he had inherited his father's artistic talent. The younger Condy was to become an art teacher in Plymouth and later to develop his artistic skills enough to exhibit in London concurrently with his proud parent.

Nicholas Condy had painted a series of six watercolours depicting the results of the great storm which had blown through Plymouth on 22 and again on 24 November 1824. The idea of depicting an event at sea by a series of small, accurate, and carefully considered illustrations became a familiar technique for the Condy family. Nicholas Matthew Condy was later to become the artist whose work illustrated some of Harris' books on lightning. Before his early death in 1851, his dramatic and accurate series of small pictures of HM Ships being struck by lightning helped convince the government that they should reward Harris with a substantial sum for his invention of the marine lightning conductor.

After his marriage in 1824, Harris had more freedom to take up the interests which were to become his life's work. The new science of electricity had already become his field of research. His carefully controlled observations would make him a scientist whose reputation was respected nationally and internationally. In a room at the back of his home in George Street, he gradually accumulated the apparatus he required for experiments. A very careful and fastidious worker, he had a feeling for the design of an instrument and for perfection of movement in its working parts. He would have been able to find help from local instrument makers and watchmakers but a majority of his apparatus was manufactured solely by himself. He gave an annual lecture for 48 years to the Plymouth Institution on his research, commencing in 1819. His reading of past papers and experimental work on any subject was thorough and he became interested in developing Henley's original idea of a permanent form of lightning conductor for ships.

By 1820, Harris had proposed his practical, albeit ambitious, plan for the protection of HM Ships from damage by lightning. His idea was to replace the inefficient temporary rigging of long chains hanging from the masts as conductors and instead to have a conductor permanently available. The plan was ambitious because it would require work on the masts and yards so as to allow them to take a copper conductor let into a groove in the wood. Protests against his idea were immediate as many felt the masts would be weakened. Most opposition would come from a man[9] who can only be described as traditionalist but whose scientific knowledge and understanding was weak.

Supporters[10] were many and included those who were critical of the small capacity of the portable conductors as given to HM Ships. Captain Lord William Napier was one such important ally but had given up hope of further advancement in the Navy and become Superintendent of Trade in Macao where he died early in 1833.

By 1821, Harris had tested his idea and to demonstrate it to others used gold leaf on paper to simulate a length of a good conductor which could safely transmit an electrical current. Realising that metals differed in their powers of conductivity, he had set up a series of experiments under controlled conditions which would allow him to compare the resistance of one metal with another or between various alloys. Pure specimens of some metals were difficult to obtain due to imperfect smelting and refining techniques. Harris added a furnace to the armamentarium of apparatus at his home laboratory and was able to remove many impurities from his specimens of metal.

He began an extensive correspondence with other workers interested in the same field, not only concerning electrostatic electricity as could be stored in a Leyden jar, but atmospheric electricity including lightning. Also, he naturally expanded his interests from lightning into meteorology. He set up wind gauges, anemometers and rain gauges. He began to make observations of local weather and had records of up to three readings each day. He began work on a new compass, on vibrating magnets to investigate the magnetic currents of the earth, on a wheel barometer, an electrometer and a balance.

His fame as a careful and conscientious researcher spread. In 1826, Harris was invited by Sir Humphrey Davy to read a paper at The Royal Institution on his researches into the relative powers of various metallic substances as conductors of electricity. This was fame indeed. The lecture was well received and was published in full in *Philosophical Transactions* a year later.[11] Harris was to publish, after peer review, at least one new paper on results of his own research each year to a total of 49 in major scientific journals and many others elsewhere.

When Harris moved to 6 Windsor Villas, he set up another laboratory where he made a series of excellent studies of electrical phenomena. Of especial interest to him were magnetism and induction, and later in his life he carried on an extensive correspondence with James David Forbes at St Andrews University[12] and with Michael Faraday[13] at the Royal Institution on the subject. Another correspondent was the scientist Whewell. The latter was a meticulous observer and often picked up small points, or requested an elaboration of one, or asked for a correction. Harris was delighted to oblige and his letters to Whewell and to other electricians and natural philosophers were serious and relevant studies in the laws of electricity.

Harris was indiscreet on one occasion, perhaps trying too hard to impress.[14] He wrote down the name and the medical condition of a certain famous person then under his care, which he should not have done. Evidently he had complete trust in Whewell. Some of the correspondence alluded to studies needed and agreed by both men of the greater movements and currents of the atmosphere and of the upper atmosphere. Was this the first glimmerings of the existence of jet streams?

The Lightning Conductor for Ships

The Navy Board, whose headquarters were in Somerset House on the Strand in London, had been led since 1816 by the energetic, courageous, strong-minded Admiral Sir Thomas Byam Martin. His independence and good judgement was evident and his post as Comptroller was permanent and not subject to change on accession of a new government.

Martin received a letter from Harris dated 1 January 1821.[15] It described the new lightning conductor and hoped for the interest of the Navy Board. Martin set in motion what was to become his regular response to the best of the innovations put to him. First, ask for all the details possible and assess it himself. Then demand a live test or experiment. If successful, check by obtaining an independent opinion from a government scientific adviser or from The Royal Society itself.

Martin's own ship, HMS *Pegasus*, had been struck and damaged by lightning so he and its then captain, the Duke of Clarence, could be said to have had first-hand experience of the aftermath of a strike by lightning. Martin agreed to a live demonstration to take place in Plymouth. On 16 September 1822, despite wind and rain, a very successful demonstration of the transmission of an electric current safely down a copper conductor was made. Many senior officers were present and all agreed that Harris had made a significant step towards solving the problem of the inadequate chain or wire conductors. These were so often missing, frayed and broken, and mostly, but not invariably, they were inadequate to discharge the electrical current when struck by lightning at sea.

The attempt to get a fair trial for the new plan was then suddenly stopped by a recalcitrant Admiralty after information received from the jealous neighbour of Harris. The considerable benefits of the fixed conductor were not to be tested until 1830–1. After that, and as discussed in previous chapters, a campaign of obfuscation and deceit within the administration of Dockyards and at the centre of the Admiralty ensured that the results of the trial were never brought to discussion.

Harris' career as a scientist became more and more constrained. Real research became less after 1835 and his published papers became a defence in response to attacks on his credibility and learning. The scientist became occupied in writing to the Admiralty, to local MPs and to members of the aristocracy influential in politics, as to the unfair way his invention had been treated. After 1839, he was to find out that not only had there been suppression of information about his invention but also that the core of its design had been stolen by an unscrupulous shipwright, John Edye.

Basic research in his laboratory was replaced by collection of observations about the weather from passive instruments. Harris' prolific scientific correspondence continued with letters to and fro from Michael Faraday, Reverend Whewell, Andrew Forbes, Charles Babbage and others. His scientific endeavours had resulted in the award of the prestigious Copley Medal of The Royal Society of London in 1835 and he gave the Bakerian lecture in 1839.

The Committee of Enquiry into Lightning Conductors had been set up by the Admiralty in 1839. Such was the political temperature raised by nearly everything done or not done at the Admiralty, that the subject of lightning protection nearly became a matter for a Committee of Parliament. The result of the deliberations at the Admiralty was a resounding and unequivocal endorsement of Harris' invention and a strong recommendation to adopt it for HM Ships without further delay. Unfortunately for its inventor, but more so for those killed and hurt from their acts of omission, the administration at the Admiralty preferred to dally with plagiarised and unimportant, inadequate hybrid schemes for the protection of ships and of their men from lightning.

William Snow Harris was a kind and temperate man who responded well to fair debate or to fair criticism of experimental method. His career as a scientist was subfusc but this man of gentle persuasion began to be altered by forces which he could not control. Indeed, many of the acts against him were outside his knowledge, desires and interests. The simple matter of his technological innovation became enwrapped with the fallout from the anger and despair of disappointed shipwrights and trainees in naval architecture. Many people appeared to believe that political posturing was a cre-all. Anyone not for them was against them. If it was a naval officer hoping for employment in the reduced fleet, he first had to hold up his Party ticket. As for what the other Party had achieved when in office, let us put it aside and with good fortune it will be forgotten. Harris' innovation of the fixed marine lightning conductor, which was a life-saving development, was to be dependent upon and in step with the fortunes of the Tory Party. During the long time it took to compile his careful analysis of the facts about lightning, he was ignored. When he finally published it as a Parliamentary Return,[16] there was consternation.

Harris had to search over many years through the dusty files of day-by-day routine records in ships' logs for any mention of strikes by lightning. As he wrote to Faraday, 'it was a Herculean task'.[17] The master's log tended to be the official one which the commanding officer would then use to obtain information for writing up his own log. Mostly mundane matters were recorded in the logs: stores and their consumption, disciplinary matters, courts martial if at anchor or alongside and navigational details and course if at sea.

The weather was the most important record and one of crucial importance to a sailing ship. The orders were to record wind, its strength and direction, clouds, sea state and, of great importance, any sightings of other ships, as their movements were forwarded on this way. The introduction of the Beaufort scale[18] and its shorthand nomenclature for weather conditions in 1838 must have assisted Harris in his tedious and boring search. He had to look for 't' for thunder heard or an 'l' for lightning seen, or both, in one of the left-hand columns, then read the log carefully for comment and if he was fortunate find evidence of a strike by lightning and any consequent effects. The details of the type of lightning conductor, or if a movable one, whether it was in use, may or not have been recorded. Later, such was the publicity about lightning protection that all ships' captains had to make separate reports about any incidents.

Not even Harris, its inventor, knew which ships had been fitted to trial his fixed lightning conductor. Some he was told about from within his increasingly wide circle of friends in the Navy. Often he got no help from the officers in the Yards for most were politicised and were against any change they had not initiated.

Harris later wrote to Faraday that the Admiralty simply did not believe him when he found clear evidence and multiple cases of damage from lightning in unprotected HM Ships.[19]

Certain areas of the world, those we now call 'high thunderstorm areas', such as off Java with 223 days of thunder per year, formed the bulk of the reports of lightning strikes in the logs. Because the number of ships was likely to be at a maximum in warmer seas, such as the Mediterranean, but contested for domination by the major maritime powers, the number of cases of lightning damage to naval ships was correspondingly higher on that station. On the other hand, a solitary ship on a distant station was important too and if damaged beyond local repair would have to leave its station with unknown but potentially important results.

What were the reasons for the Admiralty failing to progress a tried and proven system of protection from lightning damage for their ships? Some indications were given in the bland records of the administration of 1835-41. The First, or Civil, Lord was Gilbert Elliot, Second Earl of Minto. Lord Minto appeared to believe that as his education had included some scientific foundations, he was capable of understanding the technical points of the flow of current after a lightning flash to Harris' fixed conductor of high capacity. It was true that Minto had at least some scientific aptitude[20] and, as noted earlier, had recorded observations as to changes in barometric pressure on ascending mountains in the Alps. Deductive logic had occurred to him but his knowledge of the new phenomenon of electricity was too little for him to understand the discharge to earth of the massive strokes of lightning. Something more formal and in-depth was required. Minto's numerous drafts of his planned speech to the House of Commons were revealing.[21] As ever, for a politician, double-speak was an imperative. His first drafts had tried to calculate the risk of injury or death from lightning to a sailor exposed to thunderstorms managing sails on a spar of a sailing ship.[22] One in 4,000 was the chance of death, he felt. That was not too great, surely? Caution prevailed and even the ambivalent Minto decided against making that point in the House. Also revealing was that his Board of Naval Lords was of no help to him.

Admiral Cockburn had left the Board to take up a position as Commander in Chief of the West Indies station. His successor was Admiral Sir Charles Adam. Variously described as amiable but traditional,[23] the main memory of his stewardship of the post of First Naval Lord was that nobody, including himself, could read his handwriting.[24] Since some primary sources in a private collection were not available to the author, it has proved impossible to understand why Adam appeared unable or unwilling to offer a reasoned opinion: except that he was against Harris' plan because it was a technological change. Adam may not have sought expert advice on the matter. He may never have known that the original plan had been agreed in 1823 by the Navy Board after a recommendation and inquiry by The Royal Society. But that was years before and the Navy Board had been almost forgotten.

The successive Whig administrations were to prevaricate and

dissemble for many more years before Admiral Cockburn, during a Tory tenure of the government in 1842, was to give the Order to fit all ships with Harris' lightning conductor.

Harris had never ceased his efforts to get his plan for his fixed lightning conductor adopted but he must have come close to despair. What sort of man was he? He had found he had to suffer fools and enemies but it was only after many years that his patience with his opponents finally snapped. In an effort to push his case forward he circulated pamphlets and letters to those in authority, including some foreign Ambassadors. That cannot have endeared him to the government but it had behaved unscrupulously to him and had even allowed Admiralty employees to steal his work. But Harris was not a traitor and declined to give away the information to foreigners as to how he fixed the system in place to withstand everything the weather or the flexing of the masts of the ships could throw at it.

Harris had deduced long before that an open and public debate would assist his case. He proceeded to lobby almost every member of each Admiralty Board but especially the First Lords and their political secretaries. He also wrote to any politician he met or was introduced to through contacts. Sir C. Lemon, a Whig MP for West Cornwall, interceded on his behalf and arranged for Harris to meet the then First Lord at the Admiralty, Minto. Another West Countryman, The Earl of St Germans (Edward Granvile Eliot) and a protectionist for the old order during the upheavals caused by the Corn Laws, moved a debate on the subject of lightning conductors in the House of Lords. Harris wrote to Lord Lampton, to the Earl of Durham, the Earl of Derby and direct to each First Lord including Graham, Minto, Auckland Haddington and Ellenborough. His letters to prominent politicians, at first diffident, were always polite and devastatingly detailed as to facts. His punctilious attention to protocol as well as to the limits of scientific method were contrasted in his letters by his accurate accounts of indifferent administration. He was able to highlight intemperate, muddled and illogical decisions by permanent staff at the Admiralty and by the politicians dealing with naval business. Each letter was polite but obdurate and it must have been evident to the recipients that the matters he raised would not go away.

There was evidence that Sir John Barrow, the Permanent Secretary to the Admiralty, was not an impartial and objective civil servant with respect to projectors such as Harris. Barrow was in a unique position as he bridged the time when the administrative subsumption of the former Navy Board took place. According to Sir Byam Martin,[25] the last Comptroller of the Navy Board, it was Barrow who actively delayed and interfered with the process of introduction of Harris' lightning conductors for HM Ships. Barrow had become well known for obtaining official naval support for exploration and especially for the search for the North West Passage (see Chapter 5). Less well known were his bouts of arrogance and of obfuscation. In reply to Harris' enquiry as to the fate of the trial of ten ships with fixed lightning conductors, he wrote in 1838, 'not usual to transmit reports'.[26] No summary of the situation was offered or even a promise to correspond further.

A year later in 1839, the administration at the Admiralty,[27] controlled by Barrow, failed to disclose a letter from Dockyard Superintendent Admiral Warren which in effect admitted that the fixed lightning conductors originally tried in *Caledonia*, *Druid* and in *Forte* had been 'lost' on recommissioning the three ships.

Harris was in regular correspondence with many naval officers, including Fitzroy and Beaufort. Instead of relying upon copies of letters which only occasionally reached him from the Admiralty, he made direct efforts to find evidence as to the efficacy of his invention. He wrote to the captain of any ship that he knew or had been informed was bearing his fixed lightning conductors. In addition, he sent a stream of letters to opinion-formers and especially to prominent scientists who could help his cause: Faraday at The Royal Institution, Babbage, Wheatstone, Daniell, Whewell, Forbes, electrical and meteorological researchers, and many others. Some scientists such as Airey, the Astronomer Royal, appeared to believe that electrical matters were simple and were to proffer advice after minimal exposure to the subject. The majority of Harris' fellow scientists accepted his ideas, approved of his research and after peer judgement of his papers asked his advice on atmospheric electrical matters and printed his contributions as chapters in major texts.

Harris was an excellent communicator and seemingly blessed with reserves of patience exceeding those of most men. He was known to be a good conversationalist and had the skill of a musician and that of a craftsman as regards his manual dexterity. Certainly he appreciated that visual illustration would underpin his ideas. As soon as he began to illustrate his papers on the effects of lightning on HM Ships, he began to win his case for recompense for his financial outlay and a grant and pension for his invention. Most telling of all was a depiction in one of his books of the difficulty of tricing up the wire or the flexible chain conductor. The conditions of a blow at sea are immediately understood and almost felt. To add to the effect, a stroke of lightning is seen to be about to maim or kill the sailors who are attempting to deploy the conductor. This one line drawing identified the folly of reliance upon the old style of inadequate protection from lightning and foretold the requirement for something permanent in its place (Fig.4a).

Harris had used laboratory demonstrations of his scientific work all his life. In setting these up he was known to rely upon meticulous preparation and trial so that the experiment always worked. This was particularly so for the life-sized demonstrations of the conductivity of the electric current by use of connecting wires to boats from masts. His capacity for being a showman became a strength for his demonstrations were not tame but ended with an explosion of some gunpowder to show beyond doubt that continuity of conduction had been achieved. Perhaps surprising to those used to modern conditions of restricted access to military bases and to materiel were the opportunities he was given to visit the Dockyards. He supervised the fitting of his conductors on the masts of warships, knew the movements of ships and was informed as to their design changes and development. Strange to us now was a habit of sharing some new scientific information with foreign nations. Perhaps the British were comfortable with their dominant Navy and felt they could afford to be relaxed. But they lost Erikkson's propeller to America, and effective armour plate for warships was developed first by France, even though Britain had led in the production of iron for armour. In the case of Harris' fixed lightning conductor of high capacity, the Russian Navy had installed it some years before its general use in HM Ships. The Russians had long been building up their fleet as a serious competitor to the British. They had noticed at least one ship bearing the new system of lightning conductors and had asked for details which they copied. In 1845, Csar Nicholas presented Harris with a commemorative vase and a ring.[28]

The failure by the Admiralty to proceed with the adoption of Harris' lightning conductor system or even to ensure a fair trial of it during 1832-41 apparently defies any explanation except that of political will. This will was missing during the Whig years in power and was exacerbated by apparent manipulation of information from the scanty records. The interregnum exactly paralleled the absence from the Admiralty Board and from Parliament of Admiral Sir George Cockburn,[29] who declined to stand again as an MP when abroad in the West Indies and, after three years on foreign service, returned but failed to get elected for Devonport. He was later returned for Ripon in the 1841 election. The vacuum due to his absence and the loss of his executive power to lead the Admiralty was enough to delay some of the progress in technological matters.

In 1841, after a sustained campaign for his recognition, Harris was awarded a pension by a Tory government of £300 p.a. for his attainments in science. The architect to the government, Sir William Rennie, asked him to place his design of lightning conductors on the chimneys and clock tower of the Royal William Victualling Yard building. Having been granted permission, it was then mysteriously withdrawn. Just before the meeting of the British Association of Science in 1841 in Plymouth, the building was struck by lightning and damaged. Harris took great satisfaction in showing it to his scientific colleagues. His book *On the Nature of Thunderstorms* was published in 1843 but did not attract much publicity. In it, he had calculated that repair of damage by lightning to national public buildings cost about £50,000 each year.

Harris was knighted by Queen Victoria in 1847, having placed lightning protection on Osborne House, Isle of Wight.[30] The recommendation came during a Whig government and perhaps was an apology for their earlier mistreatment of Harris. He had by then learned to patent any new idea and after he had invented tubular lightning conductors for iron ships with wire rigging and upper masts of wood he became the sole patentee.

The Great Exhibition of 1851 was a triumph for Sir William. After some exertions and double-speak, the Admiralty Surveyor's Office allowed Harris to borrow an exhibit from their collection. This was his lightning conductor as set up on the mast and hull of a cutaway wooden model. Harris was awarded The Council Medal for his exhibit.[31]

In 1856, Harris was granted a capital sum of £5,000 by Sir James Graham. The grant was half of what he had asked for and deserved but was obtained as a result of a long and sustained campaign run by Harris with the support of powerful friends.[32] He insisted that his point of view be heard and evaluated and in the end won his case.

He won through attention to detail. His lists of ships struck and damaged was the truth.

The summit of Harris' fame came in 1860 when he was appointed Scientific Referee in Electricity to the Government.[33] He personally supervised the fitting of lightning conductors to royal palaces, the Royal Mausoleum at Frogmore, powder magazines and just at the time of the build-up to the Crimean War, to the Houses of Parliament. This was to be his last task as he became ill with iritis (inflammation of the iris of the eye) for six months between 1861-2 and not even outings in his beloved schooner helped it. He lost all vision in one eye and had but partial vision in the other. He died on 22 January 1862 and was buried in a vault at the upper northern end of Plymouth Cemetery.[34] His widow applied for a pension to support her after his death and she survived until 1886. Only his eldest daughter married.

7

The Surveyor and His Opponents

The post of Surveyor to the Navy by precedent was a civil appointment, selected from one of the well-educated naval architecture graduates or from the pool of established shipwrights. In 1832, in a seemingly political gesture, the Whig First Lord of the Admiralty, Sir James Graham, recruited Captain William Symonds.

Captain William Symonds had begun his interest in naval architecture as an amateur constructor of small yachts and ships. When Captain of the dockyard at Malta, he was left a bequest from Admiral William Cornwallis which allowed him to design and build what became his very successful yacht, the *Nancy Dawson*. The outstanding handling and the speed of the *Nancy Dawson* was the original basis of Symonds' reputation as a ship designer. Later, his two Whig patrons, Lord Vernon and the Duke of Portland, were able to persuade the Tory Admiralty of 1827 to purchase the experimental brig, HMS *Columbine*. This ship was fast, weatherly and roomy and became an outstanding success. This established Symonds as an expert in the design of fast ships and changed his naval career from that of a sea-going officer with an uncertain future on half pay to the holder of a permanent office-based position.

Symonds, although still in the Royal Navy, was given great freedom in his new post from administrative oversight by the Admiralty. He was also given a mandate to design ships according to his own best ideas. On his appointment, a storm of controversy surrounded him, led by 41 disappointed graduates from the School of Naval Architecture who felt rejected by the appointment of an 'amateur ship designer'. The School had just been closed by the Whig administration. The trained naval architects must have felt unwanted and to have lost their future chances of preferment. Even ship designers of great experience such as Fincham, Lang, Roberts and Blake had apparently been discarded.

About his appointment, Symonds wrote that 'many frigates and brigs on the old principle were suspended. These and other necessary alterations were at the bottom of the violent enmity with which the disappointed followers of Sir George Cockburn and Sir Byam Martin, and the admirers of my predecessor, pursued me.'[1]

In the debate in the House on the Naval Estimates[2] on 29 June 1832, Sir Byam Martin said Symonds had no practical knowledge of shipbuilding and was unable to make the necessary calculations. Sir James Graham replied that the Surveyor did not need to be a practical shipbuilder.

It was true that Symonds had no experience of large shipbuilding and thus he was forced to rely upon his assistant, John Edye, a trained master shipwright, to supply detailed calculations and draughtsmanship: 'Mr Edye was appointed assistant to the Surveyor. He was one of the best practical shipbuilders; familiar with scientific calculations and unbiased by theoretical dogmas.' This eulogy to Edye,[3] which appeared in Symonds' autobiography, did recognise his several excellent achievements. Later Edye was to achieve more. The autobiography omitted that both he and his deputy were envious if not jealous of achievement by others. This defect was to lead both into plagiarism on at least two occasions.

The duo worked well as a team and later Edye was to be responsible for the famous 'Agamemnon' class of line of battle ship. The most obvious changes in Symonds' designs (so called 'Symondite') for sailing warships were increases in breadth in proportion to length and a rising deck. The beam ratio of Symondites was 3.1:3.3 as compared with the older style of 3.6:3.9. The undoubted success of his designs of ships led to Symonds being appointed a Fellow of the Royal Society in 1835, although for him this was a pleasant honour rather than a tribute to his scientific ability.

It was these qualities of design of 'short fat ships' which were to become the focus of uninformed and then of political debate and to lead to Symonds becoming obsessed with a need to prove himself right. It may also have had the effect of diverting his attention from new ideas such as that of the fixed protection from lightning. The political pressure upon him, to which he could not reply in person in the House, led to every aspect of his work being questioned. It also led to a search by his opponents for matters with which to taunt him. Despite this antipathy from many others, Symonds' career and credibility prospered.

One ship he designed, HMS *Pique*, a frigate, was still serviceable over 20 years later. By then carrying 40 guns, she was saved by her fixed lightning conductors in 1858 near Singapore. Her captain, Edward Seymour, wrote:[4]

> one night in middle watch one of the worst thunder storms I ever saw, and on that occasion at the ends of two spars aloft were what are called 'St Elmo's lights'; they look just like bright lanterns burning there, and are indeed electric lights, things then not invented by man, being caused by the immense amount of electricity in the air.

The same ship, then new, had previously been struck and damaged in 1839 whilst bearing no conductor.

In 1835, Admiral Hon. George Elliot was persuaded to join the Admiralty Board. He seems to have been placed in charge of the technical subjects but became disinterested in administration and preferred practical work. Although he had previously backed Symonds' appointment, later he took exception to the system of wide-beam design for ships brought in by the Surveyor. At the same time, he wrote demi-officially to congratulate him. The Surveyor's designs had added to the draught of the wide-beamed fast ships and this deep draught Elliot felt was not necessary for fast sailing. He had experience of the shallow-draught fast sailing *Modeste*. Elliot then spent two years building HMS *Eurydice* to his own design. His ship successfully beat all comers. The Board, to his astonishment, failed to thank him and in fact remained perfectly silent on the matter. This single departure from the ships designed by Graham's protégé, was later to become one more reason to discredit Symonds, even by his own supporters amongst the Whigs. It formed the first of a complicated pattern of issues which would eventually lead to Symonds' resignation.

When Gilbert Elliot, Second Earl of Minto, took office when aged 54 in 1835, he became the main protector of the Surveyor, both at the time of his administration and many years later. Minto, like Symonds, was made a Fellow of the Royal Society as a form of recognition of his public career. Minto was publicly to oppose Symonds, then apparently to support him, but only so as to ensure the demolition of a disliked new political aide. As we have seen, he also persisted in opposing, without credible cause, Harris' plan for lightning protection for HM Ships. Many thought Minto's accomplishments as First Lord at the Admiralty were few. Most agreed, including his political aides and his fellow Cabinet Ministers, that he was so immersed in local Scottish differences and feuds that he had little inclination or talent left to consider wider matters. Minto left political office altogether in 1852 but continued his vendetta against Tory critics and his loyalty to the Whig Surveyor, William Symonds. He tried to protect his unsustainable position against adequate permanent lightning protection for HM Ships in the House of Lords but came to be ignored as a politically motivated mountebank. He died in 1859 after a long illness, aged 76, leaving five sons and four daughters.

In 1836, after only four years in post, the energetic Surveyor, William Symonds, proposed and had adopted a new establishment for masts and spars. He had reduced the number of classes of masts held by the Yards as replacements from 92 to 18. He achieved this by classifying lengths and widths of masts and spars and demanding compliance with his catalogue. The consequent saving of money ensured the great success of his scheme. For this and for his other services he was knighted in 1836. The reduction in expenditure for masts and spars was possible only to a limited extent as a demand was ever present for the existing fleet and for new-builds. To be asked to deface them by allowing a groove to be cut for a lightning conductor to 'his spars and masts' would be likely to have been met by resistance from the Surveyor.

Symonds asserted that he was the founder of the naval architectural museum at Somerset House, although the former Navy Board also had a serious claim. The museum was an important repository for models of ships, for woods used in shipbuilding, for designs of masts, of rigging and for proper records of the lines used to build a ship. Correspondence confirmed that the Surveyor had indeed received new ideas for improvements and inventions. It was noteworthy that Harris never corresponded directly with Symonds or with the Surveyor's department.

Symonds does seem to have had some insight into the deficiencies of his education and training. On taking up his post in 1832, he had proposed to the Admiralty Board that a Naval Committee should be formed and sit ad hoc so as to advise them as to the merits of all new inventions or scientific work. His foresight was not rewarded by swift action as even minimal activity would have cost money which the government did not wish to grant. Eventually, a Committee for Inventions was formed and became active by 1834. Prior to the Committee sitting, it had been the Admiralty's newly reformed policy to ask the Surveyor and the Storekeeper General to file any submissions from inventors and, with permission, to arrange to test their proposals. This new system evidently had not worked and by May 1834 the two departmental heads[5] were peremptorily ordered to produce 'a statement from Somerset House of all the new models and plans for experiments in ship building – fitting steam machinery'.

The list included a patent capstan, a topmast, a fid for a topmast, a new system of naval architecture, a new mode of caulking, a gun carriage, paddle wheels, a compressor, various other paddle wheels and capstans, etc. Unfortunately, the list did not include the results to date of the trial of Harris' fixed lightning conductor.

There was a great interest in new inventions and developments by the Admiralty Boards of the 1830s and their overall view was committed to progress rather than the status quo of a 'wooden walls' Navy. In those circumstances, it was even more surprising that Harris' excellent lightning conductors did not receive more support and a faster rate of progress towards their eventual universal fitting in HM Ships.

By 1839, the Whig Board at the Admiralty was showing signs of wishing to rein in the wide influence and remit of the Surveyor. According to Charles Wood's briefing paper to his successor: 'It was the intention of the Board to have made an alteration in the constitution of the Surveyor's department at Somerset House. The papers and memoranda with them entertained the view but the Board did not think it right to proceed further after the resignation of HM Minister.'[6]

The office of the Surveyor was thought by the Board to be too weak to deal with the troublesome ways and working practices of the carpenters in the Yards. The amount of work they performed varied widely between Yards. Loss of the necessary files of the history of the subject was admitted, as was a lack of direction by the Surveyor.

Meanwhile, Symonds' own supporters had become uneasy over his confrontational style. Minto wrote to Wood in 1839 and conveyed his unease about Symonds' reaction to criticism of HMS *Pique* and of *Vanguard*.[7]

The Surveyor's expertise as to masts and spars would later give him undue influence as to the adoption of lightning conductors for HM Ships. He contended that fixed conductors let into a purpose-made groove on a mast and then lined with double plates of copper weakened the masts and any spars fitted with them. Symonds had personal experience in 1806 of the severe damage lightning could cause to his ship, which at the time was without any form of conductor. Yet he was unwilling to ask permission for experimental work, which his department should have sponsored, to support his view that masts and spars perhaps could be weakened by the proposed new conductors. By contrast, Mr Rice of Chatham Yard, without waiting for official permission from the administration was able to demonstrate, with figures obtained after controlled experiments, precisely the opposite view: that the masts and spars were actually *strengthened* by the presence of the fixed conductors.

Symonds, like his predecessor Seppings, was a determined and opinionated man who reacted badly to criticism. Both were to lose their post as Surveyor for mainly political reasons. Unlike Seppings, Symonds found it a strain to have to compete his ships in sailing trials against other designs. He became a target for George Cockburn's[8] wrath, who said he could not understand Symonds becoming upset about constructively-put criticism. At the same time, Cockburn maintained he had no personal prejudice against him.[9] Indeed, he had praised certain aspects of the new ship to the then First Lord (Graham): 'praise HMS *Vernon* fairly but had unfavourable opinions'. He went on to give his opinion about 'short fat ships', 'but only let him know *if you* can'.

Raikes,[10] in his Journal of 1832, according to Symonds' biographer, reported that Sir G. Cockburn was so inveterate in his opposition to the Whigs that he was appointed at the King's express desire to the American station, so as to get rid of him from the House of Commons. Later, this opposition referred in particular to Cockburn's remarks about the unweatherly qualities of his flagship on that station, HMS *Vernon*. Thomas Raikes was a dandy and a governor of the Bank of England and had excellent social connections, so no doubt heard and then passed on gossip.

The Surveyor's most powerful patron had been the Duke of Portland, a moderate Canningite supporter of the Whig ministry. After the Duke died in 1840, his protection was missed and as Symonds' supporters moved on from the weak Admiralty Boards led by Minto, he became more and more exposed to criticism. Poor and hurried drafting[11] of the Surveyor's mandate on appointment ensured that verbal sniping continued during the whole time he was in office.

A Tory government, led by Sir Robert Peel, had taken office in 1841. Peel was the son of a self-made industrial magnate. His family's fortunes had been made in calico printing in Blackburn and other interests were in farming and in weaving. Peel appointed the inexperienced Earl of Haddington as his First Lord at the Admiralty.

The new Admiralty Board was dominated once more by the powerful and experienced Admiral George Cockburn. Cockburn was no friend of the Symondite ship design and had with justice criticised some but not all of the sailing qualities of his flagship on the West Indies station, HMS *Vernon*. In office, Cockburn set about ordering Courts of Inquiry and sailing trials with the sole aim of discrediting the Surveyor's school of wide-beam ships. These ships, when of larger lines, in his opinion, made unstable gun platforms especially in a head sea. From 1841, the Surveyor's work was subject to ever-increasing scrutiny by the Admiralty. Cockburn was eventually to be proved wrong in his criticism of the sailing quality of the Symondite form. Meanwhile, he refused to be thwarted in his endeavours to destabilise the Surveyor's department.

Cockburn authorised that a Committee of Master Shipwrights be appointed and this met on 23 December 1841. The remit of the Committee was 'to consider the best modes of strengthening ships of war and to recommend improvements to give greater power of attack and defence without interfering with the power of sailing'. In other words, Cockburn felt that the Surveyor's ship designs were yachts rather than warships and wanted something better. The Committee met at Woolwich and as Symonds justly remarked 'it was like inviting subordinate officers to sit in judgement of their superior'.[12] The Chatham Committee was composed of three graduates of the former School – Read, Creuze and Chatfield. Their work was similar to Edye's but was written down rather than learnt by word of mouth.

Symonds meanwhile had been on a long trip to the Mediterranean and the Black Sea commencing in February 1841. On his return in about June or July of that year, he found the government had changed. Sir Robert Peel was in power for the next five years. The Tory old guard had always (according to the Surveyor's autobiography) viewed the (previous) radical changes at the Admiralty with a strong dislike. The First Lord (Lord Haddington) was a stranger to everything naval:

> Cockburn ruling with an imperious and overbearing hand; interfering with my duties, setting up the Master Shipwrights, and the mechanics, in judgement of my works; clipping my wings, and depriving me of all power and respect in the Yards. A system of the most flagrant jobbing was now exhibited while merit was unrewarded, a hateful partiality was shown to those who had political influence. The Chatham Committee was composed of those from Naval School who had written anonymous papers [against Symonds] in the press.

According to Morriss,[13] the experiments as regards paddle or screw propulsion had begun before Cockburn's return to Admiralty as Senior Naval Lord in September 1841. Admiral Codrington (then C in C Portsmouth) had pushed Brunel's plans for steam propulsion for deep-sea vessels before the previous Board. Sir Edward Codrington was a Whig admiral and known to be 'difficult' in that he refused to allow politics to interfere with naval professional matters and would be likely to continue to lobby for the cause.

Haddington's new Board took up the thorny matter of advances in steam power and its suitability for warships. A meeting was arranged and the Surveyor invited to attend in his position as chief constructor for HM Ships. Symonds then showed his vulnerability and his lack of scientific knowledge. With a certain naivety, he produced a cut-away model of a line of battleship's stern. This purported to show Brunel's method of application of the steam-driven screw propeller. Brunel, who fortunately had also been invited to the meeting, denied it was his model or anything like his plan. The meeting was then abandoned. Symonds had failed in his attempt to mislead the Board as to his own scientific credentials and his degree of comprehension about screw propulsion.

As a result of this very obvious fiasco induced by Symonds, Cockburn decided he had to reduce the Surveyor's strong influence against developments in steam power. He achieved this by at once retaining Brunel as an impartial, unpaid adviser. Brunel gained from the arrangement, as he was able to use Admiralty facilities and ships as test-beds for his developments in screw propulsion for commerce.

This suited the Admiralty which took the view that it was interested in the screw *as an aid to sail*, not as the chief means of propulsion and was also constrained by economic considerations.

Had his production of a cut-away model in fact been another attempt by Symonds (and perhaps Edye) to revert to plagiarism to retain credibility? After all, both had done this with respect to lightning conductors in 1839. After this second episode, Symonds found that he had lost his former influence and was required to minute all matters pertaining to his department for decision by the Board. Meanwhile, Cockburn continued to do his best to demonstrate that the Surveyor had been promoted above his abilities and that he could not keep up with modern ideas.

Another Committee drawn from graduates of the former School of Naval Architecture was appointed on 23 April 1842 'to provide a series of designs for a ship of each class to be accompanied by an explicit statement explaining the method used for preparing them'.

Cockburn was aware that Symonds could not understand the complex mathematics and calculations necessary for ship design and that his deputy, John Edye, had been appointed to assist Symonds in this respect. Therefore, to demand that the mathematics must be produced and explained meant that Symonds could not even begin to compete as Edye was out of the loop.

Cockburn went even further in a memorandum of 1845. He suggested a Board of Construction be appointed, chaired by an admiral with a special interest and knowledge in shipbuilding – such as Rear Admiral Elliot (this would have brought the Whigs on side), along with Professor Inman for his mathematical knowledge and two or three of the most distinguished graduates from the School of Naval Architecture as well as two naval captains. Such a Board, he surmised, need not meet more than once a fortnight and the extra task and responsibility could be recognised by £200 p.a. for members and £300 for the chairman.

This constant undermining of the Surveyor's authority and that of his department, was soon to bear fruit. Symonds' continued and obdurate opposition to all scientific progress began to cause immense suspicion between on the one hand the naval officers who sailed Symondite ships and enjoyed their excellent sailing qualities, and on the other, the displaced ex-Naval School architects.

The final blow to the Surveyor's reign came when a Committee of Reference on all shipbuilding for the government was appointed on

26 May 1846. The formal Committee was set up under Captain Lord John Hay with Inman, Fincham and Abethell. They at once altered each of the Surveyor's designs for ships which were not too advanced in their building.

The Committee of Reference drew up an elaborate report on naval construction. Symonds was kept in ignorance about its conclusions until it was complete and he was then asked to comment on it. He protested it was made up of speculative theories, that it was condemnatory of his designs which had been reported upon favourably. The report had noted that the following vessels had failed in speed, handiness and capacity: *Acteon, Volage, Sapphire, Comus, Electra, Fly, Harrier, Larne, Orestes, Rose, Icarus* and *Prince Regent*. Symonds' reply was to challenge their competency and he rejected the reports. It was noteworthy that not one of the ships mentioned had been designed by Symonds and hence the report was a tribute rather than a criticism. Edye, his assistant, was to remark: 'We are plagued to death by the great number of theorists in naval construction, but there is no one in twenty that knows anything about it.'[14]

That several of these vessels had permanent lightning protection fitted instead of his plagiarised version, must have been a further blow to Symonds.

A month later, in June 1846, the decision to reinstate a Naval School of Architecture was effectively taken by ordering the higher forms of mathematics be studied at a superior school. The series of decisions were interdependent and were adopted by The Admiralty Board and so ordered.[15] Cockburn thus eliminated Symonds and Edye but without causing a political row with the Whigs who had made the original appointments. The struggle for a new regime to replace that of Symonds in the design and construction of warships might have been stopped short in 1846 with the return of a Whig-appointed Admiralty Board. However, its First Lord, The Earl of Auckland, was to prove no friend of the Surveyor. The Committee of Reference on Shipbuilding[16] had been formed and now it reported with a more reasoned critique of the Surveyor's designs.

Events Leading to the Resignation of the Surveyor

Minto was a friend and had protected Symonds. He realised that Symonds tended to attack and then lose a contest by over-representation. Minto wrote to him on 19 December 1844, when out of office, and congratulated him on the success of the trials of his design of his gun brigs.[17] Symondite ships had clearly won:

> the foundation of all the attacks upon you – the clamour was raised by the scientific, against what is called the intuitive, school of shipbuilding ... you have signally defeated, not only one, but the whole collective skill and science of the School of Architecture and shipwright officers: We all know that you have a powerful enemy [Admiral G. Cockburn] to contend with authority over you and that there are many jealous rivals bent on running you down, but you have strength in the undeniable merit of your work ... if I were you, wholly refrain from any attack upon my adversaries' conduct, confining myself entirely to what regards the ships, not their constructors.

The jealous rivals were singled out by an anonymous author writing in defence of Symonds, as 'a clique from the defunct Naval School of Architecture'.[18] They were but 'dockyard libellers and overpaid mechanics. They were insubordinate. They uttered falsehoods and calumnies and were malignant and slanderous insinuators'. These terms as printed in reply to critics demonstrated the strength of opinion and a need for a robust reply to the unjust treatment which had been meted out to Symonds.

Admiral Sir Charles Napier was the leading Whig spokesman on Naval matters. Even he was attacked in Parliament on 13 February 1845. He allowed that the Surveyor's ships were superior to their predecessors but still complained as to *Pique*, *Vanguard*, *Queen* and *Albion*. The steamers *Gorgon* and *Cyclops* were the real failures, he said.

The former Whig administration at the Admiralty could not help but be greatly interested to the point of paranoia as to the fate of their projects. Their appointees, such as the Surveyor, were still in the public eye and exposed to criticism in the press and in the House. The belief of the former First Lord, Minto, in the Surveyor's ability and integrity was loyal and great but misguided. For a time, the Whigs imagined that the office of Surveyor remained an oligarchy with much discretion left to the expansionist incumbent. Minto was optimistic when he wrote: 'I was glad to see how completely Cockburn seems to be beat in his department with regard to Symonds. He is a considerable humbug owing much of his authority to a peremptory manner.'[19]

In fact, Cockburn was busy tightening the snare for capturing the remit and the responsibility of the Office of the Surveyor to one whereby a proper line of management could be substituted for tradition. Symonds, no doubt with input from Edye, persisted in his campaign to force adoption of 'his' cheap and cheerful wire rope conductors for lightning protection for HM Ships and at the same time take any active steps he could to discredit Harris and his plan.[20] He wrote privately to Minto in April 1845 to discuss the exciting possibility that at last he could prove he was right: two ships bearing Harris' fixed system of protection had been struck by lightning. Early but mischievous reports had suggested that the ships had been damaged despite the fixed copper plate conductors which led the lightning into the hull and out through the keel and keelson to the sea:

> 'I have not yet seen reports of lightning conductors on *Scylla* and in *Electra* but have called for them. I feel convinced that wire rope lightning conductors are as much superior to Harris' as they are cheaper to the country in the proportion of £80 to £400 or 1/5 besides the injury imposed upon the masts by the latter. But I imagine it is considered a proper remuneration for Mr Snow Harris' political services at Devonport and Plymouth'.

As will be seen elsewhere, Symonds was to be disappointed but neither he nor Minto could let the subject go and concede with grace they were wrong. Minto wrote that his son had told him:[21]

> 'the *Spartan's* masts were taken out (in the most perfect condition) in order to be fitted with Harris' lightning conductors, in lieu of the wire rope conductors which, he assured me, were never in the least in the way, or otherwise inconvenient: whilst their efficacy has been tested in the *Electra*, in a thunderstorm, of which a report went to the Admiralty. It seems rather a

Above: HMS *Dido* struck by lightning when off Java Head in May 1847. The fixed conductor acted as a complete safety valve. *Painting by N M Condy.*

Below: The lookout brig sloop HMS *Surinam* had no lightning conductor up when she was struck and had two men killed. The ship was set on fire; deck stove in and the broken mast went overboard in three pieces. Shown sending out distress signals, 11th December 1806 off Belleisle, France. *Painting by N M Condy.*

Above: HMS *Thisbe* also had no conductor. She was set on fire from lightning on 4th January 1786 when off St Mary's, Scilly Isles. She was left a mere wreck with many men disabled. *Painting by N M Condy.*

Below: HMS *Fisgard* anchored in the Nisqually River, Puget's Sound, Oregon during the boundary crisis with the USA. On 26th September 1846 the warship was struck by bolts of lightning to the top of the mainmast and at deck level. The enormous surge of electricity was safely led to the sea by Harris' capacious conductor. *Fisgard* later became the training ship for naval engineers at Woolwich. *Painting by N M Condy.*

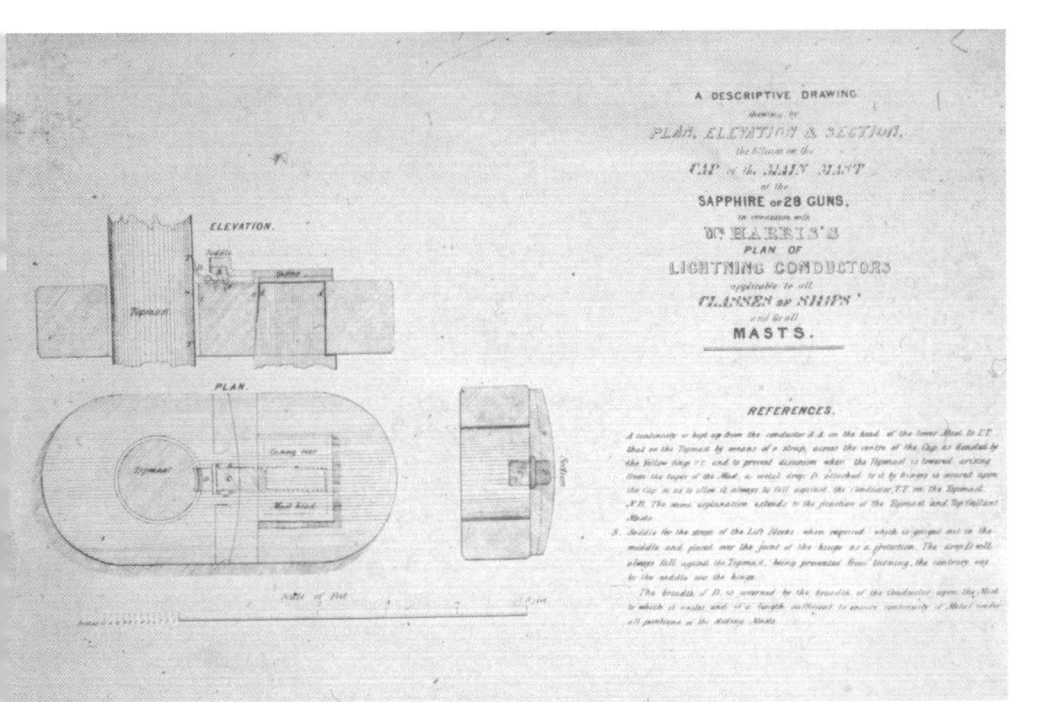

Above: Harris' clever solution to the problem of conducting a large electrical current safely down flexing, twisting and moveable masts. Pairs of overlapping copper plates set in a groove were led over the fids to the next lower mast.
Admiralty Library, ESB. Drawing by H L Peake. Plans for fitting Sapphire of 28 guns with fixed conductors. Printed for the House of Commons 11th Feb. 1840.

Below: Lightning struck 174 HM sailing ships between 1793 and 1838. Hundreds of men became casualties.
Illustration redrawn from Harris' Thunderstorms, *1843, frontispiece.*

Left: Sailors were often killed, blinded or maimed when tricing up this type of lightning conductor. When thunder was heard a thin wire rope was led from a short iron rod placed on the cap of the mast and thence dangled into the sea. It had to be reset each time the ship tacked. The wire was able to carry only a small fraction of the electrical current from a lightning strike and the ship carrying it was often damaged despite it.
Redrawn from Harris' use in publications on lightning including Thunderstorms, *1843, p.136 and 'The Danger Attendant on the use of small wire ropes as lightning conductors for ships', 1841.*

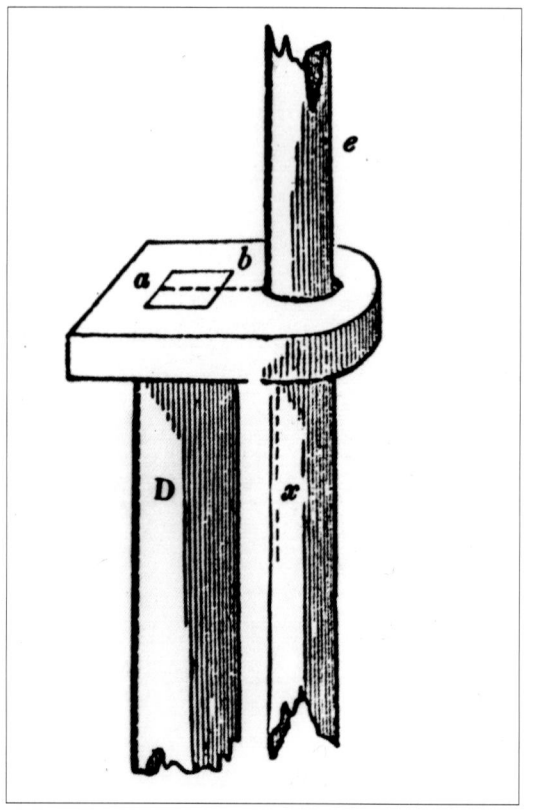

Left: By contrast Harris' system of overlapping copper plates was always in place, required minimal maintenance and was of sufficient capacity to carry off the lightning to the sea.
Redrawn from Harris' Thunderstorms, *1843, p.143.*

Left: The inventor of the fixed permanent lightning conductor system for ships.
Photograph reproduced with thanks to the Western Morning News Ltd (9.2.84)

Below Left: Lt William Pringle Green, RN. A practical seaman who incorrectly believed his talents extended to all other matters including the new science of electricity.
Illustration from his book Fragments, *etc, 1833*

Below Right: Just before its completion, this monument to Sir John Barrow was heavily damaged by lightning. Harris' conductor for buildings was fitted, since when no further damage has occurred.
Illustration from A Memoir to Sir John Barrow *by his son, 1851.*

Above: The lightning rod terminal from the French battleship *L'Orient*. Later used as a hat-stand by Admiral Nelson after the Battle of the Nile.
_{Photographed with permission of the National Maritime Museum, Greenwich, London.}

Below: Part of the original lightning conductor system installed after 1842 and recently discovered in the hull of HMS *Victory*, Portsmouth.
_{Photograph reproduced by permission of the Commanding Officer HMS Victory and of the Ministry of Defence (N).}

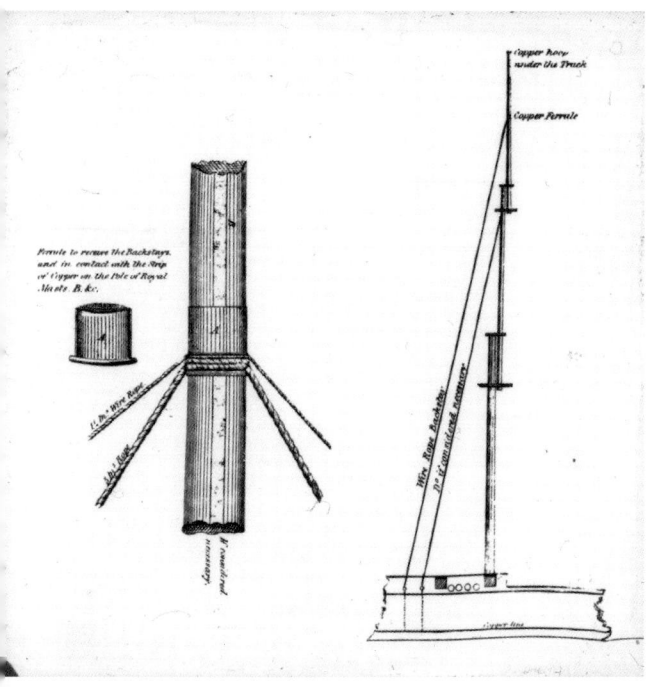

Left: The ineffective wire rope conducting system. John Edye partly plagiarized Harris' system and submitted his version to the Committee at the Admiralty in 1839. Edye was unable to answer questions about its electrical capacity.
Drawing and plans submitted by John Edge, Assistant Surveyor, Somerset House. The National Archives (TNA), ref. ADM1/607.

Below: HMS *Conway*'s mast was struck by forked lightning but saved from any damage by Harris' conductor when moored off Port Louis, Mauritius on 9th March 1846. Later she became *Conway* the school ship and eventually, as *Winchester*, an RNVR drill ship at Aberdeen.
Painting by N M Condy.

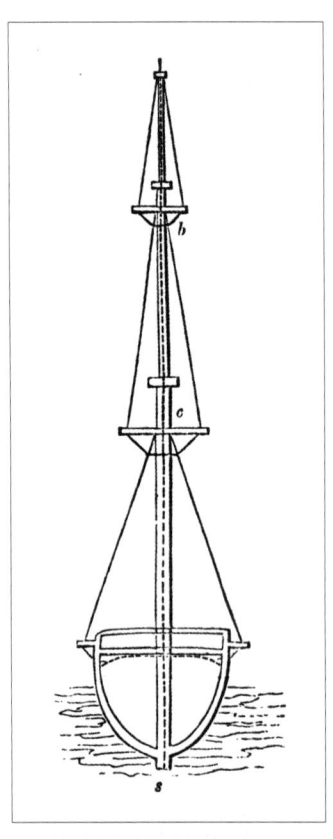

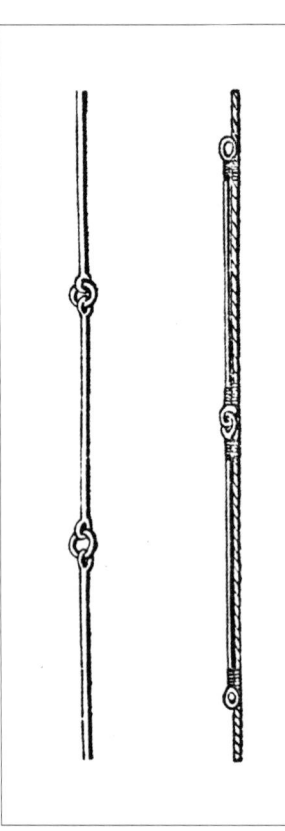

Top Left: Drawing of Harris' system of a lightning conductor from truck to keel and with lateral branches on the hull to avoid flashover to guns or other metal.
Redrawn from Harris' Thunderstorms, 1843, p.145

Top Right: The very first lightning conductors used on ships were long links of thin metal chain sometimes fastened to a rope. They were too troublesome to use.
Redrawn from J L Winn.
In Phil. Trans. 60, 1770. pp.185-9.

Below: Lightning.
Photograph by Mr J Bunyan.
Reproduced with permission.

strange thing to have dismasted a ship in order to throw away £2-300, in giving protection which was already complete'.

Minto then revealed his own deficient and ignorant opinion: 'I doubt if any member of the Board has yet taken the trouble of making himself master of this subject of conductors.' Minto was wrong. The Board, and certainly its naval leader, Admiral Cockburn, was master of the subject whereas Minto never had been. Instead, he had been swayed first one way then another by unfortunate 'advice' from Barrow and from Symonds and Edye.

A footnote by Symond's editor was in fact an apology.[22] It read:

The conductors of Sir W S Harris were tried in a ship of war, for the first time in 1830. However alarming it may seem to pass lightning through a ship, down her masts on this plan, yet their superiority and perfect safety have been shown on many occasions, in which both masts and vessels have escaped. In fact, to carry lightning off in this way is as harmless as letting water down of a pipe.

Symonds by now needed any support he could obtain from Whig friends in Parliament. Friends were few, although Sir J. Graham, Minto and Wood remained his constant supporters. Mr Hume advised the House of the restoration of the School of Naval Architecture. Cockburn acknowledged in reply that the Surveyor had brought great benefit to the Navy. But the Admiralty Board had made up their minds not to trust any one person with building ships.[23] At the same time, nothing would be done to hurt the feelings of Sir W. Symonds who had 'rendered great service'.

The first iron steamers, *Birkenhead* and *Megaera* were built on Cockburn's instructions, without the Surveyor's approval as it was well known that Symonds had no love for steamers, or for screw propulsion. Much of the criticism about the Surveyor and his ships was printed in the *Morning Herald* and Minto was anxious that Symonds should not try to reply via its columns. One of the grounds on which Symonds was criticised was that the cost of building to his designs was too great. Symonds preferred a fight to be in the open and replied in kind to criticism. An old friend, Admiral Bowles,[24] wrote to hope that Symonds 'would refrain from newspaper controversy - there was a stream of envy, hatred and malice which is running strongly against him, and ended by saying the worst defect of his ships was superior to the best of those built by the old school, (of Naval Architecture). Much was made of comparative costs. Symonds devised a table from which Table 7.1 has been modified.[25]

Table 7.1 Costs of ships and materials

HMS	£/ton	Built by
Queen 110g.	26.97	Symonds
Albion 90g.	24.70	Seppings
Vernon 50g.	23.29	Symonds
Raleigh 50g.	23.75	Fincham
Acteon 26g.	30.57	Inman
Sapphire 28g.	32.72	School
Pique 36g.	20.35	Symonds
Thetis 36g.	27.98	School

The costs per ton were calculated from total cost of the hull divided by the tonnage.

Cockburn[26] said the Surveyor had made ships broader and better capable of carrying large weights and he defended the *Queen*. Sir William, he said (with a forked tongue), was entitled to the support and protection of the Board. The Committee of Shipwrights at Woolwich had drawn up their report and most of their recommendations, modified by the Surveyor's remarks, had been adopted. Cockburn was obviously a consummate politician and well versed in double-speak, as well as being an excellent First Naval Lord and seaman.

In their most interesting book on Brunel's ships, Griffiths, Lambert and Walker[27] point to their conclusions that the Admiralty was a plagiarist of technological breakthroughs. Putting it as kindly as possible, the Admiralty had become, through economic necessity, experts in the selective appropriation of the ideas of inventors and of designers. Also, patents were feared by the successive naval administrations from 1830 to 1860, as royalties to civilian owners of an invention could soon consume small budgets. The Naval Estimates, debated each year in full, had long become a knock-about, point-scoring opportunity for the Tories in their battles to wrest power back from the Whigs.

Part, but only a part, of the Admiralty's monopolistic stance was forced upon them due to their own poverty of funding for research and development. The advances in technology which followed the Industrial Revolution could have bypassed the military and the fossilised 'wooden wall' navy. It is to the credit of several far-sighted Lords such as Hardy, Cockburn and even, to a minor extent, Adam, that sailing ships were recognised as outmoded and that naval tactics had altered for ever, once steam power had allowed warships to make progress directly into the wind.

The administration of the Navy had not failed completely to carry out research. The former Navy Board also had a long history of encouragement to innovators, even of minor works, and eventually recommended a reward for their endeavours. After 1830, the annual sum set aside for research and for rewards to improvers was only £1,000. For major advances such as machinery design and trial, that sum was clearly too little even for a start-up grant. Large capital cost items required corresponding finance, as the civilian companies floated to build steamers for commercial success soon found out. When the age of sail was at a static phase, the amount possibly was adequate. Once propulsion by manmade means was desired, the spending power available to the Admiralty for in-depth research was to prove, de facto, a famine.

Lord Minto continued to show immense loyalty to Symonds, who was eager for his support. The Committee on Naval Construction of 1846 had reported adversely on the Surveyor's ship designs, exactly as Cockburn had intended. On thanking Minto for his advice and support, Symonds referred to five years of 'hateful conspiracy' against him from the Tory administration.[28] In another letter to Minto he wrote, 'I regret to inform you that at no former period was the Admiralty left in such a state of confusion and difficulty, as in the accession of the present Board. All system having been destroyed and the reckless measures of extravagance.'[29]

Symonds finally resigned a year later in 1847, due to the mutilation, on the orders of the Admiralty, of his designs for further ships. His fight for recognition of his designs did not pass without several further spirited defences of his achievements, notably with yet more letters and debates and before those death throes with the publication in 1845 of a book, *Fact Versus Fiction or Sir William Symonds' Principles of Naval Architecture Vindicated by a Compilation of Official and Other Documents* by 'One who has Served'.[30]

Even after the resignation of Symonds, the bitterness between rival naval constructors and designers did not cease. Admiral Napier wrote that, 'Those rival gentleman [Edye, the locum Surveyor and Oliver Lang, Master Shipwright] put the Country to great Expense and ought to be brought up with a round turn.'

Symonds used his own money to finance his travels so as to assess the strength and supplies of foreign navies. Ever with Admiralty interests and business at heart, he visited the Baltic, Russia, Copenhagen, Brest, the Black Sea, Genoa and many forests used to supply timber for the construction of ships. He claimed he had ended the job and task routines in the Yards which were responsible for so many problems with progress of the building of a ship, but carpenters' routines seemed to have evaded him. His success as Surveyor between 1832 and 1847 was not as an administrator but undoubtedly was for his designs which advanced the tonnage that could be carried by warships, and improved some of their sailing qualities and speed. His political skills were negligible and his scientific knowledge even less. It was his refusal to acknowledge that steam power would replace sail and to react accordingly that isolated him in the decade up to his retirement on reaching the age of 65.

His lack of scientific knowledge was also responsible for his duplicity of conduct with respect to the progress of fixed lightning conductors. He bore line management and partial personal responsibility for his and Edye's plagiarism of Harris' ideas in 1839. Thereafter, it was probable that he attempted to defend his position as the expert on masts and their protection from all the weather could throw at them by his inexpert manipulation of data and selective loss of files.

The Assistant Surveyor

John Edye had been appointed Assistant Surveyor as the Chief Draughtsman to Sir William Symonds on 1 July 1839. Thus from that date he was able to exert considerable official influence at local Yard level both by himself and through his relative, W. Edye, who was appointed Master Shipwright in succession to T. Hawkes in 1843.

The more prominent John Edye, in the author's view, set out to destroy Snow Harris' plan, not only in order to gain personal credit for his plagiarised cut-down version of it but also because he, too, eschewed the new 'science' of electricity. Evidence for this view of the hitherto well-regarded John Edye was his tabled presentation to the Committee of 1839. This presentation was for Edye's version of a permanent lightning conductor for HM Ships. It had been pilfered from Harris' plan for the topmasts, made into a hybrid of Harris' and of Martyn Roberts' plans, and lightly camouflaged as all his own. His plan was thought by the scientists on the Committee, who had courteously received it in good faith, as almost without merit and not based upon experiment or on science.

Edye's chief, Sir William Symonds, had fractured his femur in a fall from a gig in late August 1837. Edye then became responsible for the entire department during Symonds' absence, which was from August 1837 to about April 1838. If ship design or shipbuilding or materials for ships were to be considered, Edye had charge of information to and from the Yards. This information must have included any events concerning the supply and resupply of lightning conductors.

Edye's special interest had formerly been masts and timber and his advice was well received at the Navy Board before its abolition. His reputation at the Admiralty was person-dependent, for Cockburn when in office, sought his advice.

In November 1837, during Symonds' continued absence on sick leave, Edye wrote to the Admiralty as the de facto Surveyor.[31] He suggested keeping a large store of timber for shipbuilding. His main thesis was that repair of older ships was wasteful and if repairs were to be done then old or second-rate timber could be used. Better than repair old worn-out hulks would be to build new ships, whose expected life would be 10–15 years.

Minto replied that he saw 'no reason to suggest new ships of the line should be commenced' and did not agree with Edye's statements. He did not feel competent to offer an opinion with respect to the employment of inferior timber for some repairs. This was a rare glimpse of how Edye attempted to deal with departmental matters. He had managed to put forward a discussion paper[32] to his seniors but did not put it well for it lacked breadth of thought. He soon found that the First Lord was out of sympathy with him. Edye seems not to have been skilled in committee or in political matters. Indeed, he must have seemed to Minto to be solely expansionist in outlook, during a time of strictly enforced economy. Two of the ships mentioned by Edye, *Java* and *Forte*, had previously been chosen to trial the fixed lightning conductors invented by Harris. Edye was therefore well aware of the status of these two ships and it was very likely he knew of the other ships placed in the trial of Harris' conductors.

Three years later in 1840, the Admiralty Board had made the curious decision to ignore the findings of its own Committee. The Committee's findings had been in total support of the fixed permanent lightning protection system first proposed by Harris. Instead, it issued orders to fit Edye's stolen version of Harris' plan for fixed lightning conductors in grooves cut into the wood only to the topmasts of ships. From thence downwards, the instructions were to use wire rope in keeping with the proposals put forward by the Surveyor's Office. Edye had after all gained official acceptance of his curious and untried scheme. Backed by Symonds, the Yards were advised as to the new instructions without delay. Science was humbug, stated Edye. His practical scheme would solve the problem of lightning strikes on HM Ships at a fraction of the cost of other plans. Probably what he meant by 'humbug', was that he was not in a position to understand new scientific developments. This was at odds with his acceptance of a Fellowship from The Royal Society in the 1830s on publication of his book on *Calculations of Equipment and Displacement for Ships of War*.

Edye continued his campaign against new developments brought about from scientific discoveries. At about the same time as he attempted to suppress Harris' work and substitute his own, he was raising numerous objections to iron hulls for warships. He also made it plain that he disliked the over-rapid introduction of screw propellers and fought such changes. He seems to have been a focused, practically-minded shipwright who could use advanced mathematics to design the form of a ship's hull, yet he lacked an appreciation of anything outside his own narrow range of subjects. His apprenticeship to Master Shipwright Joseph Tucker in the drawing offices and mould lift of the Yard had been privately funded for seven years from 1803. This apprenticeship style of learning on the job even led Edye into opposition to the Naval School of Architecture. Yet he used similar mathematical techniques as had been taught there. Edye had been injured on HM service when, due to his foolish action of looking at the sun through a telescope, he had lost the sight of that eye in about 1825. He had been sent to India to find new sources for timber for shipbuilding. Perhaps understandably, he felt the world owed him more recognition if not recompense.

John Edye had been unscrupulous in his plagiarism of Harris' plan for fixed conductors and did not admit to the facts. Later events exposed his flimsy and costly plan for conductors. They did not work and were a danger to the ships. The facts of the failure of his copper wire ropes as lightning conductors were obscured or lost until published in the precept for the House of Lords in 1850. Edye was fortunate that he had avoided any public criticism as none of the ships bearing his pallid ideas for protection from lightning had been set on fire or destroyed by lightning. He resigned his post, was awarded a CB and a pension and took his retirement in 1848. Thus, as an inventor or as a developer of ideas, he achieved almost nothing beyond recording traditional ways of calculating the lines for ships' hulls. Certainly he did not deserve to retain the status of a Fellow of The Royal Society, as he continued to scorn science, which, he asserted, 'retarded the commonplace duties of the dockyard, producing a correspondence that the service may said to be paralysed and the ships delayed'.

An objective view as to the number of HM Ships struck by lightning in any one year is afforded by Table 7.2 below. In one sense, the risk was small for any one ship. The exceptions to this rule of thumb were that the degree of risk increased, as we have seen, in Chapter 1, in areas of high thunderstorm activity. The reason for a warship being in a particular place at a certain time was the orders of the Admiralty on behalf of the State. Matters such as the security of the country, of its trade routes and of the prevention of or the prosecution of war, were examples. It must have been well known in naval circles that there were several instances when valuable warships were prevented from taking up their stations due to damage from lightning or due to foreseeable defects in their portable lightning conductors, such as Edye's version. In wartime, such excuses for delay would not have been acceptable. Edye was most fortunate that for once 'dockyard delay' without a precise reason worked in his favour despite the affected ships being moored out in Plymouth bay rather than the Yard at Devonport.

The appointments of the Surveyor, Symonds, and of his deputy, Edye, were the direct result of Graham's need to be a new broom, to sweep away any chance of Yard peculation, to centralise Admiralty administration and to confound the Tory old guard. The results of Graham's decision was years of vicious criticism and plain bad behaviour by his own political party and that of the opposition. The finding that neither appointment proved successful became also a matter of concern that merit was once more of little use. Political reasons for the appointment of public servants inevitably led to their failure.

Table 7.2 Number of HM Ships struck by lightning in wartime and in peacetime

War			*Peace*
1793 *1*	1805 *4*	1817 *1*	1829 *2*
1794 *5*	1806 *6*	1818 *1*	1830 *6*
1795 *1*	1807 *4*	1819 *1*	1831 *2*
1796 *2*	1808 *6*	1820 *3*	1832 *3*
1797 *1*	1809 *6*	1821 *1*	1833 *1*
1798 *2*	1810 *5*	1822 *5*	1834 *2*
1799 *5*	1811 *14*	1823 *0*	1835 *2*
1800 *4*	1812 *16*	1824 *1*	1836 *0*
1801 *7*	1813 *9*	1825 *1*	1837 *4*
1802 *9*	1814 *9*	1826 *0*	1838 *6*
1803 *6*	1815 *6*	1827 *0*	1839 *4*
1804 *3*	1816 *2*	1828 *4*	1840 *5*

The number of ships struck by lightning is placed after each year in italics.

Note: Total of 142 cases in all. Between 1820, when Harris first suggested his system for protection against lightning, and 1840, there were another 52 unnecessary cases of damage by lightning to HM Ships. His plan was finally adopted for many HM Ships in 1842.

8

1841: The Phoenix Rises

The year 1841 opened with yet more demands from the Cabinet for parsimony. The mania for unacceptable economy by the Admiralty was made worse by imposition of still further demands upon the Fleet. The costs of bases abroad had been cut down to less than the bare minimum.[1] For example, Trincomalee was run at a cost of a mere £1,350 p.a. and the base at Simonstown at the Cape of South Africa on £1.000 p.a. The important base at the entrance to the Mediterranean at Gibraltar was run on a miserly £400 p.a. Whilst the Admiralty was responsible for carrying mails abroad, the size of the fleet was not increased accordingly and together all overseas establishments cost only £44,000. As far back as 1837 all home establishments together cost a mere £527,000. Naval supremacy had not been achieved. Most ships on foreign duty were sloops and brigs rather than liners. Any improvements were said to be at a cost-effective price and amounted to 'short-term measures' so beloved of politicians. These measures were without benefit to those manning the fleet or to those attempting to develop and maintain it.

The Navy was being run on the proverbial shoestring but outside events were beginning to pressurise the naval economy and made it plain that further spending on defence interests was to become vital to the interests of the country. At peak mobilisation of ships in response to the crises in Syria and the warlike acts and demonstrations of the French in the Mediterranean, Britain had 26 liners in commission.[2] It had taken six months[3] to man the ships brought out from ordinary. Impressment was not used and the 4,000 extra seamen required were not found until 1841 when the crisis and threat was all but over.

The bombardment of the strongholds of Mehmet Ali had been effective and the local Sultan became a collective ward of the Great Powers and this had negated any Russian influence on him. Capt.

Baldwin Walker,[4] like many naval officers, had despaired of finding employment in the British fleet and had lent his services to the Turkish Sultan and defied Egyptian expansionism. For this he was knighted and returned to service in the Royal Navy in 1844.

The indefatigable Harris had not given up hope of justice and of a fair hearing. He wrote once more at length to the Admiralty and detailed his operations for lightning protection, and simply asked to be compensated.[5] He enclosed many papers in support of his application. The Admiralty replied that it was 'willing to admit he has the merit of drawing attention to the subject, but do not see sufficient reason for giving him the compensation sought by him'. This was an incredible reply to someone who had spent so much time and effort on the case for fixed lightning conductors for HM Ships. Harris had allowed his drawings to be copied and had helped and supervised others to fit his fixed lightning conductor to at least ten ships.

Why did the Admiralty take this view? The Board was Whig and was mature. Perhaps Harris had become known to them as a Tory. Perhaps they wanted to continue to be thought to be economical in all things. Minto and Wood, and even Barrow had, according to some of the official papers, replied to Harris at various times and had tried to be fair. This reply was grossly unfair and characteristic of an administration which was unable to form a policy and to carry it out. Money mattered and that is what Harris was asking for in some recompense for his expenses and efforts.

Lord Minto meanwhile prepared to answer his critics in the House. He knew he would be questioned in detail as to any hint of a volte-face. How could he justify his lack of decisive action on the plan for protection of ships and men from injury from lightning? Would he dare condone in public the plagiarism of Harris' plan by his Surveyor and open up yet another avenue by which the Tory opposition could attack him? Minto drew on his memory and on his resources in office. He wrote various drafts for the anticipated speech. Amongst the jottings in his papers were drafts in his own hand such as:[6]

> The Report and Evidence upon the subject of Mr Harris' Lightning Conductors lead to an satisfactory and somewhat unexpected conclusion viz. that the danger to be apprehended from lightning even in the most stormy regions is but inconsiderable

as compared with any casualties to which the seamen [*sic*] is exposed. Mr Harris has collected with much research a list of 141 cases, extending over a period of 40 years, of damage done to King's ships by lightning. That so few examples be found of injury sustained during so long a period and amongst the numerous ships composing our fleet during a considerable portion of that time is in itself not a little remarkable. But when we find that *the loss* of only one ship is recorded, as supposed from the effects of lightning – the *Resistance*, in which all hands perished when she blew up, and that with the exception of the doubtful case of that single ship, not above 50 men have been killed, and perhaps twice as many hurt on board the 140 ships which had been injured by lightning we may well be surprised with the insignificance of the danger so much dwelt upon – assuming that upon an average the number of persons employed at sea during these years to have been about 50,000 – the annual loss of life would be about one in 5,714, or excluding the catastrophe of the loss *Resistance* about 1 in 40,000 – and the casualties of all kinds slight severe and fatal collectively would not be found to exceed the proportion of 1 to 4,000 men. Whether this can be correct or not it is at least obvious that loss of life to be apprehended from the effects of lightning at sea has been marvellously exaggerated – Another most satisfactory conclusion also follows from the investigation of this Committee viz. that the danger such as it is, always may be effectually warded off by the use of conductors either of the old construction or upon Mr Harris' improved plan – all that remains to consider therefore is in what manner a metallic communication may be best established from the mast head to the water – it should be permanent-secure as a conductor, as little as possible in the way and not very liable to injury. I believe Mr Harris' conductor would satisfy these conditions, but they are extremely expensive, and there seems no reason to doubt that equal security may be obtained at infinitely less expense.

Minto had surpassed himself. His passion for the oratory of economy justified the loss of lives. The damage and the absence or destruction of a ship on station in the national interest was not considered. Fortunately, something must have crept into his conscience and he made amends. He did not use this carefully written draft, whereby he had suggested the loss of a life was unimportant. He suddenly realised that his minder, now More O'Ferrall and also probably Barrow the Permanent Secretary, were not being fair-minded or open with such information as the Board had in its possession. He had taken the precaution of obtaining his own brief, probably through his private acting secretary, his son Viscount Melgund[7] in early 1840. Melgund was not under Barrow's control as he was an MP and his post was a temporary one (he was replaced in April 1841).

The brief that Minto received was unequivocal: Harris' plan was the best, most economical and efficacious. Minto cannot before that point have received such firm rational advice. Possibly this was so because the release of any historical information was as usual controlled by Barrow. For the first and only time in his career as a Cabinet Minister, Lord Minto spoke the truth about the subject as he saw it and he gave his objective opinion. He was courageous enough to disregard any previous briefings and to forget snide remarks about 'projectors' from Barrow. He relied upon his instinct for what was right, rather than what might have been politically correct. Minto's speech[8] was a surprise to his own Whig Party and a denouement to his other departmental advisers at the Admiralty:

> Lord Eliot [sic] recollected to the House that in 1839 he had moved for a Committee of the House to enquire into the merits of Mr Snow Harris' lightning conductor for HM Ships. Sir Robert Peel had suggested that a proper place for a technical enquiry such as this, was in the institution concerned – in this case the Admiralty. The Commission concluded that 'there was no nautical inconvenience or scientific objection' to the fixed conductors and they earnestly recommended their general adoption in the Royal Navy. The Commission had come to a unanimous decision. Lord Eliot 'found it quite impossible for anything to be more conclusive than the Report'.

Now, Minto enquired, what steps had been taken in consequence of the recommendation of the Commission? If his information was correct, it appeared that the experiments which had taken place over a period of ten years were not enough. He understood further experiments were planned. Moreover, the fitting of ships with the original fixed conductors had been unjustly made more expensive as Harris had not been allowed to supervise that fitting. To make things worse, Mr Edye appeared to have pilfered Harris' plan and said that his invention was to be tried. The question of expense had been considered by the Commission and this amounted to £300 out of the total cost of £100,000 for a line of battle ship.

He went on to describe Harris' eminence in scientific matters and that The Royal Society had commended the plan; also that recompense to Harris should be granted. Harris' invention of a new compass now in use was mentioned. It was rather hard, Minto said, that Harris was treated with unjust cruelty by the Admiralty, which had declined to recognise that he had any merit beyond drawing attention to the subject.

He moved that a humble address be made to Her Majesty that 'this House be informed as to what measures have been taken for Harris' plan as recommended by the Commission'. Mr J. More O'Ferrall, Lord Minto's official political secretary, said that 'the Lord Minto's speech seemed to imply a considerable censure upon the Admiralty'. The House must have appreciated at once that there was a schism between Minto and this newly-appointed politician. Why should Minto, otherwise the master of obfuscation and of dissembling, have suddenly spoken with such candour? Why did he let it be known that he, the Minister, felt embarrassed at his former actions or lack of them? Had something happened at the Admiralty to harden Minto's stance from his usual indecision to one of confrontation of an inequity? To be fair, Minto had long been used to Charles Wood, later to become Lord Halifax, being the prime mover of the Admiralty Board and its conduit to Parliament. Wood had the knack of achievement in the face of difficulties. For example, he obtained a packet service from Dover by at first asking for two line of battle ships! Minto, his Minister and in the Cabinet, was content to let things take their course, to allow Wood to manage affairs. Certainly Minto could not fight the deprecatory views against technological changes so often put forward by the naval Lords. O'Ferrall was different. Appointed in October 1839, he had little experience but much self-importance. He did not know how to manage the scion of an important and long-established aristocratic Whig family. His mistake was to assume that he could. In the House, his offering was antagonistic and derisory. He said:

> any kind of conductor appeared efficacious as had happened to the New York packet which escaped a second lightning strike

even though she had an imperfect [chain] conductor. The Commission had stated that Harris' was the best of the three types of conductor considered. The expense was high however. The cost could be reduced by giving credit for return of old copper to £119. The Board adopted part of a French plan, part of Harris' and part of Edye's. Later it was discovered that no part of Harris' plan need be used and the cost would be £30 and equally efficient.

With respect to the award claimed by Harris, his Board had only £1,000 for inventions and he could claim a small portion of this. In any case, the matter was still under experimentation and it would be premature to award Harris anything.

O'Ferrall had been badly briefed. There was no evidence that a conductor costing £30 was equally efficient to a fixed system. He failed to mention that the Admiralty had allowed the Surveyor's department to steal Harris' plan. His speech was one of overwhelming conceit – one conceit being that he understood the subject. Another conceit was to his political ability and as to his position. It was also an open display of contempt for his Minister in front of the House.

The political establishment could not allow such overt discourtesy to a senior Cabinet Minister. His arrogant behaviour to the father-in-law of Whig grandee Lord John Russell was not forgiven. O'Ferrall was never trusted again. The Member for Co. Kildare was probably glad later to accept the sinecure of the Governorship of Malta and thereafter he did not offer any contributions to political life.

Lord Ingestrie said, with massive understatement, 'there was some undercurrent of proceeding towards Mr Snow Harris, which would not bear exposure'. He went on to assert that Harris did not support the views of the (Whig) government and he could not help feel it was political rather than scientific opinion which existed as a prejudice against Harris. He said that Harris had written to Lord Minto and received a caustic reply in a scarcely civil letter and no compensation. He felt the difficulties created by the government might be found in political causes and others who entertained different political beliefs had influence enough to get their plans adopted. Mr Warburton then spoke to expose the fallacy in O'Ferrall's statement as regards the strikes of lightning on the New York packet. O'Ferrall replied by saying that he meant to have stated that any metallic conductor afforded a degree of security in a storm. To this statement the rejoinder was made: hence the need for a permanent conductor of good capacity.

Sir Robert Peel, ever the complete Tory politician, felt that the Admiralty had an opportunity to object to the Commission but had chosen not to do so. He quoted Captain Fitzroy's letter of support from his time as captain of HMS *Beagle*. He trusted that Harris could be recompensed for his outlay of time and materials. He concluded by saying that the Admiralty incurred great responsibility in refusing to adopt the recommendations of the Commission. Although there were other cheaper conductors, the Commission had investigated those and rejected them.

Sir T. Cochrane said he has personal experience of lightning strikes on ships and the expense was trifling compared to the preservation of men and of ships.

Support was given by Sir R. Inglis and Sir C. Lemon. Lemon, a West Countryman with copper mine interests, stated he could not understand the answers given by Mr O'Ferrall. He stated that: Mr Harris had lost £2,000–£3,000 over ten years, as a result of delays in rewarding him for his excellent invention. As to the new experiment, there were eight ships to be sent out with Harris' conductors and eight with other types.' This decision to send out on trial eight of each type had not been promulgated and must have been inside information or a guess. 'Supposing that Harris had taken out a patent? The Admiralty would by now have been forced to pay royalties.'

Captain A'Court said that the conductors should be fitted to every naval ship or the Admiralty accept the consequences.

Sir Charles Adam, the Senior Lord, then at last intervened in the debate. He must have felt anxious that his Minister had departed too thoroughly from the recondite view so carefully and artfully inserted into the Board's thoughts by the permanent official. Attempting to defuse a situation now bound to cause anger and dissension within his own department, he said that Harris only asked for the gradual introduction of the conductors into the Navy. Harris had obtained 20 patents and the introduction into the Navy would not have infringed them (this was not founded on the facts as known at the time or was misinformation; Harris had always believed, without good cause, that the Admiralty would reward him). 'Mr Harris thought his labour and invention worth £7,000 in his letter to the Admiralty but had been refused any compensation. Both members for Devonport (Whig and Tory) had written strongly in his favour.' 'Lord Eliot [sic]' again rose and, anger temporarily assuaged, resumed his normal diffident and indecisive mumbling manner. As usual, he tried to abrogate responsibility: 'If the Government considered £7,000 [as a reward to Harris for his work] too much, how much did they propose?' He expressed great satisfaction in the unanimity of the House on the issue of lightning conductors as proposed by Harris. Bravely, Minto[9] then denied any political motive for the actions taken, but even the least cynical observer would have found the statement hard to accept.

At last, the exposure of the previous shenanigans had exploded onto the political scene. Lord Ingestrie, a forthright speaker, completed the disclosures. He asserted that Harris was a Tory and that the Whigs including Symonds and others were against him.

An overview to a disinterested observer would likely have been that Symonds and Edye had produced their 'plan' for lightning protection for HM Ships to the Commission of 1839 apparently out of thin air and without research. They were persistent in their attempts to get it adopted by the Board. So a cabal was formed which must have involved cooperation from Barrow and O'Ferrall, at the Admiralty, Symonds and Edye at Somerset House together with Blake of Portsmouth Yard. Acting in concert, they had created a momentum against Harris' plan for their own unspecified reasons. Perhaps connected with a desire to be at the forefront of the adoption of wire rope rigging and 'their' invention of lightning protection for ships using copper wire, together with any rewards or preferment. The cabal must have been stunned when Lord Minto stood up and in effect admitted to the House that he had lost control of his own Board. Even more so when he criticised his Board's previous decisions. Lord Minto came out of the debate as refreshingly honest, on that occasion at least. He soon retrenched to a more usual diffidence and an interest in purely Scottish affairs, thus leaving it to others to infer and to expose shallow dealings at the Admiralty. He must have recognised too that the impartiality of his Permanent Secretary, Barrow, was now suspect as the latter had deferred or reduced the flow of information to the Board and then obstructed it when decisions not of his liking were taken.

The decisions with respect to Harris' conductor and with respect to the trial of wire rope may or may not have been made by the whole Board, which included the industrious and fair-minded Sir William Parker.[10] Certainly the decisions were being implemented during January and February of 1841. What could have happened? What influences were responsible for ill-thought decisions? Some of the pressures were financial as the government's revenues fell. According to Briggs' first-hand account, the political views of the Board were saturated by parsimony and pushed to absurd extremes.[11]

By 24 February, Harris began to make good his plan for involving friends in the House of Lords in his campaign for recognition of his work and some recompense. Lord Mount Edgecumbe was well known to Harris in Plymouth as the Earl and owner of the estate just across the Hamoaze from Devonport, in Cornwall. The Earl announced that he would ask for the papers from the Admiralty.[12] Also that he understood that Harris' case for remuneration was being considered.

Lord Minto replied[13] and admitted that no negotiations were in progress: 'The Admiralty was open to his claims but he himself was not favourable to them.' Once again, Minto had changed his mind. The reply was at complete variance with his speech to the House of Commons earlier that month. Or had he then played the devil's advocate? What had happened to make him so confused or could he ever make up his mind?

A significant clue to Minto's state of mind was given by a minute[14] dated one day later (25 February). Minto must have been persuaded that the Board had agreed to a further comparison of the two types of lightning conductor, Edye's and Harris', and that sea trials were to take place at once. The minute was to become de facto evidence of plagiarism by John Edye and should have been used to release both him and his line manager, Symonds, from their posts.

Instructions were sent out to all Yards (excepting Pembroke) for wire rope lightning conductors, the wire to be 3/8in from cap of lower masthead secured to the truck, 7/16in thick lower down from copper screw eye bolts to copper plate of 2 1/2in broad and 3/10in thick and so to the hull. Tellingly, attached to this minute in Minto's papers were ten pages of draft criticisms of Harris' conductor. The criticisms were at variance with his previous privately obtained brief and must have been supplied to the Board or direct to Minto by the secretariat. The main grounds of the critique were those of expense or, more exactly, one interpretation of the cost of fitting the two plans to various ships.

The astounding feature of the archive[15] was the limited amount of information made available to Lord Minto. How was it possible for his secretariat not to know the costs of building Harris' conductor into each of the sixteen ships listed? The information had already been provided by the Yards to the Admiralty on a number of occasions. It did confirm that the records and especially those involving the Surveyor's Department at Somerset House were not available. Later, complaints were made that Symonds had destroyed some of the papers when he moved into his offices there. It also meant that returns and correspondence to the Admiralty about the matter had been selectively retrieved for the First Lord.

Minto had been given the cost of only six out of sixteen ships fitted with Harris' plan and four out of twelve with the wire rope plan. The costs of the former included the development costs and the initial cost of manufacture of copper plates and nails. The costs of the latter group included no development costs, no costs for royalties for the patented wire rope and did not mention the failure of those materials and the cost of replacements. In addition, Minto did not appear to know that much information had been suppressed about five ships bearing Harris' system.

On 24 February, the Superintendents of the Yards were sent instructions[16] by Symonds with respect to the fitting of wire rope conductors. On 25 February, HMS *Impregnable* and *Belleisle* were ordered to be fitted, the mainmasts on Plan 1 and their mizzens on Plan 2. Thus, the Surveyor's orders were that the foremasts were not to be protected at all. Moreover, not content with one plagiarised version of Harris' plan, he proposed to trial yet another variant without authority. Whilst at anchor in Cawsand Bay, the two ships were fitted with the variant plan (Edye's) for wire rope lightning conductors on 1 March. The new lightning conductors had broken on 2 July but the Surveyor's department denied that this had caused any delay. *Belleisle* sailed on 22 July but unexpectedly had to return to Plymouth in September. Her new lightning conductors, which were now 1/16in larger in diameter, had proved unusable and had again chafed through. The copper wire was ordered to be replaced and the ship finally sailed for Malta in October. Unfortunately, the page of the master's log for 6 September, the date of her return to Plymouth, had been torn out, thus no true reason for her return was recorded.

Was protection from lightning held to be important enough to delay a sailing time by the captains of an HM Ship? Injury and mental instability after lightning strikes to seamen were a fact in the sea-going fleet. Certainly it was taken as a cause of bizarre behaviour and the log showed that Able Seaman William Taylor, although admittedly drunk on two occasions, had his number of lashes remitted as he had since been injured by lightning and could not hold his liquor.

The Surveyor had felt it necessary to question the Yard at Plymouth with respect to the new lightning conductors.[17] Perhaps they had failed almost at once. Symonds wrote that the Superintendent was to report whether an examination was made of the lightning conductor of HMS *Belleisle*; whether they were fitted in three distinct parts and what steps were taken to place the conductors in an efficient state.

In May, Symonds demonstrated beyond all doubt that his knowledge of electricity was negligible.[18] He gave an order which put HMS *Dublin* at risk of sinking if struck by lightning: he ordered that the ship was to be fitted with Harris' conductors but that the continuity of the copper conductor was not to be carried through to the keel – the expense to be reported. Was this an attempt to discredit Harris' design once and for all? It was an astonishing order and no reason was given for it. Perhaps he hoped *Dublin* would be lost or damaged and he would benefit.

Also to the discredit of the Surveyor[19] was another attempt at plagiarism or worse. Brunel had been attending the Admiralty in an advisory capacity with respect to steam propulsion using a screw propeller. A cut-away model was produced by Symonds which purported to show Brunel's method of application of the screw propeller. Brunel denied it was his model or anything like his plan and the meeting was abandoned.

This was another clear example of how far Symonds, evidently a desperate man, was prepared to go to achieve his ends. Of concern, too, was a letter from Andrew Smith to the Admiralty.[20] Smith was by then the sole official supplier of wire rope. On 11 March, he requested and obtained approval for a copy of the drawings and of the method of fitting the wire rope lightning conductors for his use to sell to the Merchant Service. This was a strange reversal of the more usual role of the Admiralty of abstraction of inventors' ideas and the using of them without leave. The Admiralty actually gave Smith the necessary information and technical drawings. Was there some form of understanding between Smith and certain officials? In mitigation, the Admiralty had to comply with the request, as Smith had taken out a patent for his wire rope.

The wire rope conductors as proposed by the Surveyor's department had not been able to withstand conditions at sea. In July 1841, the captain of *Impregnable* had sent in a written report on the state of the wire lightning conductors, which had failed.[21] This report was contained amongst other papers but was not indexed or recorded.

Later, Symonds manipulated the facts. The Return to the House of Lords of his wire rope conductors on ships did not show any of HM Ships fitted before 1842. *Impregnable* and *Belleisle* had both been given trial wire rope conductors in February 1841. In both, they had been returned to store as unfit for purpose.

Further fiddling with the use of Harris' plan for fixed lightning protection was then suggested by Admiral George Elliott. He asked Edye to send out the order for HMS *Aigle* to be fitted with Harris' conductors but 'with a riding bit on topmasts according to Admiral Elliot's plan'.[22] In August, in the absence of Symonds, Edye exceeded both his authority and ability.[23] He ordered 'all ships to be brought forward, with wire rope lightning conductors, unless others were applied for, when the request was to be referred to their Lordships'.

9

Exposure of Whig and Admiralty Manipulation of Facts

The administration of the Whigs had long been unsteady and by early summer of 1841 was under pressure. Eventually the Tories were elected as government and Minto and his Board at the Admiralty retired from office on 6 September. On 8 September, the Earl of Haddington took over as First Lord with Admiral Sir George Cockburn once again at the Admiralty and once again as the Senior Lord. Minto had been thoughtful enough to write a memorandum to his successor. He had asked for another Lord to be appointed 'to take on some of pressure of business'.[1] The Senior Lord who carried overall responsibility for all naval matters also now had to oversee the department of the Surveyor 'which is quite impossible'.

On learning of the membership and leadership of the new Board at the Admiralty, Harris immediately made preparations to establish once again his case. He knew by experience that it would be necessary to convince a new regime. He was certain also that he could not rely upon the permanent civil servants to bring the matter to the attention of the executive.

Only one month later, Harris, perhaps in expectation of fairer treatment than he had obtained from the Whigs, had sent Haddington several printed papers and a long letter.[2] As was by now his usual tactic, he gave a briefing and a truncated chronology of events since 1820 in relation to his work on lightning protection for HM Ships. The printed papers were a complete rebuttal of unfair criticisms of his system. One paper dealt with the actual costs of fitting his system of copper plates and compared it with those for copper wire rope and topmast copper plate partly plagiarised from his invention by John Edye and Symonds. The manipulated versions of the costs of the various forms of lightning conductors which had been presented to Parliament by Minto's administration were then exposed in detail.

Harris asserted that *at Edye's request*, all ships were to be fitted with wire rope conductors except for those who applied especially for another type. Edye's line manager, Captain Sir William Symonds, the Surveyor, had been away on a long information-gathering trip to the Black Sea and Odessa from July to September of 1841. It seems to have been during this time that the Order to fit all ships with wire rope conductors was signed by Minto, probably at Edye's suggestion and most likely with Barrow's connivance. Harris' overwhelmingly detailed case was a complete denunciation of the cozenage.

Harris also reported to Haddington, for it was very unlikely that the Admiralty Board had been given the information officially, that the wire rope conductors designed by Edye and fitted on *Impregnable* and on *Belleisle* had been shown to be unserviceable and that the commanding officers had returned them to store.

Harris was careful to deny that he was setting out 'to be troublesome to the executive by a species of agitation' but felt that matters should be made public. 'Lord Eliot (*sic*)', he wrote, had been impressed that he, Harris, was entitled to fair attention for his scientific labours.[3] Harris then pointed out that a gentleman in a subordinate position in the Admiralty 'had contrived to arrest the progress of a great scientific measure and throw aside a most valuable body of evidence put forth in the Report of a Commission for the House of Common' as was 'within his reach'. This forthright but well put and fair-minded letter cannot have been a pleasant start of his business at the Admiralty for the new First Lord but the problems had occurred under the Whigs and it was up to his administration to put them right, if it could.

Harris was right to assume that Lord Haddington would be troubled by any suggestion of inappropriate conduct or interference with official business or by publicity. According to Briggs,[4] the Reader to many Boards, Haddington 'was a kind and courteous nobleman' who expected similar treatment from others. Harris had thoughtfully included his latest pamphlets which showed the true expense of fitting his lightning conductor.

One of the pamphlets described *'The Danger Attendant On the Use of Small Wire Rope or Lines for Lightning Conductors for Ships and Practically Shewn'*. Harris also enclosed the 1840 reprint of *The Report of a Committee of the House of Commons* from the *Nautical*

Magazine & Naval Chronicle. In addition, he enclosed a copy of his book, *Shipwreck by Lightning*'. The first-hand evidence presented to Lord Haddington allowed him to be fully briefed as to Harris' plan for the fixed lightning conductor. Also of Harris' request for compensation and of his desire for public recognition for his saving of lives and of the public purse. Haddington deferred the matter until he could obtain firm advice from Admiral Cockburn.

Just before the change in the government in early September 1841, Harris had written to the Admiralty and asked for the return of his models[5] which displayed his plan for lightning protection and with the construction of which he had been assisted by the Surveyor's department in 1839. He received the reply: 'nothing is known of them'. This was unhelpful and obstructive and seemed typical of the behaviour of the senior civil servant who long before had made up his mind not to progress proposed technological improvements. The Tory Board treated Harris very differently. His explanation of expenses of £730 was accepted at once and his offer of attending gratuitously to ships fitting his system of conductors accepted.

Meanwhile, the new Board began to gather evidence as to the status of the protection of HM Ships from lightning. The Surveyor and Storekeeper General were asked (again) at which ports several types of lightning conductor were fitted and what the expenses were. A list was to be provided but was not readily available. It was noteworthy that the Board was not offered the past papers where all this information had been carefully garnered on several occasions over some years and for the use of several different Naval Lords. Perhaps those in the Records Office at the Admiralty, scenting criticism, denied responsibility for them. The former Comptroller of the Navy Board, Byam Martin, later correctly identified the administrative oversight for records as belonging to Barrow, the Permanent Secretary. The result once again was that disclosure of the bundle of papers known to have been gathered for the use of former Boards was obstructed and scanty.

That the Board had difficulty in collective decision-making was partly due to pressure of business. It was also due to its defective structure and lines of authority. Morriss,[6] in his elegant appreciation of the times, considered in summary that:

> although there were apparently clear line management pathways made possible since reform, in fact there was too little

time for discussion between the Naval and Civil Lords or between departments. Admiral Cockburn felt this most keenly and wrote that it was inappropriate that a Lord responsible for a single department should issue instructions in the name of the Board. As a result, business was conducted in an unconnected and disjointed manner sometimes without any communication with colleagues.

It was highly likely that some of the records from the Yards of the technical aspects of Harris' system for lightning conductors had been sent to the Surveyor. As we have seen, his department at Somerset House was insufficiently managed, had been under threat for years and had been neglected by Barrow. It appeared to have had no separate facility for archiving and none for safe-keeping. Indeed, many papers of interest as to technological developments appeared to have become 'lost' there.

Harris' earnest attention to detail and his unremitting courtesy had gained the respect of the Tory Board. When he suggested[7] that a certain number of ships in each class should be fitted with his conductors, the Admiralty replied at once: 'Inform him that HMS *Minden* is ordered to be fitted and when done my Lordships wish to know the exact expense'. The Yard then reported the ship could be fitted without taking out lower masts.

Harris approached the Admiralty and, mindful of the expense of fitting his conductors to HMS *Minden*, argued the costs would be greatly reduced if two cast-iron rollers could be fitted to a copper milling machine in Yard.[7] This simple request illustrated the decay in the infrastructure at the Yards and their relative inability to respond with flexibility and increased output in wartime.

The debates on naval estimates in the House continued to be conducted as factionalism and as a fairground battle.[8] The new administration at the Admiralty nevertheless applied common sense to the issues of the day rather than the 'economania' of the former Whig Board.

Despite the murmurings and political turbulence expressed in the House, the combination of Haddington the politician and administrator and Cockburn the very experienced and able naval professional at the head of the Admiralty proved to be a happy one, even though Cockburn had to brief the Earl as to every naval matter. Haddington's Board became a strong one. The profound depth of

Cockburn's knowledge, his quick mind and his ability to dissect a problem led to his being a towering presence as the senior naval officer. Evidence as to the inadequacy of the Records Office at the Admiralty was given independently.[9] The new First Lord 'was not slow to investigate possible cases of ill-usage, but inevitably had to rely upon permanent civil servants to produce the relevant documents'.

Lists of ships fitted with each type of lightning conductor had been produced in 1841 by the Surveyor's Office in response to an enquiry from the Home Office, although not without a delay.[10] During 1841-2, there were 21 ships fitted with Harris' system. Two of these had modifications made unilaterally by the Surveyor's department and 13 less fortunate ships had been fitted with the hybrid, part-plagiarised wire rope of inadequate capacity.

After 11 July 1842, all hulls were ordered to be fitted with Harris' system for lightning conductors. In fact, that Order had already been made by Minto's administration but it was likely that Edye delayed its implementation. A month earlier, all lower masts, while being made, were ordered to be prepared with a groove pre-cut for the expected overlapping copper plates of the conductor.[11]

The long-awaited breakthrough for Harris had finally happened. In 1842, many further ships were fitted with his system for lightning protection. By October, Harris had modified his system so as to ensure that the copper bolts were always fitted right through the keelson to the copper sheathing and hence to earth (sea). Moreover, others who tried to gain the interest of the new Admiralty Board in their form of lightning conductor were firmly but courteously advised not to bother.[12] Steamers with iron rigging and hulls were becoming even more important and much information was sent to the new First Lord, including books on the subject.[13]

Detractors of Harris' plan were always on the lookout to abuse him and his works. A chance came when a merchant ship, *Underwood*, was struck by lightning and seriously holed in two places at the bottom of her hull where some copper bolts had been fixed. At last, clear evidence to his opponents that Harris' system must be no good if not dangerous, for did he not advocate just such a system? Analysis of the incident was then published. There had been no form of lightning protection fitted to *Underwood*.[14]

Admiral Cockburn then made sure that the Surveyor and his men were excluded from decisions to do with lightning conductors and ordered to work on certain projects only as first determined by the Board. The Commander in Chief of Portsmouth, a supporter of Harris' system, himself, [15] sent reports and diagrams as tried by Mr Harris[16] of experiments on HMS *Orestes*, as well as views on the disadvantages of wire rope conductors, direct to the Admiralty Board. The Board began a series of discussions[17] and active collaboration with the ever-keen Harris. The continuity of the conductor through to the keelson was discussed. The height of the vane spindles and the remedy was another discussion. Lt. Pringle Green[18] had long asserted that lightning would be attracted to the vane spindles. Now Harris dealt with the subject in detail. The metallic vane spindle housed a small wooden pivot on which the vane, a piece of bunting as a pennant, turned.[19] The height of these was altered and his copper lightning rod placed slightly higher. Even many years later there was still some fear and superstition due to Green's successful fear-mongering and propaganda about vane spindles.[20] Finally, and of much more significance, there had been a report of that rare occurrence: a lightning strike to a ship's bowsprit. Harris wrote that he would travel to London at once to discuss and analyse the problem.[21]

Harris was still collecting data of lightning strikes to ships, by now both HM and merchant ships. He wrote to his mentor Faraday in October and related the status of his lightning conductors. 'I consider the question quite settled, by my perseverance. The Admiralty has lately had some fine notions of the effects of conductors in parrying and rendering harmless such discharges'.[22] He quoted the case of:

> HMS *Acteon*. In Central American waters lightning had enveloped the ship for an hour. There had been a fearful shock on the mainmast conductor. Vivid light had taken a man's sight away for several minutes, the horrid crash was simultaneous and like all the ships' guns fired at once. The conductor was undamaged and not even a rope yarn touched. Think of the damage if only a chain conductor had been up.

Further cases of HM Ships being struck by lightning and incurring damage were now being reported openly. One of the most interesting reports was from Captain Hon. F. William Grey.[23] Grey was brother-in-law to Charles Wood, the leading Whig politician and lately political secretary to Lord Minto. Grey had plenty to lose by implied criticism of the Whigs. He was formerly commanding officer of *Acteon* and his report of his ship's successful protection by Harris' conductor had been 'lost' during the recent Whig Admiralty Board. Now in command of *Endymion*, of 44 guns, his ship sustained damage from lightning on 21 March 1842 at Calcutta and was delayed in taking up her station in consequence. The ship's only protection had been a small chain conductor for one mast.

The hard work of amassing accurate extracts from ships' logs now began to pay off. Harris had evidence of what amounted to negligence: the failure of the Navy to adopt adequate protection of their men and ships from lightning. Tellingly, he had been able to be specific about places and times. His case for change was unanswerable. His new book, *On the Nature of Thunderstorms*,[24] was published on 1 May 1843. The book was dedicated 'to Admiral Sir George Cockburn and referred to his kind consideration since 1830 of the fixed conductor. Candour, fairness and enquiries into the many objections urged against them'. Table 9.1 shows the list as published in Harris' book on thunderstorms. To this list, if he could have held the press, he would have added that HMS *Scylla* had previously been struck by lightning and severely damaged in 1835 and was then struck again on 17 October 1843. The later strike resulted in almost no damage because the ship had the fixed high-capacity conductors fitted. It then became apparent that significant damage was claimed solely by those seeking to justify their previous indecisiveness. Immediate correspondence with the Admiralty followed the news. By 5 November, Harris had replied with a full objective assessment of the incident but based upon what limited information was available to him.[25] In February 1844, Harris was sent a copy of the Commanding Officer's (Captain Sharpe) report on the damage to the conductor of his ship.[26] After much consideration Harris was able to convince the Admiralty that by referring to evidence from those on board at the time, only the most minor damage to a few topgallant mast copper plates, easily repaired, had in fact occurred.

Admiral Adam[27] had been commander in Chief in the West Indies where the incident to *Scylla* had occurred. He replied with fairness to an enquiry from his father-in-law, Minto, received on 1 December 1844 as follows:

I do not think there was any appearance of fusion on the lightning conductor of *Scylla*, nor have any reason to believe that there was any want of control (although no doubt that might happen easily). I understand it was when the conductors are fixed at the upper end of the topgallant mast [Royal Pole] and when the [electrical] fluid was first supposed to strike the conductor that the conductor was slashed from the mast. From Cdr Sharpe's account the lightning was more severe when the *Scylla* was struck.

This is some slight but concrete evidence that Sir Charles Adam was trying to help Minto as to any actual or possible flaw in the efficacy of the fixed system of lightning conductors. Later, the extremely partisan Surveyor, Symonds,[28] still in post but under a Tory administration and under increasing scrutiny and criticism, wrote to his former First Lord, Minto:

'I have not yet seen reports of lightning conductors on *Scylla* and in *Electra* but have called for them. I feel convinced that wire rope lightning conductors are as much superior to Harris' as they are cheaper to the country in the proportion of £80 (£5,610 at current prices compared to 1845) to £400 (£28,053 at current prices) or 1/5 besides the injury imposed upon the masts by the latter. But I imagine it is considered a proper remuneration for Mr Snow Harris' political services at Devonport and Plymouth.'

He then referred to the costs of protection for 23 liners, 19 corvettes, 71 brigs for relief of stations for three years as £23,071(£1.62 million at current prices).

Propaganda against Harris' efforts to gain recognition for his services continued to be published. By contrast with such anecdotal cant, the methodical Harris now sought official permission to continue his garnering of hard facts.[29] Presumably his efforts before 1843 had been demi-official as they had been carried out with the help of the Hydrographer's Office at Somerset House.

Table 9.1 The number of HM Ships known to have been struck by lightning, 1829-42

	No fixed conductors Ships damaged	Fixed conductors No damage to ships
STATION		
MED.	14	3
E. IND.	6	5
W. AM.& W. IND.	8	7
S. AM.	1	9
CAPE	7	2
General	5	4
Totals	41	30

By 1843, the Admiralty was cooperative and sensitive to former defects in its administration. Harris' reputation then received a timely boost when the Royal yacht, *Victoria and Albert* was ordered to be fitted with his system in May. The yacht had been fitted with wire rigging and whilst this posed a new problem for Harris, he was careful to take an objective stance and consider the best possible outcome. He then made arrangements to inspect the fittings after Chatham Yard had completed them.

Five further ships,[30] *Moderate*, *Cormorant*, a wooden paddle sloop, *Larne*, a steamer, *Vengeance*, of 84 guns and *Vanguard*, of 78 guns were fitted with Harris' conductors during 1843 but none with the wire rope type. One of these ships, *Vanguard*, had previously been fitted in 1841 with Edye's wire rope system[31] at a cost of £62/4/11. The total cost of fitting *Vanguard* twice with new types of conductor was never formally admitted or published.

Harris carried on with his campaign to publicise his project by a continuous barrage of articles in peer-reviewed journals and via books. As much as possible, he demonstrated the scientific points with simple diagrams. About the time he was preparing his books and articles, he sponsored a local artist and friend, Nicholas Matthew Condy, to commence painting a set of watercolours from which engravings could be made of HM Ships being struck by lightning. Harris thus drew attention to his already well-made case by these beautiful paintings. Was he a self-publicist in self-defence or in frustration? He kept his enemies informed too. Even though Minto had long left office at the Admiralty, Harris, from his home at 6 Windsor Villas, Plymouth, wrote to him and explained his analysis of the holes blown in the hull by lightning striking the merchant ship *Underwood*.[32] He also sent Minto reprints of his recent papers.

Minto pretended he was spoiling for a debate in the House and wrote[33] to Charles Wood: 'I do not believe that Lord Haddington and Cockburn, the two men who most dread public discussion, would willingly expose themselves to attack.' This informs us of something of the Whigs' assessment of the abilities of their Tory political opponents. Cockburn had always been described as definite, ruthless and domineering at his public duties. It was always accepted, too, that his knowledge of naval and of legal issues was vast. His weak point, according to these Whig politicians, was obviously public debate. The ability of a department to obfuscate or even to deny absolutely was mentioned as part of the usual partisan warfare of politics by Minto to his confidante and erstwhile political secretary Wood: 'indeed I feel perhaps even more strongly then you, an insuperable objection to the administrative muddling of Parliament in departmental papers. On reflection a discreet or becoming course would be to call for a Ct. of the House. I am quite aware of the advantages which a department has in its resources for defence or attack.'

Table 9.2 Ten HM Ships struck by lightning between 1830 and 1843[34]

Acteon	*Dryad*	*Scylla*
Asia	*Daphne*	*Talbot*
Beagle	*Minden*	
Druid	*Racer*	

Note: Only *Asia*, *Beagle* and *Druid* were struck by lightning before the original formal trial, commenced in 1830, was discontinued. In two cases, *Asia* and *Druid*, the results were not reported to Harris. Thus, for some time he had to rely solely upon *Beagle* as an example of the complete efficacy of his invention.

The relevance of the risk versus cost benefit comparisons for non-enemy action losses can be assessed by checking the causes, so far as they were then known, for warships of HM Navy. According to Hepper,[35] warship losses in the Napoleonic war were 61 per cent by wreck or foundering as compared with 37 per cent by enemy action. In the French Revolutionary War, nearly the same proportion: 62 per cent by wreck or foundering but compared with only 27 per cent by enemy action.

During the period 1820-59, a total of 104 HM Ships were lost.[36] If consideration is given for enemy action and special circumstances, then only four were lost by enemy action, three against the Chinese forts in 1859. Seven more ships were lost through ice in the Arctic. The remaining 93 ships lost give a mean, over the 39-year period of relative stability with no major wars with fleet actions, of 2.38 ships lost through wreck or foundering each year. Of the total of 93 ships, 19 were described as missing in storms or had just disappeared. It was very possible, but only conjecture, that lightning contributed to or caused some of those losses. Most were of small ships of under 500 tons and many were brigs or packets. If a ship disappeared and no survivors found, then there was no direct evidence of its loss from any particular cause. Eleven of those lost were steamers, mostly paddle steamers, but each of these was known to have been wrecked on rocks and not in association with lightning strikes. That is not to suggest that lightning did not strike steamers, merely that most ships were wrecked or foundered through other of the many hazards faced by mariners.

Table 9.3 Types of ship in British Navy in 1832 and 1869[37]

Wooden sailing vessels		Steamers
1832	552	20 (paddle)
1869	64	671 (8 classes)

Harris' new book,[38] published in 1844, showed that his researches had found 142 cases of lightning strikes to HM Ships over many years, including when at war. His system of lightning protection, if fitted from 1830 onwards, could have prevented damage in 52 cases. The statistics he quoted make interesting reading as a litany of the preventable. Some 315 masts and spars had been damaged in time of war and 108 in peace. Of these about 5/6 were destroyed or rendered unserviceable. Fire occurred in 133 cases during wartime and 70 seamen were killed with 158 badly hurt or crippled. Twenty-one others recovered from their injuries.

Harris went on to describe how the ships struck by lightning and disabled were prevented from carrying out their naval missions, the most telling instance being 5 out 12 line of battle ships disabled by lightning when off the estuary of the Rhone in September 1813, all on the same night. The blockade of Toulon was thus placed in real jeopardy. Other examples were that of HMS *Glory* which missed

Admiral Calder's battle through being disabled by lightning and HMS *Guerriere*, which was damaged before her battle with USS *Constitution*, although never before admitted. There were many other examples.

A year later, one problem surfaced. A Chatham-built 18-gun sloop HMS *Fly* had Harris' fixed lightning conductors applied for successfully by her captain, Captain Blackwood,[39] in October 1841. In May 1845, her then commanding officer, Commander Warden,[40] reported that the protection of the masts was broken when the ship had been struck by lightning.

Strangely, Harris did not react to this apparent calamity, then or subsequently. Up to that time, he had responded in great detail as to what had might have occurred in each and every case reported to him. It can only be concluded that for some reason Harris was not informed about the matter. Barrow, almost certainly the arch obstructor of Harris' plan, could not be blamed as he had retired on 28 January 1845, to be succeeded by Mr W.A. Baillie-Hamilton. Mr Henry Bedford, the Head of the Record Office and First Class Clerk since 1826, had retired in May of the previous year. New promotions within the permanent staff of civil servants were to allow a new and cooperative approach to replace the previous irrational failures in the production of documents for the Board.

10

House of Lords Misinformed: The Whigs Again, 1846-52

Lord John Russell became Prime Minister in 1846. His new Whig administration at the Admiralty was headed by Lord Ellenborough. Sensibly, Ellenborough had retained Admiral Sir George Cockburn, albeit a Tory, as the Senior Naval Lord. Cockburn's retention also made sure that his deep knowledge of recent discussions about technological changes in steam and in the propulsion of ships would contribute to the success of the department. Sir W. Gage, Admiral William Bowles and the Hon. W. Gordon completed the naval membership of the Board.

The subject of lightning conductors and their performance was kept under review but it seemed to have been accepted that Harris' system should continue to be applied to all ships. Papers and letters of the era once again forecast an increased risk of war, probably against America. Renewing fears of the unsettling effects of the former 'traitor colonists' of the Benjamin Franklin era, one letter mentioned that an American spy was active in England. The reality for the Admiralty was also an increasing frustration with French (as well as with American) naval activity.

Shipwreck was still a common event for the merchant fleets of the time. For warships, shipwreck remained a hazard but increasingly accurate charts of home and distant waters produced by the Hydrographers Department had done much to reduce navigational errors. Protection from shipwreck after damage by lightning had been achieved after Harris' conductors had been installed on most HM Ships, including on *Avenger* in 1846 and again a year later! She was a paddle steam frigate of six heavy guns. Captain E. Napier and her crew must have been confident of their protection even though there was much lightning around them during a storm on 20

December 20 1847. Later that night she struck the Sorrelle Rocks, near the Isle of Galita off the north African coast, having been set off course by a strong current. Only four men survived. Table 10.1 describes the losses of men and ships from shipwreck by all causes.

Table 10.1 Losses of RN men and ships from shipwreck, 1820-49[1]

Men lost	1,235	(this is a low estimate)*
Ships wrecked	49	(including four steamers)

*In two cases, the number of men manning the ship and lost was not recorded

These losses of men, as now for fishermen, were accepted as a hazard of their employment at sea. Public conscience, however, had been set alight by revelations of cruelty in industry. The former tolerance of the abuse of seamen, by flogging, starvation and recklessness, was ended by higher standards of training, education and by accountability. Captain Alexander Milne[2] felt it right and necessary to record in private letters in 1842-3 the death of a ship's boy from drowning and of a topman from a fall, as well as to arrange an official sickbay mess for those on the Sick List of his receiving ship, *Caledonia*. By the mid-nineteenth century, any opportunity to reduce casualties at sea was taken up by the Admiralty. If the real figures of needless injury and death from, for example, lightning, had been more widely known, they would not have been tolerated. Unfortunately, the figures were not collected except as general statistics, the causes of death or injury being given historically as killed, drowned or died by shipwreck or died of disease or accident. Later, Sir Gilbert Blane[3] recorded that during the Napoleonic War the death rate was 33 per 1,000 in the Navy. By 1856, the rate had dropped only to 21 per 1,000 as compared with the country as a whole whose figure was 9.2 per 1,000.

The statistics presented by the Medical Department were attacked in *The Lancet* during 1838 as gross and misleading. The eventual results of this public denouement were to be a standardised system for the recording of deaths and injuries and annual returns. Despite this improvement in record-keeping, the value of the more detailed data did not result in improvements in standards of seamens' health and safety until after the end of the Crimean War.

Because so many diseases were poorly understood during the mid-nineteenth century, some conditions were wrongly classified as to the bodily system mainly affected. The exact detail of deaths or of accidents leading to death at sea was non-existent unless the ship's log could be consulted. Even then, the descriptions remained vague.

Tables 10.2 and 10.3 are adapted from Harris' book and were part of his devastating rebuttal of the misinformation previously given to both Houses by dishonest politicians. The publication of the paper for the House of Commons marked the end of open opposition to the fixed system of lightning conductors. Covert opposition and jealousy continued. The case for the provision of the high-capacity permanent lightning conductor was now so overwhelming that most failed to appreciate it or to contemplate opposing it. This was because the success of the system was 100 per cent and therefore it was human nature just to accept it – an analogy being the acceptance of the wheel for transferring loads from one place to another; it is so obviously successful we no longer acknowledge it. The true experimental null hypothesis would have been: 'Permanent copper plate conductors of high capacity on each mast do not protect the ship and her crew against lightning'.

This in fact was proved, or more properly put as disproved, by the tables below. The difficulty was that what we now term Popperian logic was not defined at the time, although the criteria for experimental method and deduction were well understood by scientists but not by laymen. It must have felt to Harris as if he had to measure no damage, injuries or deaths.

Liaison between the Admiralty and Harris continued at a high level. Arrangements were made for the industrious inventor to visit the Yards twice a year to check the standards of the fit of his system of conductors. This supervision was made necessary by errors and failures to ensure continuity of the overlapping plates of copper. Their continuity was of course vital for the discharge of a lightning strike. Two ships were being built or converted and therefore at the stage best suited for the fitting of the conductors. One was the first four-funnelled ship in the Navy, the wooden paddle frigate HMS *Terrible* (ex-*Simoon*).

When Lord Auckland again took over as First Lord, Harris wrote to him at length and sent him his usual comprehensive briefing.[4] That briefing was calculated, from bitter experience, to be independent of any status report originating from the permanent civil servants to the Admiralty, although John Barrow junior had by then taken over as Head of the Record Office in 1844 and was busy cataloguing the neglected archives. Harris' letter can have left the new First Lord in no doubt as to the status of the progress of his system for lightning protection. The addition this time was a plea for another and larger reward for all his work. Auckland took the encouraging but necessary action of marking the file, 'let the papers be kept together'.

Table 10.2 Men killed and hurt by lightning at sea, 1820-49[5]

Bellette 18 gun 1825	36 men struck, 5 badly hurt	W. Indies
Bittern 16 gun 1844	8 men hurt	Africa
Despatch 18 gun 1837	20 injured	Cape Rosa
Invincible 1827	1 marine killed (prize, slaver)	Africa
Larne 20 gun 1820	2 killed, many injured	Med.
Racehorse 18 gun 1849	3 injured	S. America
Renegade 16 gun 1836	1 killed	W. Indies
Rodney 90 gun 1838	2 killed, 2 hurt	Med.
So't'on 74 gun 1832	2 hurt	Downs
Tees 26 gun 1820	2 killed, 5 hurt	Cape (Afr.)
Wasp 18g gun 1838	9 men struck, 2 badly hurt	Med

Notes
Totals were 11 incidents to HM Ships with 8 killed and a minimum of 85 injured. As a comparison, the total killed by lightning was 0.57 per cent of those lost by drowning, although the 85 injured may then have suffered from long-term disability. Most of the deaths and injuries from lightning were preventable and need not have occurred after 1820. *Bittern*, as all other ships, could have had permanent lightning protection fitted from 1842, i.e. two years previously, but was on a long commission against slave traders and had not been for a long refit since the order to fit was extant. She carried a small capacity wire rope conductor, which failed to carry off all the current from the lightning. A further 52 incidents of HM Ships being struck by lightning occurred during this period with much damage to masts and spars. The figures give a frequency of 15 per cent for deaths and injuries after lightning strikes to men on ships at sea or anchor. One hundred per cent of ships struck by lightning and unprotected by the permanent system of high capacity were damaged.

Table 10.3 HM Ships with permanent lightning protection of high capacity: incidents and injuries, deaths or damage, 1820-49[6]

Lightning strikes to protected ships	40 minimum
Deaths	0
Injuries	0
Damage	Insignificant

Owners of passenger and merchant fleets became very keen that their ships be fitted with the now proven fixed conductors. The *Great Western* was so fitted by an Order of 4 June 1847. The ship had been built for the Atlantic as a paddle steamer in 1836 of wood with copper sheeting as well as being rigged as a four-masted topsail schooner. The wheel for the paddles had blades with stepped narrow strips, the whole travelling in a cycloidal curve to minimise power loss on impact with the sea. Technological advances such as these were very modern but the paddle ship proved unable to compete against screw propulsion. Nevertheless, at least she had proper protection from lightning.

Interest from foreign ship owners and navies in the British technology of lightning protection became immense. Certain countries enjoyed favoured status due to royal connections and friendships and visits from members of the aristocracy.[7]

Russian interest in aspects of British technology may first have occurred when HMS *Acteon* was moored for some time and used as a diplomatic deterrent at Constantinople in 1832.[8] *Acteon* had a Harris lightning protection system in place on trial and it was possible, since she remained at anchor, that the Russians had noticed it. Some time later, they asked unofficially to be shown one. Harris was asked to demonstrate his system to them and in 1845 had accepted a vase from the Emperor for his trouble. The vase, which was kept on show at The Athenaeum, Plymouth, was unfortunately destroyed by bombs during the Second World War. It was strange that the Russians had been official diplomatic friends but also jealous rivals for naval supremacy in the Mediterranean. They continued to be courted by the British in 1847, but ended up as enemies in the Crimea about 20 years later.

It was in 1847 that Baron Burn of Russia was informed that a certain Lt. Alexauchof,[9] surely a euphemism for the Crown Prince, might wish to visit Sheerness and Portsmouth Yards to view masts being fitted out with the continuous system of conductors. Harris was sure that the Russian naval lieutenant was the Tsar's son and bragged in a letter to his friend Whewell in Cambridge: 'am just off to Portsmouth to meet the Russian Prince and his Admiral, and see one of their squadron having my lightning conductors on board. The Emperor has determined on carrying my plan back to the Russian Navy after his return home.'[10]

Harris had just been ill with 'an affliction of the stomach' but had found 'sea breezes restored' him. He had spent much of his convalescence in his schooner moored at Plymouth and was known for being out in it during thunderstorms, thus studying first hand any lightning nearby.

Ill though he had been, Harris' energy for the harvesting of information about his lightning conductor system remained. He received news in 1846 that HMS *Fisgard*, a 42-gun frigate, had been struck by lightning in two places simultaneously on 26 September. The ship was at anchor in the Nisqually River, Oregon. This was part of the territory disputed by America and had nearly led to war. The vane spike (spindle) was fused and the copper conductor started from its bed about 13 feet below the spindle where the second part of the discharge had struck. The current was safely carried away and the ship suffered no significant damage. When reports of some damage to *Fisgard* became widely known, Harris' old enemy surfaced at once. William Sturgeon, the impetuous editor of the *Annals of Electricity*, demanded of the Admiralty that an investigation take place.

Harris merely asked for a copy of the ship's log before he investigated the incident and ignored Sturgeon.[11] Harris' reputation for objectivity and for careful assessment of facts was now high and was still growing. The East India Company had put aside earlier misinformation from their scientific advisers and asked for Harris' expertise. His system for protection of their well-found ships against lightning was granted to them and he itemised the costs of fitting them.

The reward for his invention had not yet been forthcoming, although his expenses were freely granted. Harris gathered around him powerful friends who recognised the injustice to him. Harris himself had behaved well in the face of ignorance and prejudice: he had been statesmanlike, courteous and responsive to all, with the eventual exception of those who had made vicious personal attacks upon his scientific credibility. It was announced that a Precept[12] from the House of Lords, dated 13 May 1847, had called for reports of HM Ships which had been struck by lightning, together with extracts from their logs. Harris knew the precise type and depth of information his friends should seek to make public in the House of Lords. It was true that his books had already published some of the material but an official report would consolidate his efforts. Harris published in 1847 a second edition of his book on the protection of ships from lightning.[13] He had by then accumulated 220 cases from the official logs of ships. He dismissed the incapacious wire rope conductors by describing the damage inevitably caused when lightning struck an inadequate pathway to earth. Concrete examples were given, such as HMS *Hazard*, damaged twice in 1846, HMS *Bittern*, struck, wire rope conductor broken and men injured in 1844, *La Juno* (French), with a wire rope conductor damaged in 1838.

He published the details and dared the authorities to deny that the inadequate wire rope conductors in HMS *Impregnable* and *Belliele* had chafed through and had been returned as useless.

He presented many cases of ships fitted with his system of protection which had been struck by lightning but had sustained no damage. Some of these were HMS *Fox, Fisgard, Dido, Druid* and *America*. In his addenda he added the details of the strikes on *Conway* and *Racer*.

The watercolours by N.M. Condy must have been painted mainly after this date but those of *Dido* and of *Fisgard* had already appeared as engravings to illustrate Harris' book (Figs 1a & 2b.)

The conductor in *Dido*, according to the officers, acted as a complete safety valve for the lightning, even though the forked current had demolished the yardarm. The ship was in an area where the most thunderstorm days per year in the world were likely to be encountered. Had she not had an efficient conductor it is likely she would have been severely damaged or even wrecked.

Sir Robert Peel, ever fair-minded and open to reason, had ordered a list of ships struck by lightning since the Commission of 1839 to be prepared. Because the information was presented in a certain way it was probable that much of it may have been assisted by Harris' endeavours with the laborious grind of checking every ship's log at the end of each commission. The return of incidents of lightning strikes to HM Ships was devastating to those who sought to propose the adoption of the cheap and cheerful wire rope solution or any version other than Harris' fixed and permanent system. That did not stop those who wished to buy cheaper systems or the commercial interest of those who were determined to sell them.

For example, Andrew Smith[14] published a flyer and a pamphlet in which he manipulated the truth by clever juxtaposition of iron wire rope for rigging but used copper wire rope for conductors. His scheme consisted of a copper wire fastened at the masthead and fixed to a copper plate on the bulwark of the ship.

Table 10.4 Smith's list of some HM Ships fitted with wire rope[15]

Locust, Samson, Vixen, Terrible,   *Penelope, Bulldog, Janis, Emotion,*
Virago, Fairy, Garland,   *Vires, Hog,*
St Vincent(partly), *Victoria and Albert,*   *Ramus* (Symonds' yacht)
Also Emperor of Russia's yacht and nine of Russian Navy
Danish: 1 steam frigate
Prussian government: sailing vessel
Spanish government

The advertisement as published for Smith's patent wire rope lightning conductor 'as fitted to 50 HM Ships and a number in the Russian, Prussian and Danish Navies'.

Lord Minto had kept a copy of the pamphlet in his papers. A piece of additional information was that the copper wire rope conductor had been 'issued by the Admiralty on 25 February 1841'.[16]

To his disbelief, Harris became Sir William Snow Harris KBE after being knighted in 1847. His knighthood came from the Queen herself for, as previously noted, Harris had accepted the task of designing and supervising the fitting of lightning conductors to protect the Queen's favourite residence of Osborne House, Isle of Wight.

By 1848, Harris had published yet another book.[17] This was the first fully illustrated set of instructions made available to all by Harris for the fitting of lightning conductors to HM Ships and it was accorded the accolade of being printed by HMSO.

Harris' old but clandestine antagonist, Sir John Barrow, had retired from his post in 1845 but he lived long enough to learn of Harris' knighthood. Also, that the House of Lords was moving steadily towards a full disclosure of the truth. Indeed, it seemed likely that the debate would expose the chicanery concerning the adoption of the marine lightning conductors by the Admiralty. Especially, too, the delays which had so marred the reputation of Barrow himself and that of his inchoate department.

In May 1848, a Return[18] for the House of Lords listed the number of vessels fitted with Harris' system of protection, which had been struck by lightning. The list began without explanation only in 1842 although that was the year when Harris' plan was formally ordered to be adopted by the Admiralty. No damage had been found in the first 12 ships in the new trials; each had been fully protected by Harris' system from strokes of lightning. All the details had been abstracted from the ships' logs. The ships listed were: *HMS America*, 50 guns;

Constance, 50 guns; *Fisgard*, 42 guns; *Fox*, 42 guns; *Conway*, 26 guns; *Dido*, 18 guns; *Tyne*, 22 guns; *Favourite*, 14 guns; *Orestes*, 14 guns; *Rose*, 14 guns; *Scylla*, 14 guns; *Beagle*, 6 guns. The sole damage that even the most obdurate opponent could claim had occurred was the minor amount to *Dido*'s main royal yard.

Sir John Barrow died on 23 November 1848. With him died much information as to the pace of technological change, which he had chosen to hide or to obfuscate. His autobiography, as would be expected, claimed a worthy and industrious career almost without blemish. More recent historical research has suggested that Barrow had seriously overreached himself during his career, that his lust for fame had endangered others and had even claimed their lives, and that his actual achievements had been exaggerated, most of all by himself.

Events aimed at clarification of the politically motivated delays and the mishandling of Snow Harris' claim for recognition were by now in slow but ponderous motion. The House of Lords was determined, through its Tory majority, to settle the matter and see justice done. With great politeness, the Earl of Wilton[19] had 'wished to know whether there were any objections to comparative returns of lightning conductors'. The former First Lord at the Admiralty, Gilbert, Second Earl of Minto, had long been identified by the Tories as one of the men who had blighted the adoption of Harris' plan. In addition, Minto was responsible for creating smokescreens to hide the issues from Parliament. Now speaking in the Lords, Minto was determined to obfuscate. He replied that 'there never had been or could be the slightest doubt of the value of the invention of Sir Snow Harris'.[20] It was desirable to compare them. There had been no ships fitted with chain conductors. Merely the wire ropes or Harris'. It appeared that there was no limit to Minto's duplicitous speeches. Perhaps he was optimistic and was expecting to win any debate. In fact, he must have been thoroughly misinformed as to the facts in the past by Barrow. As First Lord, he had been disregarded by his political confidante, Wood, and had been given wrong and incoherent advice by the Surveyor, Sir William Symonds, just before the latter's forced retirement.

By contrast, there cannot have been a better prepared case than that so diligently put together by Harris. His Whig opponents had failed to take notice of the gathering weight of data. The newly-prepared illustrations by Condy would forever show the truth as drawn direct from the ships' logs. Engravings from the original paintings were prepared for publication. On 11 May 1849, a Precept[21] was issued for a Return to be made to the House of Lords of HM Ships fitted with lightning conductors and of any damage.

On 11 June, the House of Lords received the list of by then 279 ships (109 were Symondites) with Harris' fixed conductors. There was a minimum of 56 separate instances of lightning strikes. It was highly probable that there were very many more but as the dates and times were not very detailed these were counted as one. Harris' conductors had prevented any damage even in some ships struck by lightning on multiple occasions. Most of the reports merely stated that the ship and men had no inconvenience from lightning strikes.

The compilation had been produced by the Admiralty and the then Whig Board must have exerted some political pressure so as to minimise the dramatic content of the report. The riposte of the Tories was to order disclosure of reports of protection from lightning by the alternative copper wire rope conductors. This took time but was to be released a year later.

Harris continued to receive good information from his many friends in the Navy which he continued to use in his publications and as evidence.[22] He had printed an open letter[23] as a robust statement in advance of certain returns due to be made to the House of Lords. He reiterated the history of the subject and then demonstrated that use and replacement of copper wire rope was actually more expensive than his fixed copper plate conductors. This was intended to be a knockout blow to the parsimony of the Whigs who had wanted value without proper payment. The calculation was that there was a mean of 117 ships at sea per year during the years 1829-42. During this time 41 ships struck by lightning had only the inadequate protection offered by the low-capacity temporary chain or wire conductors.

This open letter included several points as follows: the early trial of the system for fixed protection in ten ships was costly to fit as shipwrights had to be employed cutting grooves for plates in masts with chisels instead of a groove cutter machine as now. Copper nails had to be made out of copper bolts. The conductors were applied to ships already in commission instead of when building. *Tweed*, a 28-gun frigate, had cost more to fit than *Caledonia* of 120 guns!

Harris then alluded to the curious decision of the Admiralty Board to ignore the findings of its own Commission, which had reported in 1840 and was printed for the House of Commons. He gave examples of the wire rope hybrid system, with the overlapping copper plates on the upper mast stolen from his original plans. Worse was to come. Examples he gave pointed to a lack of understanding of the electrical currents in lightning strikes. *Britannia*, of 120 guns, had her mainmast only fitted with a wire rope conductor, whereas other ships were given wire conductors for each mast. Those variations were then set aside for wire ropes leading from truck or head of royal mast according to drawings sent out in February 1841. Then, in July 1841, an order was given to place copper shackles and thimbles on connecting parts of wire rope to prevent friction. Then another order of 7 July 1841 was to increase the diameter of wire rope by 1/16in.

On 22 August 1840, Mr Smith was directed to supply 307ft of wire rope 7/16in diameter at 6s (£18:56p at current prices) per fathom and 301 feet of 3/8in at 5s/6d (£17.01p at today's prices) per fathom. On 27 August 1841, all ships were required to be fitted with wire rope conductors unless requested to Lordships. Evidence was produced that the *Queen* found her copper wire rope conductor defective and often out of place. *Bittern* had eight men injured due to a lightning strike inadequately carried away by copper wire rope. *Hazard* had suffered similar problems on two occasions.

Harris then went into cost considerations and showed that his conductors, because they were reusable, were actually cheaper than wire ropes, which often became lost or damaged beyond repair. The Precept for return on wire ropes was not yet available but showed the actual cost as similar or more than his fixed copper plate conductors. It was to prove a brilliant stroke by Harris to publish this open letter as it was later to allow his friends in the House of Lords to insist upon obtaining the correct detailed information rather than a censored version.

An approximation of the ships at risk from lightning at the time was that during one year in 1849, there were a total of 138 ships at sea. There were a reinforced number of 21 on the East Indies and China station and 29 in the Mediterranean, both high-risk areas for lightning storms.

Lower risk areas such as the coasts of home waters had only 8 and 'Particular Service,' 11 ships; the West Coast of America had had but 10.

Privately, Harris was still seething at the delays in granting a reward for his invention and when he wrote to his friend Charles Babbage[24] he complained 'of all the vexations and difficulties and jealousies I have had to encounter in carrying out my plan in the Navy'. The long-awaited return in response to the next Precept of the House of Lords[25] was made available in March 1850. The list was of 34 ships which had been fitted with the Symonds/Edye copper wire rope conductors. Twelve (i.e. 35 per cent) of them had been designed by Symonds. There were two instances of damage, one on more than one occasion.

The comparative expense of Harris' conductor, to no one's surprise, was shown as two to four times more expensive than the copper wire rope. Seemingly the contest was even but the item of cost, if correct, made the balance shift towards the half-plagiarised scheme. Further evidence in favour of wire rope conductors was offered by the former senior naval Lord, Sir Charles Adam. Out of loyalty to his Whig father–in–law, he misguidedly sent in a letter from Commander Darley which recorded that the wire rope conductor in his ship *Electra* worked well twice. *Electra* was an 18-gun sloop built in Portsmouth in 1837. There had been considerable correspondence about this ship and the letter from her commander may have been economical with the truth.

Of great importance was that in the Return[26] it was stated that there had been 'No damage recorded in logs' as the official reports from 6 June 1842 for *Impregnable* and from *Belleisle*. As noted earlier, both of these ships had wire rope conductors fitted according to Edye's Plan and 'Plan B' whilst at anchor in Plymouth Sound in February/March 1841. Both ships were ordered to return to port and missed their expected sailing dates in order to replace their original thin wire conductors which had become chafed through. Of course, the date after 5 June 1842 appeared to have been carefully chosen. There was no mention of or costs listed, as to the failed wire rope conductors as first 'designed' by Edye and Symonds.

These thin copper wire ropes, as the reader has been informed, had been found to be wanting and had to be replaced. The expense of this replacement for *Impregnable* and for *Belleisle* and for how many other ships was not recorded. The omission amounted to a serious breach of trust by the authors of the Return. The Return was therefore deliberate misinformation to Parliament. It was not properly exposed as such but should have been. Perhaps it was the price of his silence on the matter that Harris was awarded his final ex-gratia payment.

Of course, nothing could have angered Harris more than this selective list and the inference that his plan was so outrageously expensive. He replied in kind by publication of yet another pamphlet.[27] For the first time, he attacked the politician himself. The Return to the House of Lords by Lord Minto was, he wrote, calculated to bring his lightning conductor into disrepute. The costs of the four ships chosen as comparisons were artificially high. Three of the ships mentioned were fitted with his conductors when the plan was first tried out. No costs for the work had been made or agreed by the Yards and the work of fitting had to be taught. Harris was then specific. *Acteon* and *Tweed* were fitted under the administration of Sir Charles Adam as First Lord. The returns he made were selective, and maliciously so. Harris then criticised Commander Darley's report, or as he had been directed to make it by his Admiral, Charles Adam. The report was two years old and could not be found in the ship's log.

Harris must have been really angry because he went on to record that Admiral Adam 'was the especial patron of the wire rope conductor'. What did he mean? That Adam had an interest in purchases by the Admiralty, via the Surveyor's department, of wire rope? Harris concluded his reply by quoting four letters from his files.

First, on 18 June 1838 to Barrow. *Acteon* was refitting with Harris' conductor. This was unnecessary, destructive of the original trial and a very great waste of resources. Secondly, on 9 June 1840 he had written direct to Admiral Adam and objected to the extraordinarily high costs of fitting *Tweed*. Third, on 25 August 1840 he had again written to Barrow. He had pointed out that costs were being charged twice for moving his conductor from *Caledonia* to *Rodney*.

Finally, he had written on 18 October to the Secretary of Admiralty Board (More O'Ferrall). Wire rope conductors, he had pointed out, were of insufficient capacity, for example, in *Vanguard*, where the topmast had his conductor but the lower part of the system was made of wire rope.

Table 10.5 Costs of fitting fixed conductors[28]

Rates	1st	2nd	3rd	4th	5th	6th	Sloops	Brigs
Fitting cost	£50	£46	£43	£41	£37	£31	£20	£17
Totals	£125	£119	£111	£104	£93	£66	£51	£44

Notes. Costs included re-use of copper as old copper but recyclable or transferable intact to other ships. The Admiralty Board was sent a copy by the author, which is still obtainable from the Admiralty Library.

Part of the blitz of books, papers and pamphlets published by Harris was sent out in support of his case for recompense for his considerable work over many years. It must have been impossible for members of the Whig government, past and present, to escape knowledge of his project. It must have cost Harris a great deal to publish too. His latest book,[29] a list of ships protected by his system of lightning conductors, was published also in an abridged form as a pamphlet.

The year 1851 had brought forward preparations for the Great Exhibition at Crystal Palace. His concern for saving lives brought Harris a prize but not before he met with some obstruction at the Admiralty. Harris[30] requested that some models of his system for protection of ships from lightning be made at Portsmouth Yard in time for it. The reply was unequivocal: 'it was not customary to employ dockyard artificers on private models'. Harris sent a second letter in which he requested the models to be made at own expense. This, too, was refused. However, the newly-appointed Surveyor, Captain Baldwin Walker, relented and said he would have a model made and arrange for it to be placed in the model room. No doubt Harris was allowed to borrow this model for the Exhibition. Thus, there was the strange dichotomy between the official stance of the Admiralty, which had decided that his model to demonstrate his system of lightning protection was a private undertaking, while at the same time they were the main recipients and end users of his great invention. Despite acknowledging adoption of Harris' system, they had not thought to support his adequate reward.

11

Harris' Reward: 1852-70

Russell's government was beaten. The Tories had their chance and Lord Derby formed a government. The Duke of Northumberland as First Lord had no previous experience of the Admiralty or of Parliament but he was a retired rear admiral. His Board was to last for less than a year. In that time, he obtained increases in manpower and increases in the naval estimates to pay for vessels under construction. The achievements were remarkable as there were public demands for low taxes and economical budgets. The First Lord was assisted by Admirals Hyde Parker and Phipps Hornby and some continuity was provided by the presence of the hard working Captain A. Milne.

The Duke had suggested that Harris provide him with a Memorial in a request for remuneration for all his previous endeavours. Harris was easily able to prepare one[1] and had included with the submission many of his printed works. He received an acknowledgement at once from the Admiralty stating it would be considered. His hopes high, he also set about obtaining help from other Cabinet members.

Harris also wrote to another supporter, Thomas Grosvenor Egerton, Second Earl of Wilton,[2] and in his letter suggested a sum of £10,000 (approx. £600,946 today) as a fitting reward for all his years of work. He pointed out that he had saved the Treasury at least £25,000 (approx. £1.5 million today) within the previous six years. Perhaps, he thought, it might be inappropriate to ask Wilton[3] for a debate in the Lords over such a small sum. Wilton was kindly disposed and gave a letter of introduction for Harris to meet the Prime Minister's Private Secretary, Colonel the Hon. E.B. Wilbraham.[4] Soon, a meeting at No. 10 Downing Street took place but Harris felt overwhelmed by the occasion and had to write to Wilbraham to amplify his points.

The support of Lord Derby as Prime Minister would be crucial.[5]

Harris had corresponded with him before as plain Lord Stanley MP in 1839. Again, in 1851, Harris had written and enclosed his usual offerings of books, papers and letters in support of his case for recognition. Derby must have been reminded of the entire story as Harris had sent him two letters and increasingly importunate requests for a decision. Lord Derby then wrote in a private note[6] that Disraeli, the Chancellor of the Exchequer, was less well disposed about Harris' case, but he would raise the matter with him again.

Everything moved too slowly for Harris. It was only natural that he felt the impatience of years of neglect and of obfuscation by the Whigs and perhaps a feeling, too, that the Tory administration might not last. Autumn gave way to winter and by December the government fell, without there being a clear decision made as to Harris' reward. The Whigs were to resume office – could Harris expect any justice from them?

The Admiralty meanwhile continued to cooperate and to send Harris every detail of any of HM Ships which had encountered lightning. The steam packet *Dee*, on contract hire to the Admiralty, had been struck on the vane spindle but the current discharged safely down the fixed conductor. By contrast, a nearby Spanish packet steamer, without a permanent conductor, had her spanker boom shivered. By copying the letter to the Prime Minister[7] they were fully supporting Harris' case for a reward.

Harris mentioned later, in a private letter to his friend Charles Babbage,[8] that his recent Memorial to the government did not mention the sum of £10,000 (approx. £600,946 at today's prices as expressed as RPI), but the covering letter with it did. After all, his invention had saved £10,000 in one year alone.

The Whigs under Lord Aberdeen took office on 5 March 1853. The reformist in a perpetual haste, Sir James Graham, was asked to become First Lord once more. His earlier errors of the 1830s now visited him and became ever plainer as his Ministry matured. His new Board did have several previous members from 1849 which allowed continuity of purpose. Hyde Parker continued as Senior Naval Lord and that, too, was helpful. At last, the Boards were becoming professional rather than political in nature.

Babbage took up the cudgels on Harris' behalf. The replies to his letters were from Ralph Bernal Osborne,[9] MP for Middlesex and holding the appointment of the First or Political Secretary to the Admiralty. Babbage had not bothered to mince his words: 'no man has a chance of success unless he is a charlatan or has strong party influences to support him, Sir S. Harris has none. He therefore appealed to clear sighted scientific Government.'

Osborne[10] eventually admitted 'the Memorial had been found' after first trying to dissemble by stating the problem was Captain Milne's department. Osborne then had the audacity to suggest that Babbage (rather than himself) 'apply' to the Treasury with respect to it. This reaction by the new Whig administration can only be described as vindictive and shabby.

By this time, Harris was forced to think in political power terms. How could he further his good claim to a reward for his long services on behalf of the Crown? He had suggested in his letter[11] that Disraeli would be his choice to put his claim forward to the House of Commons. A letter of support from the Earl of St Germans would probably help and he could calculate that he could obtain support from Macgregor, Gibson, H. Stephenson, Locke and Bullen.

Harris wrote to thank his friend for writing to Osborne.[12] He went on to say that he knew Captain Milne, who served for years on the Board, and considered him a friend. Milne had put Harris' case to the Board in November. Then the Duke had requested the Memorial but the government was dissolved just as it was about to be acted upon. Harris then related how he had just been visited by Sir R. Forbes, the ship owner, who was using his influence to get the fixed conductor applied to the US Navy. He ended by suggesting that Babbage meet with him over the idea of a lightning conductor for his house.

Harris now thought[13] he must put his papers in the hands of the new Prime Minister, Lord Aberdeen (Prime Minister 1852-5), using several channels. These might include again the President of The Royal Society, then Lord Harrowby (in 1853 not in office). Harris also thought he was not without friends in the House of Commons. He would:

> operate to a fine end of a wedge on the Government. He knew he was not favoured by the late Secretary to the Admiralty, Sir Stafford as there was a misunderstanding between them on a political matter which also led to the Chancellor of the Exchequer throwing cold water on my application. He felt sure that Lord Derby and the senior Naval Lord admitted his claims but the Government fell.

He ended by suggesting that Babbage makes Osborne claim the matter is 'a liberal political one'.

Babbage[14] countered by suggesting privately to Harris that he write a letter which could, with propriety, then be forwarded to Osborne. Harris[15] wrote at once. Dated 23 January 1853, it commenced with the fate of other inventions, 'like the proposer of the penny postage, or the inventor of gas lights etc., he had run the gauntlet of an illiberal and vexatious opposition and fought vulgar and unlearned prejudice single handed'. He referred to Admiralty contracts with packets to carry the mail and asserted that those vessels had his plan of fixed lightning conductors.

He mentioned Sir Baldwin Walker, the Surveyor, who was on board an HM Ship preserved by his lightning conductor. Between March 1846 and July 1847 (16 months), ten ships had been preserved from lightning. The Exchequer had benefited by £10,000 (approx. £600,946).

Osborne (the First Secretary), he wrote, was unbiased and politically free. Surely he would help. Harris then pointed out that his invention had won the Council Medal at the Great Exhibition. Also that others had received financial recognition for their inventions and developments. For example, £46,000 (approx. £2.76 million today) for the invention of watertight bulkheads, £20,000 (approx. £1.2 million today) for the screw propeller. He, on the other hand, could not obtain patents as the plans had been made public by Naval experiments.

Harris stated his case[16] was now ready for immediate action. The Treasury had agreed to his claim but had to decide the amount. He wrote of the influence of Gibson on Wilson at the Treasury and compared awards for life-taking inventions (e.g. shrapnel) to life-saving ones. Harris thought that his title and annuity would be taken into consideration and that £10,000 the very least they could offer him.

On 4 July 1853, the good news arrived. The Treasury had agreed a grant of £5,000 (approx. £300,473 today) to be awarded to Harris. Incredibly, but in view of past experience believably, there was a delay and an argument between departments as the papers relative to 'Shipwreck by Lightning', so carefully prepared by Harris,[17] had again 'been lost'. The papers had certainly been sent by Harris to the Admiralty in a presentation format and are now in the Admiralty Library. Harris listed 240 cases of ships struck by lightning.[18] The costs in wartime over 23 years amounted to £140,000 (approx. £8:4 million today). In 23 years of war, 1793-1815, 78 ships of line, 58 frigates and 31 sloops had been damaged.

In peacetime, during 23 years, the damage caused costs of £28,000 (approx. £1:5 million today). Between 1815 and 1839, eight ships of the line, 15 frigates and 50 sloops or smaller had been damaged. In a third of all cases, men had been hurt or killed. The shy and trusty mentor of Harris, Michael Faraday, wrote to give his congratulations on the grant of money. Harris, in acknowledgement, wrote:[19]

> It was a Herculean task to hunt all the dusty ships' records deposited at the Admiralty and obtain published evidence of the terrible loss of life and property etc. by strokes of lightning at sea. 10-20 men at a time more or less paralysed whilst furling a topsail. The Admiralty would not believe all this at first and I was looked on as a sort of visionary in proposing to defend ships from lightning by a systematic application of metallic conductors of great capacity.

He then referred to difficulties of time to experiment and research while his public duties had to be fulfilled: 'The long battle was a source of great trouble and vexation to me, especially the illiberal dealing I experienced at the hands of persons who should have known better.'

The Admiralty[20] had completely accepted Harris' fixed system for lightning protection and even ensured it was fitted to contract mail packets. Soon afterwards, the Ordnance Board protected their buildings, also on Harris' plan but modified for buildings and powder magazines.

The time of wooden sailing line of battle ships was coming to an end. In 1854, screw propulsion allowed the wooden hulled *Caesar* to achieve 10.25 knots over the measured mile. Yet hybrid steam and sail paddle steamers were being commissioned as late as 1856. A wooden hull was used and a full rig as a frigate but with boilers for steam. One such vessel, HMS *Retribution* with 28 guns, was the second largest paddle steamer ever built for the Navy. She, too, had protection of the masts and spars with Harris' lightning conductors and was saved from being struck by lightning in May 1857 south of the River Plate.[21] Soon, the last wooden line of battle ship had been built and by 1861 the government suspended their building, except for the purpose of iron-plating them. A short while later, the all-iron hull became standard. These armoured ships, such as the famous *Warrior*, had been built with wooden topmasts which needed protection by fixed lightning conductors. Indeed, wooden masts were still part of many ships as late as the 1870s.

There remained many unanswered questions about thunder and lightning. In 1860, Professor Thompson[22] had outlined what was known and what remained to be discovered. He gave a lecture on the subject but it asked more questions than he or other workers could answer:

> What is atmospheric electricity? Of earth, water or particles in the air? Electricity cannot be transmitted in a vacuum and with difficulty in rarefied air. Intensity of electricity in air is always fluctuating. How is it distributed through the strata of the atmosphere? Does electrification of air near the earth's surface vary with weather? His answer: Yes, it did. Do particles of rain, hail, snow possess electric charges? He could not tell them. He discussed the water dropping collector apparatus and referred to Faraday's work. As long ago as 1824, Faraday had thought that water particles were charged with electricity under certain circumstances.

Note

Amounts at modern prices given in this chapter are calculated to the year 2004 according to data supplied by the Economic History Services as Relative Values of UK Pounds. Thus the 1d (penny) postage has a value of 31p today. The Retail Price Index (RPI) has been chosen as a descriptor as it is more easily compared as a bundle of necessary purchases of goods and services by a householder.

12

Modern Times and Barrow's Epitaph

In 1880 the Admiralty, under the signature of the Controller, W. Houston Stewart, published Official Rules for Lightning Protection:[1]

1. Wooden ships with wooden masts, according to Snow Harris' instructions.
2. Wooden ships with iron masts. The lower mast forms the conductor: connect to the sea in normal way.
3. Iron ships with iron masts. The step of the iron mast is to be made bright before fitting the mast.
4. Iron ships sheathed with wood and with iron masts. Copper bolts to hull bottom and vulcanite to prevent galvanic action.
5. Iron ships with wooden masts. The wire rigging may form alternative route for electricity. But men may be in danger. Therefore fit conductor between wire shrouds and chain plates, not rope.
6. Complete form 237, to include lightning protection and test with galvanometer.

Merchant fleets, as ever, were subject to the parsimony of their owners and many were allowed only the old-style ineffective chains of low current-carrying capacity. In 1879, D. Morgan, the master of the barque *Southern Queen*, recorded that lightning struck her mast and the fore topsail halyard chain of iron was fractured into bits.[2] Even the weight and capacity of iron chain at 2lb per foot proved not enough to allow a proper channel for the discharge of the lightning.

In 1878, The Meteorological Society met and proposed that as the French and other nations had made suggestions about lightning protection for householders and for public buildings, the British should consider taking an official view for the benefit of their citizens. The conference took scientific evidence furnished by delegates from the meteorologists, the physicists, The Society of Telegraph Engineers and of Electricians, and the RIBA.[3] Advertisements were placed in the press and a large response was obtained from the public. Many wrote in and displayed the old prejudices and fairy tales about lightning. Others were more thoughtful but, like the football supporter, imagined they had all the answers to every eventuality. Manufacturers of lightning protection apparatus were also asked by means of a series of detailed questions to describe their particular techniques for lightning protection. A complete literature search, including of foreign published works, was undertaken by the Committee. Abstracts, evidence, conclusions and advice were collated and published in a book of 261 pages in 1882.[4]

Ships and their vulnerability to lightning were given much space and Harris' work appraised. There were still some critics, mostly those who mentioned costs and others who suggested the fixed system was over capacious for the intended task. McHardy[5] wrote that in some ships with iron masts, there was also a copper strip or tube down the rigging and that the latter was unnecessary.

Priest[6] later wrote 'that there were ships in HM Navy which had for fifty years been fitted with lightning conductors according to Sir William Snow Harris' principles [and no damage had occurred]'.

Death from lightning by an indirect mechanism occurred in 1894. At the US Navy Yard[7] in Norfolk, some men were sheltering from a thunderstorm under the iron hull of *Raleigh*. There was no flash and the officers on deck felt nothing. Those underneath were killed. The cause was said to be inductive condenser discharge.

Ships and water-craft, too, continued to become casualties. In 1900, a barge on the River Thames was struck by lightning when unloading naphtha. It was set on fire. A few years later in 1903, the liner *Teutonic* was off Newfoundland. Lightning struck her wooden topmast and destroyed it and some ropes were punched into the cavity of her hollow iron lower mast.

The Admiralty regulations[8] have changed little over the years from the sailing ship Navy to the modern warship, the only significant new items being to accommodate new technology such as wireless masts or all-steel masts and hulls. In 1924, the regulations as printed were:

> Ships are particularly liable to be struck by a lightning discharge because it is frequently the only object projecting above the

general level of the sea. Therefore each mast has a conductor. For steel hinged or telescopic masts lightning conductors are not necessary unless to satisfy W/T requirements.

Wooden masts: conductors should not be recessed (although it is often necessary). Conductors should be secured by hard copper nails in elongated holes and a small loop made near [the] top of conductors to allow for expansion. Should be efficiently earthed in wooden or in composite ships to copper sheathing on hull or to an earth plate.

The masts of ships (including submarines) and flag staffs are to be fitted with lightning conductors. Where masts support wireless telegraph aerials, the insulating and earthing of the rigging must satisfy W/T requirements.

Ships in dry dock are to be earthed by connection to the water main.

Conductor to be of copper tape 1 x 1/8' thick weighing 1lb. per foot if for structure of less than 150 feet in height. If higher then 2 x 1/8' thick.

On inspection of a ship, or after refit, the conductor had to be tested for continuity by measurement of resistance. If that was found to be more than 0.02 ohm then it should be checked for a bad joint. In Appendix 6, there was an extract from Lloyds Rules (for insurance purposes) for merchant vessels:

Lightning conductors shall be fitted to all wooden vessels or steel vessels having wooden masts. They need not be fitted to steel vessels with steel masts.

Lead copper tape where shrouds leave the mast and clamp to a copper rope 1/2' in diameter. Lead down the shrouds and attach to galvanised iron plate 2sq. feet below light load water line.

Ships with wooden masts should have copper tape terminating in nearest metal forming part of the ship.

Serious incidents from the effects of lightning or a build-up of atmospheric or of static electricity could and do occur to airships and aircraft. On 6 May 1937, the airship *Hindenburg* exploded whilst at her mooring at New Jersey, USA. The airship was earthed to the tip of the mooring mast but exploded due to atmospheric electricity setting alight gases leaking from her hull. St Elmo's fire had been seen playing around the airship shortly beforehand.

Even modern warships of all-steel construction can be damaged if wooden masts or booms are part of the superstructure above deck. Lightning hit the 7,250-ton Devonport-built cruiser HMS *Leander* when at Espiritu Santos on 4 April 1943. It found its way down the conductor and went off track to split the cut-swing boom.[9]

Oil tankers,[10] due to residual gases, remain vulnerable to electrically-caused fires and explosions. Between 1950 and 1975, 12 oil tankers or barges were struck by lightning, four of them whilst at sea. Any resultant fire was snuffed out by use of carbon dioxide gas or foam. There were six dead and 30 injured in the case of the *Princess Irene* in August 1972 in ballast at Donges. The explosion also damaged her berth. Two tankers became a total loss, one, the *Ktriti Sun*, on 28 October 1975. The 122,000-ton dead weight Greek *MV oiler* was moored three miles off Singapore. Lightning touched off fires and explosions and the blasts sank a tender sent to rescue the crew. Seven were injured, two badly so. The tanker had just discharged 95,000 tons of crude oil when lightning struck her amidships thus igniting fumes left in empty tanks. Another example was the *Selco*, L-27 barge. This incurred extensive damage to her port tanks on 26 November 1975, again near Singapore. Two people were injured. The risk of fire and explosion after a lightning strike seems to be worse when the tanks of the oilers have been emptied as residual gases, even if vented, are flammable. However, to put the matter in perspective, the total losses due to fire after lightning at that time formed only 2 per cent of the causes of 100 fires with damage in tankers. Lloyds List recorded that only 7 out of 1,500 (nearly 0.5 per cent) of tanker fire incidents which had been reported to them were due to lightning.

Yachts

As late as the 1980s, many yacht builders of cruisers took advantage of the strength of modern materials and stepped the mast(s) onto the cabin roof or to the deck. This was in preference to deep into the hull or keelson, as more room was made available within the hull by the absence of the lower part of the mast. It was not altogether surprising when a local newspaper[11] reported that 'two men were rescued in the Channel at dawn after their new 34ft motor sailor was struck by lightning and set ablaze. An explosion had occurred.' The Vulcan class yacht[12] had a metal mast, stepped to the deck and was not connected to an earth plate, although an auxiliary motor was properly earthed. The mast had wire shrouds attached to chain plates and in turn to ribs on the hull with internal fixings. The hull was a glass reinforced plastic type material. All the electrics were burnt out and charge from the lightning ran out from the mast along the cables which were set on fire. Perhaps a high voltage circuit breaker for the electrical circuit would have helped to reduce the risk of damage.

The incident, which must have been very frightening for the crew, hastened the provision of adequate earthing plates for masts, wherever stepped, although Lloyds Register of Shipping reported that there were no statutory requirements for yachts to have lightning conductors in 1981. Most reputable yacht builders now include lightning protection within their specifications when building.

Some fatalistic yachtsmen are said still to rely for their protection against lightning strikes during a thunderstorm solely on an anchor chain just touching the sea. It appears to the author that natural selection may diminish their number in high thunderstorm-day areas. Bernstein[13] commented that a very high resistance would be caused as only a very small surface area of a chain would be in contact with the sea to discharge the lightning. Harris had thought out this problem many years before. He recommended that a capacious mass of metal be bonded to the lightning conductor so as to limit the chance of side flashes (lateral explosions).

The journal *Yachting Monthly*[14] carried an appraisal of lightning strikes to yachts made of glass-reinforced plastic (GRP) in 1977. Damage from lightning was quoted as occurring in five possible ways:

> 1. Voltage rise due to the resistance offered by any conductor carrying a very large current. A voltage of difference of 1 kilovolt per metre being suggested. Any instrument reliant upon electricity was therefore likely to be fused.
>
> 2. Heating may burn out small wires or metal objects incapable of carrying the full current load. Water in wood affected by the electrical current may be turned to steam and explode.

3. Air breakdown may occur if high voltages from a lightning discharge allow the electrical current to jump an air gap and cause a flash and a shockwave.

4. Coiled or even looped wire could be affected by induction during a strike.

5. Finally, magnetisation induced after lightning may wreck compasses and electrical instruments.

The magazine concluded by stating that since fresh water has a higher resistance to electricity than salt water, then damage to hulls could result from lightning if yachts were sailing on lakes and inland waters, the risk being greater if no protection from lightning and no earth plate is provided.

Lightning protection arrangements for yachts in British waters does not seem to have been a priority due to the small number of thunderstorm days, at only about 15 a year. Strikes from lightning do occur nonetheless. A lightning strike to a trimaran on trestles whilst undergoing repairs resulted in a hole blown in the hull. This incident caused a rethink. Lohman[15] then wrote an article with sound advice for the yachtsman. Regardless of mast materials, he recommended a conductor from a point at least 6ft above the mast. The conductor should be of a good size and with no sharp bends or loops in its path to the earthing plate of 1sq ft and placed well below the water line. A metal hull was considered by him to be an adequate earth. He wrote that all metal rigging should be earthed, as should sail tracks and any masses of metal which are within 6ft of the path of the conductor.

Others less concerned as to the risk of a lightning strike have felt (unwisely as was demonstrated by Harris many years before) that tinsel copper braid wire led from the metal wire rope shrouds into the sea is adequate protection from a lightning discharge.

Modern Warships

For warships of the modern era, the Ministry of Defence Ship Procurement section at Bath very kindly arranged for their advisers on lightning protection for ships, Y-Ard,[16] to release details from their draft guide. The long and very technically densely written document was adumbrated by the author and therefore excludes much fine detail.

To paraphrase: lightning is the long spark discharge of large accumulations of electrical charge contained in thunderclouds. Turbulent motion in the cloud separates the charges, which then reside on particles of dust, water, ice or snow. The turbulent motion is produced from heat from the sun's rays and hence occurs more often in tropical areas.

High electric stresses are produced which eventually lead to breakdown of the air dielectric. This produces an ionised conducting leader channel which develops away from the charge centre towards ground or another centre. When the leader channel is established, discharge of the charge centre occurs. Discharges to ground or the sea may be positively or negatively charged. Most are cloud to cloud.

Effects of lightning on warships[17]

A ship can be damaged by a direct strike from lightning or by its secondary effects, for example, ignition of flammable material. Sufficient energy may be transferred to vaporise any thin metallic conductors or to boil water in the cellular structure of wood. Pressures generated may rupture any contained conductor. Severe magnetic forces can be produced when the high currents flow in parallel paths or around sharp bends or corners and may be sufficient to rip out screws or fittings. Very high voltages of the order of one megavolt can be produced by the passage of lightning through a ship and may puncture non-conducting hulls.

Protection Against Damage

Three categories of damage:

1. Critical to existence of the ship.
2. Vital equipment damaged which jeopardises mission.
3. Minor damage.

In vessels with metal hulls, the hull acts as the earth terminal. In wooden or composite hulls (e.g. minesweepers), the earth terminal is to be permanently submerged with a connecting pillar which penetrates the hull. The earth plate is contoured to the shape of the hull, is preferably rounded, left unpainted, is at least 7mm thick and with at least $0.25m^2$ contact area with the sea.

If special arrangements for surge protectors on specialist electrical and other equipment are excluded, then the advice nowadays has altered only slightly in emphasis since 1924. Thus William Snow Harris' calculations of capacity for an adequate lightning conductor together with his recommendations for the protection from lightning of wooden masts, metal masts, for non-conducting and for conducting hulls, remain of use today. His work, originally begun in 1820, has indeed withstood the test of time.

General Advice[18]

It remains only to record the most up-to-date advice obtainable from experts when thunderstorms approach. As mentioned in Chapter 1, the risks of thunderstorms are very different for certain areas of the world. In a few places, thunder is heard daily more often than not. Fortunately, most lightning discharges take place between clouds rather than a discharge to earth or sea.

The scientific basis for traditional systems for lightning protection was questioned as recently as 1998 by a committee appointed on behalf of the (US) National Fire Protection Association. Their report concluded that 'Franklin rod air terminals had not been validated under thunderstorm conditions'. International scientists refuted this view in 2001 but specified that blunt-tipped air terminals as against those with sharp points were probably more effective but that the evidence needed confirmation.[19] Thus, interest in lightning and controversy about the efficacy of apparatus for the protection of people, buildings and ships remained of moment to many and, I submit, also justified the publication of this historical record.

The use of telephones during thunderstorms has been studied. It has been found that a lightning-induced electrical surge[20] can hurt, but more often merely frightens, telephone users. The problem has been especially studied in Australia where about 30 people a year reported injuries from lightning whilst using the telephone. The period of study was 1988 to 1990 and ten people were found about whom there was data sufficient for inclusion in the study. Half had an altered level of consciousness after the surge and two (20 per cent) had burns or other problems affecting their head and neck.

Long-term neurological problems and other symptoms occurred in three cases (30 per cent). The major risk factor associated with a lightning-induced current surge to the telephones was found to be damage to the power lines supplying electricity, even if these were underground, rather than by a direct strike partially affecting a telephone wire.[21]

For personal protection against the risk from a stroke of lightning, the experts have divided the situation into low-risk and high-risk zones.[22] Low risk were those where a direct strike was prevented by a zone of protection afforded by a building bearing a lightning conductor system, or where the person was not on the telephone and in a modern building with good bonding of metalwork to earth. Any buildings with steel frames or of ferroconcrete construction were in effect well earthed.

High-risk situations were said to be where the person was out in the open on high ground, or swimming or wading. Or, as has been demonstrated in this book, on a ship near to or on a wooden or other mast not well connected to the sea by a capacious conductor permanently in place.

For those interested in yachting, a check should have been carried out as described above as to where the heel of the mast is stepped. If the step is on the cabin roof or at deck level or anywhere else without a capacious bond to earth, then suitable action should be taken. The many items of electrical apparatus, such as satellite navigation, echo sounders or radios, should be earthed. Additionally, they each should have surge current breakers to protect them.

If caught out in the open by an imminent thunderstorm, the best (but far from complete) obtainable protection for the human body against the possible effects of lightning is said to be given by crouching on the ground, even if wet, but doing so well away from metal or pointed objects such as golf clubs, ski sticks or guns. A large wood may form a satisfactory shelter but care should be taken to be low down and well away from the tallest trees. It is thought to be unwise to shelter under a solitary tree surrounded by open spaces. Much the best temporary shelter is said to be a car, but with the sharp-pointed telephone and radio aerials retracted and other electrical apparatus not in use.[23]

A victim of a strike by lightning, if unconscious or apparently dead, should be given immediate and prolonged resuscitation and skilled help summoned.

To complete this book, it remains only to record that the opponent of technological advance in the Victorian Navy, Sir John Barrow, has a fitting memorial. The memorial has accidentally also become a permanent symbolic toast to one of his hated projectors, and in particular to the developer of the permanent and capacious lightning conductor for HM Ships. How can this be?

After Sir John Barrow died in 1848 at 84 years of age, only three years after retirement, it was natural that his sons wished to perpetuate his memory. In his will, Barrow had endowed his old local grammar school and this act had endeared him to the local people. This was despite the fact that none knew him as he had not revisited the area since leaving it as a young man. A subscription fund was set up to which the Queen Dowager, the ever-generous Palmerston and some other politicians and some naval friends contributed. The site chosen for a monument was near his birthplace at Dragleybeck near Ulverstone, Cumberland.[24] The site dominated the Hill of Hoad and overlooked the shifting, dangerous sands and the blind-ended channels of Morecambe Bay.

The foundation stone was laid in May 1850 with 8,000 people and a brass band present and the schoolchildren led a procession, singing as they went up the winding path to the summit. The design chosen was a tower in a shape of a lighthouse, a smaller version of that which guarded the Eddystone rocks. It was an odd place to put a sham lighthouse but no doubt was a useful landmark for those out on the sands at low tide. Built from ascending tiers of stone blocks, it soon rose many feet into the air. It was over two-thirds finished but roofless when, during a severe thunderstorm, the tower was struck by lightning.[25] Nine 3cwt blocks of stone were found broken and there was much other damage to the partly completed building.

According to instructions given to the builders, Harris' conductors had been ordered to be placed to guard against lightning but had not yet been fitted. A temporary conductor was put in at once and the scaffolding re-erected. The repairs cost a further £136.

According to local people, lightning frequently plays around the monument but since Harris' conductor has been in position, there has been no further damage.

There cannot be a more fitting epitaph to the civil servant who delayed the adoption of the highly effective system of lightning protection for ships, as developed by William Snow Harris.

Notes

List of Abbreviations Used in the Notes to Chapters.

ADM	Admiralty. Used for Admiralty departmental papers at the Public Record Office (now the National Archives). Also used for the Admiralty component of the Ministry of Defence Library.
BL	British Library.
CUL	Cambridge University Library.
HO	Home Office.
IEE	Institute of Electrical Engineers, holds the Ronalds collection.
ISS	Information and Service Systems.
JMR	*Journal of Maritime Research.*
KCL	Kings College Library, London.
LRO	Liverpool Record Office.
MM	*Mariner's Mirror.*
MRF	Microfiche version of record.
NMM	National Maritime Museum, The Caird Library.
NLS	National Library of Scotland.
PRO	Public Record Office, Kew, London, now the National Archives.
Pro	Promiscuous (letters or papers).
SRO	Scottish Record Office now National Archives for Scotland.
Trans Ply. Ins	Transactions of the Plymouth Institute.

Chapter 1

1. Golde, R.H., *Lightning Protection.* pub. Edward Arnold. London 1973. pp. 3-22, 147-163.
2. Met Office. National Meteorological Library and Archive. Fact Sheet No. 2 Thunderstorms. pp. 10, 13. July 2007.
3. Ibid.
4. Ibid.
5. Pierce, E.T. *Lightning Warning and Avoidance.* p.498-9 in Ed. Golde RH. *Lightning. Volume 2 Lightning Protection.* pub. Academic Press. London, 1977.
6. Ibid.
7. Taylor, A.R. *Lightning and Trees.* p.843. in Ed. Golde, R.H. op cit.
8. Ibid. p. 831.
9. Ibid. p. 844.
10. Ibid.
11. Ed. Andrews, C.J., Cooper, M.A. *et al.*, *Lightning Injuries*, pp. 27-30, pub. CRC Press, Boca Raton 1992.
12. Golde, op. cit. p. 108-117.
13. Dolley, R.H., *Meteorology in the Byzantine Navy*, pp. 5-16, *Mariners Mirror* (MM), 37(1), 1951.
14. Golde, op. cit. p. 186.
15. Golde, op. cit. p. 139.
16. Ibid.
17. Newman, M.N and Robb, J.D, *Protection for Aircraft.* in Ed. Golde, R.H. op.cit p. 691.
18. Ed. Skempton A.W. *John Smeaton FRS.* pp. 15, 92. pub. T Telford Ltd, London 1981.
19. Golde, p. 10, op. cit.
20. There are two other types of atmospheric electricity: 'ball lightning', which is a very rare but real phenomenon, and the lightning formed in the vapours of volcanic eruptions.
21. Harris, W.S., *State of the Question Relating to the Protection of the British Navy from Lightning*, p. 9, section A, pub. T.J. Bond, Plymouth 1838.
22. Golde, p. 30. op. cit.
23. Rieu, E.V., trans., *Homer's Odyssey*, Book XII, p. 200. Penguin Classics Edition. 1946.
24. The Greeks and later the Romans used to avoid a place on land where lightning had already struck. It was their common practice to surround the location by a fence and never to build there as they believed lightning would strike again at the same spot. They could not avoid known lightning areas at sea and were unlikely to be able to locate them accurately.
25. Holy Bible, e.g. Job, 37:3.
26. Clowes, W.L., *The Royal Navy: A History from the Earliest Times to the Present*, Volume 1, p. 169, pub. Samson Lowe Mast & Co., 1897.
27. Dolley, p. 12. op. cit.

28. Howarth, D., *Sovereign of the Seas: The Story of British Sea Power*, p. 61, Book Club Assoc. & W. Collins Sons & Co. Ltd, Glasgow 1974.
29. Ed. Wheatley, H.B., *Diary of Samuel Pepys*, Volume III, p. 172, pub. G. Bell & Sons Ltd, London 1922.
30. Anon, 'The remarkable effects of a great storm of thunder and lightning at Portsmouth, October 23rd, 1685', *Philosophical Transactions*, 177, p. 1212. Abridged version, p. 3, Vol. III, pub. C & R Baldwin, London 1809.
31. Marsh, A.J., 'A Frigate in Three Hurricanes', p. 188, *Mariners Mirror* (MM), 54(2), 1968.
32. Franklin, B., 'Concerning the effects of lightning', *Philosophical Transactions*, Vol. XLIV, p. 289, letter dated Philadelphia 20 June 1751.
33. Franklin, B., *The Theory of Meteors*. p. 681. Printed D Henry and R Care. 2nd ed. London 1754.
34. Watson, W., 'Some Suggestions Concerning the Preventing the Mischiefs which happened to Ships and their Masts by Lightning', *Philosophical Transactions*, p. 660, abridged version, Vol. 11, 1755-1763.
35. Watson, W., *Philosophical Transactions*, p. 201, Vol. LIV, 1762.
36. Clowes, W.L., *The Royal Navy: A History from the Earliest Times to the Present*, Vol. 3., p. 338, pub. 1897.
37. Wynne (sic) for Winn Capt. to Franklin. B., open letter, 'An account of the appearance of lightning on a conductor fixed from the summit of the mainmast of a ship down to the water', *Philosophical Transactions*, Vol. 60, 1770.
38. Nairne, E., 'Experiments on electricity being an attempt to shew the advantage of elevated pointed conductors,' pp. 1-40, read at The Royal Society, June 1778, pub. J. Nichols, London 1779.
39. IEE. Ronalds Library. Letters from Wilson and from Collinson to Franklin giving details of lightning strikes to English ships, *Oeuvres de Franklin*, Paris, 1773.
40. Dubourcq, H., pp.125 et seq., re. electrical fire, 'Franklin, B., Book of Recipes, Canopus Publishing, 2000.
41. Rushbrook, F. quoted Bathoe, J. in *Fire Aboard*. Vol.1. pub. Technical Press Ltd. London 1961.
42. van Doren, C. *Benjamin Franklin,* pp. 581 et seq., pub. Putnam, London 1939.
43. IEE. Ronalds Library, file of MSS on 'Atmospheric Electricity'. F. Duprez, *Statistics of Buildings and Ships Struck By Lightning*, Acad. Royal de Belgique 1857.

Chapter 2

1. Editorial, 'Lightning', *British Medical Journal*, 26 October 1974, p. 181.
2. Taussig, H.B., 'Death from Lightning and the Possibilty of Living Again', *Annals of Internal Medicine*, 69(6), pp. 1345-53, 1968.
3. Ed. Andrews, C.J., Cooper, M.A., Darveniza, M., Mackerras. D. *Lightning*

Injuries: Electrical, Medical and Legal Aspects, Chaps. 3-9 and pp. 28-29, 40-6, 49-55, pub. CRC Press, Boca Raton, USA 1992.
4. Ibid.
5. Ibid.
6. Ibid.
7. Ed. Golde, R., *Lightning*, Vol. 2, *Lightning Protection*, pp. 530-540, pub. Academic Press, London, New York 1977.
8. Andrews *et al.*, op. cit.
9. Taussig, op. cit.
10. Taussig, ibid.; Editorial, 'Lightning', *British Medical Journal*, op. cit; Andrews *et al.* op. cit.; Golde, op. cit.
11. Bailey, D.M. *et al.*, 'Electron paramagnetic resonance spectroscopic evidence of increased free radical generation and selective damage to skeletal muscle following lightning injury', *High Alt. Med. & Biol.* 4(3), pp. 281-9, autumn 2003.
12. *British Medical Journal*, op. cit.; Andrews *et al.*, op. cit.
13. Andrews *et al.*, op. cit.
14. Taussig, op. cit.
15. Andrews *et al.*, op. cit.
16. Cannell, H., 'Struck by Lightning: The Effects upon the Men and the Ships of HM Navy', *J. RN Medical Services*, Vol. 65, pp. 165-70, 1979.
17. Cannell, H., 'Varieties of Strikes on Men', *J. RN Med. Services*, Vol. 66, pp. 152-6, 1980.
18. Critchley, M., 'Neurological Effects of Lightning and of Electricity', *Lancet*, I, 68-72.
19. Muelberger, T., Vogt, P.M., Munster, A.M., *Burns*, 27(8), pp. 829-33, 2001.
20. van Zomeren, A.H., ten Duis, H.J., Minderhoud, J.M., Sipma, M. J., *Neurology, Neurosurgery & Psych*, 64(6), pp. 763-9, 1998.
21. Janus, T.J., Barrash, J .J., *Burn Care & Rehab*, 17(5), pp. 409-15, 1996.
22. Hawkes, C.H., Thorpe, J.W., J. *Neurology, Neurosurg, & Psych*, 55(5), pp. 388-90, 1992.
23. PRO. ADM 53/722 IMPREGNABLE, Master's Log, A.B.W. Taylor, 18 NOV 1842 & 7 MAR 1843.
24. Datta, *et al.*, *Ind J Opthamology*, 50(3), pp. 224-5, 2002.
25. Elliott, Admiral Sir George KCB, *1784-1863, A Memoir*, p. 23, pub. London 1863.
26. Veicht, R., 'On the effects of lighting on three ships in the East Indies', *Philosophical Transactions*, Vol. XII, p. 294, 1763-9.
27. Anon, *The Naval Chronicle & Nautical Magazine*, p. 65, 1809.
28. Harris, W.S., *Naut. Mag. & Naval Journ*, Vol. XXV, pp. 395, 439, 1832.
29. Murray, J., *The Description of a New Lightning Conductor*, pp. 8., 43, pub. London 1833.
30. The Report for the House of Commons, *W.S. Harris, Papers Relative to Shipwrecks by Lighting*, 5 August 1854.
31. Le Roi, J.R abridged translation. pub. Paris 1797. *Philosophical Papers*

and useful Naval Projects. pp. 197-204. Naval Chronicle. Vol.1 pub. Joyce Gold, London 1799.
32. Duprez, F., 'Statistics of buildings and ships struck by lightning', *Academie Royale de Belgique, extraits du tome 31 des memoires*, 1857.
33. House of Commons. *Shipwreck by Lightning.* Copy of Report and Evidence from the Commission into the Plan of William Snow Harris. pp. 51-3. Printed 12 Feb. 1840.
34. Martin, Sir B., *Journals and Letters of Sir Byam Martin*, Vol. 1, pp. 114-15, pub Navy Records Society 1898.
35. *Naval Chronicle,* Vol. XX p. 349, 1808.
36. Ibid. Vol. XXV p. 221, 1811.
37. Baynham, H., *From from the Lower D Deck*, p. 179, pub. Arrow Books 1972.
38. Ibid.
39. Gilly, W.S., *Narratives of Shipwrecks of the Royal Navy 1793-1849*, Preface and p. 8-10, pub J.W. Parker, London 1850.
40. Phillimore, A., *The Life of Sir William Parker*, Vol.I, p. 394, pub. Harrison, Pall Mall, London 1876.

Chapter 3

1. Harris, W.S., 'Electrical Conductors for Ships', two articles. *Philosophical Magazine,* Vol. LX, pp. 231-3, 1822.
2. PRO. ADM 1/ 4730. Pro.H 181, Harris to Navy Board, 1 JAN 1821.
3. Henley, W., FRS, XLI, 'An account of some new experiments in Electricity', 1771-2, *Philosophical Transactions*, Vol. LXIV, pp. 551-65, pub 1774.
4. Green, W., Pringle. Lt. RN, 'Selection of papers in Fixed Lightning Conductors for HM Navy', pub 1824, No.10, Lyons Court, Wales and London. Letters quoted previously published in (Plymouth) *Dock Telegraph,* p. 49,14 SEP 1822, p. 58, OCT 1822; p. 61, 9 OCT 1822, pp. 70, 25 OCT 1822.
5. DM. 4, 118ff 188, Harris to President and Council of Royal Society, 2 MAY 1823.
6. CMB 1, Minutes of the Royal Society, London, 26 JUNE 1823, unpublished.
7. PRO. ADM 1/2909. Lts. G. ff. 56 and 82. Green, W Pringle to Admiralty. 29 May and 15 Aug 1823.
8. Henley, W., FRCS, 'Experiments concerning the different efficacy of pointed and blunt rods in security buildings against a stroke of lightning', pp.512-18, *Philosophical Transactions,* Abridged Vol. XIII, 1770-6, printed for and by C. & R. Baldin, New Bridge Street, Blackfriars, London 1774.
9. Harris, W.S., 'Protection of Ships from Lightning', *Nautical. Magazine & Naval Chronicle*, XXVI, p. 453, 1837.
10. Ibid.

11. PRO. ADM 1/2909, Lts. G. ff. 113. Green to Admiralty. 5 December 1822.
12. Rodger, N.A.M., 'Commissioned Officers' Careers in the Royal Navy, 1690-1815', *JMR*, June 2001.
13. O'Byrne, I.R., *A Naval Biographical Dictionary. Comprising the Life and Service of Every Living Officer in Her Majesty's Navy from the Rank of Admiral of the Fleet to that of Lieutenant Inclusive*, pp 426-7, pub. 1849, reprint 1990.
14. PRO. ADM 1/2909, Lts. G ff. 9. Pringle Green to Admiralty, 30 JAN 1823.
15. PRO. ADM 1/2909, Lts. G ff 34. ff. 37., ff.38. Lt W P Green to Admiralty 26 MAR 1823 and 17 APR 1823.
16. NMM. JOD/48. MSS 55/030 Green WP Lt., Instructions on training a ships' crew to the use of arms. Appendix. 1805.
17. PRO. ADM 12/2909, Lts. G 90. Lt W Pringle Green to Navy Board. 20 OCT 1822.
18. PRO. ADM 1/2909, Lts. G; ff.28. 31 DEC 1822 . ff.114. 1 NOV 1823.
19. CUL. Green W., Pringle, Lt. RN, 'Fragments from remarks of 25 years in every quarter of the globe etc.', Egertons Military Library, Whitehall, London 1833.
20. Green W., Pringle, Lt. RN, *Precautions to Avoid Accidents by Lightning*, pp. 19-24, 41, pub. T Tarner, London 1837.
21. PRO. ADM 1/2909. Lts. G. ff.37. Green to Barrow. 2 APR 1823.
22. NMM. Green, W., Pringle, Lt. RN, *Ships and Lightning*, large scroll, made probably 1832 onwards, sent to Prince Albert circa 1840-2.
23. PRO. ADM 1/2909, Lts. G113, op. cit.
24. Harris, W.S., Sir, *Shipwrecks by Lightning*. pp. 47,50. Return to an Order. House of Commons, 1 June 1854.
25. O'Byrne, op. cit.
26. PRO. ADM 1/2909. Lts. G. Green to Admiralty. 5, 31 December 1822, 30 , 31 January, 2, 17 April, 15 August 1823.
27. PRO. ADM 1/4730. Pro. H 181, Digest 59.2, Dry Rot, op. cit.
28. Anderson, R., *Lightning Conductors,* pp. 140, pub E&FN Spon London, 3rd edition 1885.
29. PRO. ADM 106/1539 H Pro 322 Harris to Navy Board, 28 May and 12 July 1823.
30. PRO. ADM 1/2909, Lts. G113, op. cit.
31. Harris, W.S., XXVII, Extract of a Letter, Harris to Sturgeon, pp. 208-23, *Annals of Electricity*, V(27), September 1840.
32. PRO. ADM 106/153 filed in Pro.D.183. Admiralty office (Barrow) to Navy Board. 5 AUG 1823.
33. Ed. Hamilton, Sir R.V., *Letters and Papers of Admiral Sir Thomas Byam Martin*, 3 vols.,Vol. 1, pp. 114-15, pub. Navy Records Society 1900.
34. Ed. Guff, B. *To the Pacific and Arctic with Meechey. The Journal of Lt. G. Peard of HMS Blossom 1825-1828*, pub. Cambridge University Press for the Hakluyt Society, 1973.
35. Anderson, op. cit., p. 359.
36. Ibid. p. 171.

37. Ellis, F.E., 'Robert Fitzroy: Aboard HMS THETIS and HMS GANGES 1824-1828', *MM*, 75(1), pp. 21-38, 1989.
38. Phillimore, Rear Admiral A., *The Life Of Sir William Parker*, Vol. I, pp. 445 and 464. pub.Harrison 59 Pall Mall, London 1876, 1879, 1880.
39. Harris, *Shipwrecks by Lightning*, op. cit.
40. Hamilton, J., *Faraday: The Life*, p. 204, pub. Harper Collins 2003.
41. Ed. Symons, G.J., *Lightning Rod Conference*, pp. 61, pub. E. & F.N. Spon, London 1882.
42. PRO. ADM 1/596, Superintendent Ad. Brooking to Lord High Admiral, 15 AUG 1827.
43. PRO. ADM.1/596, in letters to Sec. Admiralty. G Denyer to Croker 8 JAN 1827 and ADM.1/4537 PRO D 247.
44. BL. Martin Papers, Add. MSS 41397, ff.151, Martin to Lord High Admiral, HRH Duke of Clarence, 28 AUG 1827.
45. Barrow, Sir John, *An Autobiographical Memoir*, pp. 386-7, pub. J. Murray, London, 1847.
46. Cockburn, P.P., MSS 17,576, Washington, MRF/D/7 NMM, Cockburn to Hindmarsh, 24 September 1829.
47. Pack, A.J., 'The Board of the Admiralty', in *Notes*, pp. 174-7, *MM* 75, 1989.
48. Cockburn, op.cit., Cockburn to Morgan, 7 October 1829, 11 NOV 1829.
49. Anderson, op. cit., p. 123.
50. IEE. Ronalds Library, Harris, W.S., *Utility of Fixing Lightning conductors in Ships*, pub. J. Bond, Plymouth 1830.
51. Hore, P., 'Lord Melville and the Coming of Steam Navigation', *MM*, 86(2), pp. 157-72, May 2000.
52. SRO. MINTO Papers, MSS 12226, 1823.
53. PRO. ADM 7/538, Daily Returns to First Naval Lord of Ships and Stations, 2 AUG 1830.
54. Symons, op. cit.
55. PRO. ADM 1/4748, Pro. H. 31, Harris to Ad. Cockburn, 24 JAN 1830 and Order on obverse.
56. PRO. ADM.1/4748, Pro. H 271, 24 JAN 1830 and obverse.

Chapter 4

1. Williams, H.N., *The Life and Letters of Admiral Sir Charles Napier. KCB*, p. 390, pub. Hutchinson & Co, London 1917.
2. Torrens, T.Mc., *The Life of Sir James R.G. Graham*, Vol. I, pp. 324-33, 408-96, pub. Saunders, Otley &Co., London 1863.
3. Ibid.
4. Sainty, J.C., *Office Holders in Modern Britain IV: Admiralty Officials 1660-1870*, pp. 28, 49-62, Univ. of London, Athlone Press, 1975.
5. Torrens, op. cit.
6. Ibid.

7. Ed. Lady Briggs, Briggs, J.H., *Naval Administrations 1827-1892*, pp. 42-4, pub. Sampson Low, Marston & Co., London 1897.
8. Torrens, op. cit.
9. Ibid.
10. Ibid.
11. Savours, A., *The Search for the North West Passage*, pp. 126-7, pub Chatham Publishing, London 1999.
12. Barrow, J., *An Autobiographical Memoir of Sir John Barrow, Bart. late of the Admiralty*, pp. 424, pub. John Murray, London 1847.
13. Pool, B . 'Navy Contracts after 1832', *Mariner's Mirror,* Vol. 54, No, 3, pp. 209-14, 1968.
14. Murray, Sir O.A.R., 'The Admiralty, Pt. VII, Naval Admin from 1832 onwards', *MM*, 24(4). p. 458 et seq., 1938.
15. Ibid.
16. PRO. ADM 87/2, Out Letters, Storekeeper General then Surveyor from Yards, 26-31 AUG 1833.
17. Sainty, op. cit.
18. PRO. ADM 12/291, Digest. Adty. to Yds. ff., 321, 4, 5, 1833.
19. Ed. Hamilton, Sir R.V., *Letters and Papers of Admiral Sir Thomas Byam Martin*, Vol. III, p. 168, pub. Navy Records Society 1900.
20. Pool, op. cit.
21. Lambert, A.D., 'Preparing for the long peace: the reconstruction of the Royal Navy 1815-1830', pp. 41-54, *MM*, 82(1), 1996.
22. NMM. ELL 275, One of several undated drafts for a speech. Also drafts found in Halifax papers, Borthwick Inst., York.
23. Ed. Hamilton, op. cit., pp 384-90.
24. Ed. Lewis, M.A., Sir W.H. Dillon, KCH, *A Narrative Of My Personal Adventures (1730-1838)*, Vol.II, p. 487, pub. Navy Records Society 1956.
25. Torrens, T.Mc., op. cit., Vol. II, pp. 602-8.
26. PRO. ADM 53/35, Log HMS ACTEON, 27 Aug to 2 Sep 1834.
27. PRO. ADM 88/2, Ships' Registers, Adty. Materials Dept, Items 210, 717, 953, AUG.-DEC 1834.
28. Whewell Papers, Trinity Coll. Cantab. Add., MSS 205/147. Harris, 12 AUG 1834.
29. PRO. ADM 12/299, Adty. Out Letters to Yards, To Ply. Yd. 20 OCT 1834.
30. Green, Lt. W.P., 'Fragments from Remarks of 25 years in every Quarter of the Globe etc.', Egertons Military Library, Whitehall 1833.
31. BL. Auckland Papers. Add MSS 34460, ff140. BL. Auckland to Hardy 3 JUN 1834.
32. NMM. ELL 239 Minto MSS, 1835.
33. PRO. ADM 12/310, PRO C 301. Adty. to Yards, 12 MAY 1835.
34. Ibid.
35. Cockburn, MSS MRF/D/6 , MSS 17, 576.
36. BL. Martin Papers, Add. MSS 41404, pp. 151, 1835.
37. Gosset, W.P., *The Lost Ships of the Royal Navy 1793-1900*, pp. 105-6, pub. Mansell Publishing Ltd, London 1986.
38. SRO. Minto Papers MSS 12226 Gen. Correspondence on Scientific

subjects, Vol. VIII, No 11., pp. 249-51. Observations on the temperature of the atmosphere made by means of balloons by the Earl of Minto.
39. KCL. ISS archives, Daniell Papers, 1/50 Minto to Daniell. 20 July 1822.
40. NMM. ELL 268, Miscellaneous correspondence, 1840.
41. *An Autobiographical Memoir of Sir John Barrow, Bart. late of the Admiralty*, p. 434, pub. John Murray, London 1847.
42. PRO. ADM 7/889, Admiralty Circulars and Memos, July 1836.
43. SRO. MINTO papers, MSS 12226, 1823.
44. Hamilton, J., *Faraday: The Life*, p .283, pub Harper Collins 2003.
45. NMM.. ELL 276., Minto PP, various unfinished drafts for speech, 1840.
46. Ed. Lloyd, C.. Blane, Sir G. *The Health of Seamen*, Vol. CVII, pp. 198-9, Navy Records Society, 1965.
47. Ed. Lloyd, C. & Coulter, J.L.S., *Medicine and the Navy*, Vol. IV, 1815—1900, pp. 271, pub E&S Livingstone, Edinburgh and London 1963.
48. Lloyd and Blane, op. cit.
49. Ibid.
50. NLS. Minto PP. MSS 12050ff., 207,209, 211, 212, 1839.
51. Sainty, J.C., op.cit.
52. Ibid.
53. NMM. ELL 236, Naval Correspondence 1835-1842, Hamond to Minto JUN, 1836.
54. NMM. ELL 236 Naval Correspondence 1835-42. Grey to Minto JUN 1836 re. ACTEON 1831-1834.
55. Colomb, P.H., *Memoirs of Admiral Rt. Hon. Sir Astley Cooper Key*, pp. 27, pub. Methuen, London 1898.
56. Parl. Papers, Return for the House of Commons,13 MAY 1847, returned by Admiralty 2 JUL 1847.
57. NLS. Minto Papers. MSS 12067, ff.207, Adam to Minto, 20 DEC 1844.
58. PRO. ADM 12/445, Digest 59.9 P47, Darley to Adty. 8 JAN 1845.
59. Parl, op. cit.
60. MOD. ADM Library, Letters, W.S. Harris to Sir C. Lemon. Bart, 11 MAR 1837.

Chapter 5

1. Lloyd, C. *Mr Barrow of the Admiralty*, p. 77, pub. Collins, London 1970.
2. Barrow, Sir John, *An Autobiographical Memoir*, p. 411, pub. J. Murray, London 1847.
3. Ed. Lady Briggs, Briggs, J.H., *Naval Administrations*, p. 85, pub. Sampson Low, Marston & Co., London 1897.
4. Pool, B., 'Navy Contracts in the Last Years of the Navy Board', *MM*, 50(3), pp. 166, 174-5, 1964
5. BL. Halifax Papers, Add. MSS, 4,9572, 1839.
6. Lloyd, op. cit., p. 195.
7. Barrow, op. cit., p. 446.

8. Bonner Smith, D., 'Some Remarks about the Mutiny of the Bounty', *MM*, 22(2), pp. 200-37, 1936.
9. Lloyd, op. cit., p. 98.
10. Barrow, op. cit., p. 416.
11. Ibid., p. 405.
12. Byam Martin, Sir T., Ed. Sir R.V. Hamilton, *Letters of Sir T. Byam Martin*, Vol. I, p. 115, Navy Records Society 1903 .
13. Murray, Sir O., *The Admiralty*, reprinted from *Mariners Mirror*, Vol. XXII, No 1, Jan 1937.
14. NLS Minto Papers MSS 12058ff, 106, Barrow to Minto, 3 SEP 1838.
15. Lambert, A.D., 'The Reconstruction of the Royal Navy 1815-1830', *MM*, 82(1), p. 54, 1996.
16. BL. Macvey Napier PP Add Mss 34624 f.94, dated 26 SEP 1843.
17. BL. Martin Papers. Add.MSS 41378. General section for 1839.
18. Ibid.
19. Barrow, op. cit., p. 334.
20. Rodger, N.A.M., *The Admiralty*, ch. 'Unity and Simplicity', pp. 93-106. The Offices of State Series, Ed. M.N. Reese, pub. T. Dalton Ltd, Lavenham Suffolk, 1979.
21. Lloyd, op. cit., pp. 30-47.
22. Harris, W.S., *Shipwrecks by Lightning*, pp. 1-88. An Order for the House of Commons, pub. 1854.
23. Lloyd, op. cit., p. 25.
24. Fleming, F., *Barrow's Boys*, p. 306, Granta Publications, London 1998.
25. Ed. Hamilton, Sir R.V., *Letters and Papers of Admiral Sir Thomas Byam Martin*, 3 Vols., Vol. III, p. 132, Stopford to Martin July 1835, pub. Navy Records Society, 1900.
26. Fleming, op. cit., pp. 6, 12.
27. Ibid.
28. BL, Martin Papers, Add. MSS 41378, General 1839.
29. Parl. Debates, Vol. 45, 3rd Series, House of Lords, Safety to the Service 1839.
30. Fox. G., *British Admirals and Chinese Pirates, 1832-69*, pp.19-24. pub. Paul, Trench & Co., London 1940.
31. Ibid.
32. Ibid.
33. NLS Minto papers, MSS 12050. ff. 207, 209, 211, 212, General 1839.
34. Phillimore, A., *The Life of Sir W Parker*, Vol.II, p. 411, pub. Harrison, London 1879.
35. Ibid.
36. PRO. ADM 83/4, Adty. to Surveyor, 1832.
37. Parliamentary Debates, 3rd Series, Vol. 17, p. 130, 1833.
38. Barrow, op. cit., pp. 418-9.
39. Ibid., pp. 417, 421.
40. Briggs, op. cit., p. 157.
41. Cockburn, P.P., MSS 17, 576, Washington, MRF/D/8 NMM No.4 for 1832, Cockburn to Admiralty 25th December 1832.

42. Beeler, op. cit. p. 221.
43. Rodger, N.A.M., 'The Dark Ages of the Admiralty, 1869-85', *Mariners Mirror*, 61, p. 131, 1975.
44. PRO. ADM1/6873, Minute, Hamilton, 5 DEC 1887.
45. BL. Barrow MSS. 43244. ff.254. Barrow to Aberdeen, 4 June 1845.
46. SRO. Haddington Muniments, GD 249/1, Box 17. Memorial, Lt. Hill to Haddington, 28 FEB 1842.
47. BL. Halifax PP, Add. MSS 49572, 1839.
48. Ibid.
49. Griffiths D., Lambert, A., Walker, F., *Brunel's Ships*, p. 156, reference 76, pub. Chatham Publishing 1999.
50. Ibid.
51. Rodger, N.A.M., *The Command of the Ocean,* pp. 103, 377, pub. Allen Lane, London 2004.
52. Barrow, op. cit., pp. 274, 333.
53. CUL. Graham Papers. Microfilm 52. Unsigned memo. Barrow to Graham and Graham's response, 12 MAY 1832.
54. Hamilton, op. cit., Vol. I, p. 115.
55. *Shipwreck by Lightning*. Return to House of Commons. Report and Evidence from the Commission appointed to inquire into the Plan of William Snow Harris relating to the Protection of Ships from the Effects of Lightning. p. 74. Printed 11 February 1840.

Chapter 6

1. Longmate, N., *The Breadstealers*, pp. 8-58, pub. Temple Smith, London 1984.
2. Hilton, B., *Corn, Cash , Commerce*, p. 233, pub. Oxford 1977.
3. Lambert, A.D., 'The Reconstruction of the Royal Navy 1815-1830', *MM*, 82(1), p . 42, 1996.
4. Hobsbawm, E., *Industry and Empire*, pp. 40-2, 84, diagrams 4, 15, pub. Penguin Books, revised edition, C. Wrigley 1999.
5. Greenhill, B., Giffard, A., *Steam, Politics and Patronage*, pp. 88-9, pub. Conway Maritime Press, London 1994.
6. Woodward, Ll, *The Age of Reform 1815-1870*, p. 493, pub. Book Club Assoc., 2nd edn, 1979.
7. Personal communication, Edinburgh University Library, Special Collections, 12, 27 July 1988.
8. PRO.HO.50/294, Cheshire Militia, 5 SEP 1812.
9. CUL. Green W. Pringle, Lt. RN, 'Fragments from remarks of 25 years in every quarter of the globe etc.', Egertons Military Library, Whitehall, London 1833.
10. BL. Martin Papers Add. MSS 41397 ff151, Martin to Lord High Admiral, HRH Duke of Clarence, 28 AUG 1827.

11. Harris, W.S., 'On the relative powers of various metallic substances as conductors of electricity', *Philosophical Transactions*, pp. 18-24, 1827.
12. St Andrews University Library, NRA 13132, Forbes Correspondence, Harris to Forbes and replies, 1831-42.
13. IEE. Faraday Collection, NRA 20573, Harris to Faraday, 1839-60.
14. Trinity College, Cambridge, Whewell MSS, Add. MSS. 205, 147-54 and MSS 89.12, 1832-55.
15. PRO. ADM1/4730 Pro H 181. Harris to Navy Board, 1 JAN 1821 (mis-filed to May 1821).
16. Harris, W.S., *Shipwrecks by Lightning*, pp. 1-88, an Order for the House of Commons, pub. 1854.
17. IEE. Ronalds Collection, Harris to Faraday, 22 December 1855.
18. Courtney, N., *Gale Force 10*, pp. 241, pub. Headline Publishing, London, 2003, and ADM 7/889 Adty. Circulars and Memos, C. Wood, 28 DEC 1838.
19. IEE. Ronalds Collection. Harris to Faraday 22 DEC 1855.
20. NLS. Minto Papers, MSS 12226, General Correspondence on Scientific Subjects.
21. NLS. Minto, PP. MSS, 12058 ff.188R+V, 1837-42.
22. NMM. ELL 276, undated draft speech, probably 1839-40.
23. McTeer, W., 'Admiral Sir Charles Adam', *MM* 63(3), pp. 271-2, 1977.
24. Ed. Lady Briggs, Briggs, J.H., *Naval Administrations 1827-1892*, p. 57, pub. Sampson Low, Marston & Co, London 1897.
25. Ed. Hamilton, Sir R.V., 'Letters and Papers of Admiral Sir Thomas Byam Martin', 3 vols, Vol. I, p. 115, pub. Navy Records Society 1903.
26. PRO. ADM 1/4764, PRO H 578, Harris to Wood, 6 December and draft reply by Barrow, 12 December 1838.
27. PRO. ADM 1/3433, Plymouth Yard (Ad. Warren), to Adty. 8 JUN 1839. Initialled by Barrow.
28. Trans. Ply Inst., Vol. XVII, 1922-36, pub. Devon Press 1937.
29. Morriss, R., *Cockburn and the British Navy in Transition*, pp. 224-5, pub. Univ. of Exeter Press 1997.
30. *Western Morning News*, BB Harris, 9 FEB 1984.
31. Harris, W.S., *A Treatise On Frictional Electricity*, Ed. and with a Memoir of the author, C. Tomlinson, pub. Virtue & Co, London 1867.
32. Forbes MSS, St Andrews Univ. Library, NRA 13132, ff.446, Forbes to Harris 12 OCT and Reply, 22 DEC 1831.31, trans. Ply Inst., Vol. XVII, 1922-36, pub Devon Press 1937.
33. Harris, W.S., op. cit.
34. Ibid.

Chapter 7

1. Ed. Sharp, J.A., *Memoirs of the Life and Services of R. Ad. Sir Wm. Symonds*, pp. 90-2, pub. Longman, Brown, Green, Longmans & Roberts 1858.

2. Sharp, op. cit. in Report of Ct. on Naval Estimates.
3. Ibid.
4. Seymour, Ad. Sir Edward, My Naval Career and Travels, p. 72, pub. Smith, Elder & Co., London 1911.
5. NMM MRF/87/5. Admiralty, in Letters from Surveyor, from Symonds, No. 240, 15 May 1838. Lists and reply.
6. BL. Halifax papers. Add. MSS 4,9572, 1839.
7. Borthwick Inst. York, Halifax Papers, A4/53, General Corresp., Minto to Wood, 24 OCT 1839.
8. Morriss R., *Cockburn and the British Navy In Transition,* p. 210, pub. Univ. of Exeter Press 1997.
9. Cockburn MSS, MRF/D/8, No. 544, Cockburn to Graham, Private, 1 MAR 1833.
10. Sharp, op. cit., p. 141, footnote.
11. Lambert, A., 'Captain Sir William Symonds and the Ship of the Line 1832-1847', *Mariner's Mirror,* Vol. 73(2), pp. 167-78, 1987.
12. Sharp, op. cit., pp. 290-1.
13. Morriss, op. cit., p. 249.
14. Sharp, op. cit., Evidence to Ct. on Naval Estimates, 1847-8, by Mr Edye.
15. ADM 3/265, 1841-57, Adty. Special Minutes.
16. Morriss, op. cit., p. 241.
17. Sharp, op. cit., pp. 326-7. Minto to Symonds, 19 December 1844.
18. Anon, *Facts versus Fiction etc.,* 'Introduction', pp. i-lx, pub Parker, Furnivall & Parker, Military Library, Whitehall 1845.
19. Borthwick Inst., York, Halifax Papers, A4/53, Minto to Wood, 17 FEB 1845.
20. NMM. ELL 237, Symonds to Minto, Private, 24 APR 1845.
21. Sharp, op. cit., pp. 341-2, Minto to Symonds 17 SEP 1845.
22. Ibid., p. 342, editor's footnote to letter from Minto to Symonds, 17 SEP 1845.
23. Morriss, op. cit., p. 239.
24. NLS, Minto Papers, MSS 12067, ff. 231, Ad. Bowles to Minto, 31 DEC 1844.
25. Sharp, op. cit. p. 366.
26. Morriss, op. cit.
27. Griffiths, D., Lambert, A., Walker, F., *Brunel's Ships,* p. 52, pub. Chatham Publishing 1999.
28. Minto Papers, MSS 12068 ff. 123, Symonds to Minto, 17 OCT, 1846.
29. Ibid., ff. 119, 10 DEC 1846.
30. Anon, op. cit.
31. PRO. ADM, 3/264 Special Minutes, Edye to Adty, 21 NOV 1837.
32. NMM. MLN, 155/4, Copy of a paper by J. Edye on the 'Subject of Dockyards and the construction of Ships' sent to the Earl of Auckland Oct. 1847.

Chapter 8

1. Padfield, P., *Rule Britannia*, p. 84, pub. Pimlico 2002.
2. Ibid.
3. Sondhaus, L., Naval Warfare 1815-1914, pp. 32-4, pub. Routledge, London & New York 2001.
4. Ibid.
5. PRO. ADM 12/385, Pro. H 56 1, FEB 1841, Harris to Adty.
6. NMM. ELL 276, draft Memo, Lord Minto 1840-1.
7. Sainty, J.C., *Admiralty Officials. 1660-1870*, p. 65, Athlone Press, Univ. of London 1975.
8. Parliamentary Debates, Vol. LVI, 18 February 1841, pp. 708-22.
9. Ibid.
10. Phillimore, A.V. Ad., *The Life of Admiral of the Fleet Sir William Parker*, Vol. II, p. 419, pub. Harrison, London 1879.
11. Ed. Lady Briggs, Briggs, J.H., *Naval Administrations*, p. 62, Sampson, Low & Co. 1897.
12. Parl. Debates, Vol. LVI, House of Lords, p. 1019, 24 FEB 1841.
13. Ibid.
14. NMM. ELL 276, Minute and Diagrams, 25 FEB 1841.
15. Ibid.
16. PRO. ADM 53/722, Ships Logs, Masters, HMS BELLEISLE, 1841.
17. PRO. ADM 12/385, Surveyor to Supdt., B 312 1 MAY 1841.
18. PRO. ADM 88/4, Surveyor General, 7216, 12 MAY 1841.
19. Morriss, R. 'Cockburn and the British Navy in Transition' pp. 250. pub. Univ. of Exeter Press, Exeter. 1997.
20. PRO. ADM 12/385 59.9 for 1841, 3 FEB 1841. Minutes 18-22 FEB, 1841, PRO S 123, Smith to Adty, 11 MAR 1841.
21. PRO. ADM 12/385, CO. IMPREGNABLE to Surveyor, 2nd JULY 1841.
22. PRO. ADM 88/5, Surveyor Out Letters, 391.
23. PRO. ADM 12/385, Minute 27, AUG 1841.

Chapter 9

1. Memo. to Adm. by Earl of Minto, 6 Sep, 1841, First Lord, on retiring from Adm. BNDOC, 1204-1960, pp. 654.
2. SRO. Haddington Muniments, GD 249/1, Box 6, Harris to Haddington, 28 OCT, 1841 and supporting papers.
3. Ibid.
4. Ed. Lady Briggs, Briggs, J.H., *Naval Administrations, 1827-1892*, p. 69, pub. Sampson Low, Marston & Co., London 1897.
5. PRO ADM 12/385 Pro. H 91, Harris to Adty, 1 SEP 1841; Pro. H 709 1 DEC 1841; ibid. Adty. to Surveyor, 8 DEC 1841; ibid. Pro. H 771, 27 DEC 1841.
6. Morriss, R., *Cockburn and the British Navy In Transition*, pp. 228-35, pub. Univ. of Exeter Press 1997.

7. PRO. ADM 12/398, PRO H, indexed 59.6, 2 JAN 1842.
8. Parl. Debates, Vol. LXI., H. of Commons, MAR 1842.
9. SRO. Haddington Muniments, GD 249/1 Box 17, Memorial, Lt. Hill to Haddington, 28 FEB 1842.
10. PRO. ADM 12/385 Sec. of State Home Dept. enquiry 22 JUL and reply by Surveyor with lists 27 JUL 1841.
11. PRO. ADM 88/5 3495 9 JUN.; and ADM 12/398, Portsmouth Yard to Admiralty, 16 JUL. and reply, Digest, 59.6; and ADM 88/5, Surveyor General 4512, 6 OCT, 1842.
12. ADM 12/398, Pro. D 191, Poad Drake to Adty, 1 JUN, 1842 and Pro. R 269, Reece to Adty, 8 AUG 1842.
13. SRO. Haddington Muniments, GD 249/1 Box 17, Hoblyn to Haddington, 30 MAR 1842.
14. Harris, W.S., 'On the effects of lightning on the British ship *Underwood*', *Nautical Mag.. & Nav. Chron.* (reprint), JUNE 1842.
15. PRO. ADM 12/398, Digest 59.6, C in C Portsmouth to Adty. A 1553. 16 OCT 1842
16. PRO. ADM 12/398, Pro. H 566, Harris to Adty, 26 AUG & 6 OCT 1842.
17. Ibid. Pro. H 656, 666, 683, Harris to Adty, 6, 31 OCT & 7 NOV, 1842.
18. CUL. Green W. Pringle, Lt. RN, 'Fragments from remarks of 25 years in every quarter of the globe etc.', Egertons Military Library, Whitehall, London 1833.
19. Smyth, Ad., W.H., *The Sailor's Word Book*, pp. 710, pub. Blackie & Son, London 1867.
20. IEE. Ronalds Collection, Harris to Faraday, 26 OCT 1842.
21. PRO H 656, 666, 683, op. cit.
22. IEE. Ronalds Collection, op. cit.
23. Harris, W.S., *Shipwrecks by Lightning*, p. 22, An Order for the House of Commons, pub. 1854.
24. Harris, W.S., *On the Nature of Thunderstorms*, p. 175, pub. Parker, London, 1st May 1843.
25. PRO. ADM 12/413, Digest 59.9 for 1843, Pro H 359, 17 OCT and 5 NOV 1843.
26. PRO. ADM 12/429, Digest 59.9 for 1844, Capts S. Sharpe to Adty, 10 FEB 1844.
27. NMM. Minto Papers, MSS 12067, ff. 207, Adam to Minto, 20 DEC 1844.
28. NMM. ELL 237, Symonds to Minto, Private, 24 APR 1845.
29. PRO. ADM 12/413 Digest, 59.9 for 1843, Pro. H 99 Harris to Adty, 22 FEB 1843, ibid., Pro. H 318 30 MAY 1843, ibid. Pro. H 191, 315 5 APR & 27 MAY 1843, ibid. MAR to NOV 1843.
30. Ibid.
31. NMM. ELL 276, Minute and Diagrams, 25 February 1841.
32. SRO. Minto Papers, MSS 12226ff. 158, Gen. Corresp. Scientific Subjects, Harris to Minto 9 MAR 1843.
33. Borthwick Inst. York, Halifax Papers, A4/53 Minto to Wood, 30 NOV 1844.
34. Harris, W.S. *Remarkable Instances of the Protection of Certain Ships of*

HM Navy from the Destructive Effects of Lightning, pub R. White Stevens, Plymouth 1844.
35. Hepper, D.J., *British Warship Losses in the Age of Sail, 1650-1859*, pp. 157-70, 213, pub. J Boudriot Publications, Rotherfield, East Sussex, 1994.
36. Ibid.
37. Watts, A.J., *Pictorial History of the Royal Navy*, Vol. 1., 1816-1880, pub. Ian Allen, London.
38. Harris, W.S., *The Meteorology of Thunderstorms*, pub. R. Hunt, London 1844.
39. PRO. ADM 12/385, Capts. B. Blackwood to Admiralty, 19 October 1841.
40. PRO. ADM 12/445, Capts.W. 252, Warden to Adty, 9 MAY 1845.

Chapter 10

1. Gilly, W.S., *Narratives of Shipwrecks of the Royal Navy 1793-1849*, pp. 299, 312-31, pub. J.W. Parker, London 1850.
2. Ed. Beeler, J., *Milne Papers*, Vol. 1, pp. 165, 169, pub. Navy Records Society, Vol. 147, 2004.
3. Lloyd, C., Coulter, J.L.S., *Medicine and the Navy, 1200-1900*, Vol. IV, 1815-1900, pp. 266-7.
4. PRO. ADM 12/477, Pro. H 603, 22 MAR 1847.
5. Harris, W.S., *Shipwrecks by Lightning*, pp. 1-82, An Order for the House of Commons, pub. 1854.
6. Ibid.
7. Lees-Milne, J. *The Bachelor Duke: A Life of William Spencer Cavendish, 6th Duke of Devonshire, 1790-1858*, pub. John Murray 1991.
8. Mends, B.S., *Life of Admiral Sir WR Mends*, pp. 29-32, pub. Murray, London 1899.
9. ADM 12/477. Pro H 254, 22 MAR 1847, General 78.,4 JUN 1847, ibid., 256, ibid., 48.1.
10. Whewell Papers, Trinity Coll., Cantab., Add. MSS. 205/157 Harris to Whewell, 9 AUG 1847.
11. PRO. ADM 12/477, PRO H 497, ibid., PRO S 1034, ibid. Precepts, 13 MAY 1847; ibid. PRO M 452 East India, ibid. PRO H 603 22, MAR 1847, ibid. PRO H 613, 1 AUG 1847, ibid. PRO H 76.
12. Ibid.
13. Harris, W.S., *Remarkable Instances of the Protection of Certain Ships of HM Navy from Lightning*, 2nd edition, pub. R. Clay, London 1847.
14. Smith, A., Wire Rope [for Lightning Conductors], printed 15 SEP 1847.
15. Ibid.
16. NMM. ELL 276, Smith A., *Patent Wire Rope for Rigging, Lightning Conductors etc.*, pub. Poplar, London 1847.
17. Harris, W.S., *Instructions for Application of Conductors of Lightning in HM Ships*, pub. W. Clowes, London 1848.

18. Return, House of Lords 4 MAY 1848, moved by Earl of Wilton.
19. Parliamentary Debates, House of Lords, Vol. CV, 1849. pp. 257.
20. PRO. ADM12/509. 34, PRO H 346 Harris to Adty, 10 May 1849.
21. Return, House of Lords in compliance with a Precept of 11 JUN 1849. Vessels fitted with Sir W. Snow Harris' Lightning Conductors and Damage or Remarks.
22. ADM 12/509, Capts. M 27 Maxwell to Adty, 13 FEB 1849.
23. IEE. Ronalds Collection. Harris to Earl of Wilton July 1849, pub. R Stevens, Plymouth 1849.
24. BL. Babbage Correspondence, Vol. XII, Add. MSS 37194 ff. 327 Harris to Babbage, 21 NOV 1849.
25. Parliamentary Papers, Precept, House of Lords 15 Mar 1850.
26. Ibid.
27. IEE. Ronalds Collection. Harris, W.S., *On the Relative Cost and Efficiency of Permanent and Temporary Lightning Conductors*, pub R. Stevens, London 1850.
28. Ibid.
29. Harris, Sir W.S., *Remarkable Instances of the Preservation of Certain Ships of the Royal Navy from Lightning*, abridged version as pamphlet, pub. Stevens, Plymouth 1850.
30. PRO. ADM 12/541, PRO 70, 92, Harris to Adty, FEB 1851.

Chapter 11

1. PRO. ADM 12/557, Pro H. 710, Harris to First Lord, DEC 1852.
2. LRO. Derby MSS, Box 163, NRA, Harris to Second Earl of Wilton, 28 April & 17 May 1852.
3. Ibid., Harris to Earl of Derby, 22 May 1852.
4. Ibid., Harris to Wilbraham, 31 May 1852.
5. Ibid., Wilton to Wilbraham 29 May 1852.
6. Ibid., Wilbraham to Derby and reply, undated but circa 31 May 1852.
7. LRO. Derby MSS, Box 163, NRA, copy of Hay to Harris, 21 July 1852 and copy of letter from Lt. RN.
8. BL. Babbage correspondence, Add. MSS 371295, ff. 7 & 9, Harris to Babbage 19 Jan 1852.
9. BL. Babbage Correspondence, Add. MSS 371295 ff. 3, 4 & 5, Babbage to Osborne (copy) and Harris to Babbage.
10. Ibid.
11. Ibid., ff. 189, Harris to Babbage, 29 Dec 1852.
12. Ibid., ff. 214, 276, Harris to Babbage, 16 Jan 1853.
13. Ibid., ff. 216. Harris to Babbage, 20 Jan 1853.
14. Ibid., ff. included with 228, Babbage to Harris, Private, 21 Jan 1853.
15. Ibid., ff .228, Harris to Babbage, 23 Jan 1853.
16. Ibid., ff. 315, Harris to Babbage, 2 Jul 1853.
17. PRO. ADM 12/573, Pro. H 124, Harris to Adty, 12 Feb 1853.

18. Harris, W.S., 'Papers Relative to Shipwrecks by Lightning', presented to the Admiralty 1853.
19. IEE. Ronalds Collection, Harris to Faraday, 22 Dec 1855.
20. PRO. ADM 12/605 for 1855, Southampton, Lt. to Adty, 22 Aug 1855.
21. Fitzgerald, P., Admiral, in, *Memories of the Sea*, pp. 57, 79, pub Edward Arnold, London 1913.
22. *Illustrated London News*, 18 Nov 1854, pp. 520-1, Thompson, W., 'Questions about Atmospheric Electricity', Library of Science, pp. 334-47, 1860.

Chapter 12

1. Stewart, W.H., Controller, *Admiralty Rules*, p. 507, pub. 1880.
2. Liddell, J., *Evidence to Lightning Rod Conference*, pp. 202, 205, pub. E & F.N. Spon, London 1882.
3. Ibid.
4. McHardy CML, op.cit. p. 200.
5. Ibid.
6. IEE. Priest, Sir William, 1889.
7. Hedges, K., *Modern Lightning Conductors*, p. 93, pub. Crosby, Lockwood & Son, 2nd edition 1910.
8. Admiralty, DEE Department, *Instructions for the Protection of HM Ships and Naval Establishments from Damage by Lightning*, pp. 12, 20, 71, S. 3484/24, 1924.
9. Harker, J.S., *Well Done, Leander,* pub. Collins Bros. & Co., New Zealand 1971.
10. 'Jurong add their standard fore body to a blasted tanker's stern', *Shipbuilding & Marine Engineering International*, July/August 1978. p. 324.
11. *Southern Evening Echo*, Wednesday, 20 May 1981.
12. Sanders, D.G.M., Westerly Marine, personal communication to author, 29 May 1981.
13. Bernstein, T., personal communication to author, 1981.
14. *Yachting Monthly*, Cross, J.A., 'Lightning Strikes to GRP Yachts', pp. 1093-4, July 1977.
15. Lohman, D., 'How to Prevent a Lightning Strike', *Yachting Monthly*, p. 1096, July 1973.
16. 'Lightning and its Effects', Y-Ard Memo, YM 3056/78, *Guide to Lightning Protection in Surface Ships*, Final draft, 28 Dec 1979.
17. Ibid.
18. Andrews, C., Cooper, M.A., Darveniza, M., Mackerras, D., *Lightning Injuries: Electrical, Medical and Legal Aspects*, pp. 155, 178-85, pub. CRC Press, Boca Raton 1992.
19. Report of the Committe on Atmospheric and Space Electricity of the American Geophysical Union, *The Scientific Basis for Ttraditional Lightning Protection Systems*, June 2001.

20. Andrews *et al.*, op. cit.
21. Ibid.
22. Ibid.
23. Ibid.
24. Barrow, J., *Memoir of Sir John Barrow Bart* (printed 1852). 3 Jan 1851.
25. Ibid.

Index

Adam, Admiral Sir Charles xii, 59, 67, 68, 141-2, 159
   intervenes in debate 129
   wrote re *Scylla* 142
Admiralty 61
   Admirals Unemployed (AU) 86
   Boards 1830 40-64
   Digest and synoptical table 61
      steam 64
   Official Rules 167
   1924 regulations 168
Airey, Astronomer Royal 99
airship *Hindenburg* exploded 169
Andrews *et al.* 5
   lightning flash 5
      amperage 5
      people 5
      volts 5
Auckland, Lord 98

Babbage, Charles 95
   correspondence with Harris 95, 164
   Harris confides 158
   suggests memorial 162
Banks, Sir Joseph 76
Barrow, John xiii, 48, 55, 64, 66, 69-88
   administration 72
   amount of correspondence 81
   Arctic expeditions 77-78
   autobiography 49
   bigoted views 27
   centralisation of Admiralty courts 79
   crotchets of inventors 49
   dangerous projectors 86
   decade of Orders missing 81
   dry rot doctors 49
   epitaph 176
   exposed by Harris 136
   failure to archive 55, 71

   honorary degree 75
   lost files of trial 2
   missing files 66
   monument struck by lightning 176
   nepotism 84
   obstinate man 45
   passenger on ship struck by lightning 76
   power base confronted 86
   projectors 49
   publications 72, 79
   Records Office 71
   refuses results of trial 99
   rejects Harris' plan 45
   retires 146
   Royal Society and Royal Geographical Society 87
   salary 72
   saw all communications 69, 73
   schooling 77
   second secretary 69
   shows his power 80
   sparks from his kite 76
   travels 76
Barrow, John Junior 72
   head of record office, 1844 149
Bathoe, J. 14
   wind vanes on masts 14
   wire on hats 14
Bedford, Mr H., head of record office 146
Berkeley, Capt. Hon. M. 81
Blake 103
Blane, Sir Gilbert 148
Bowles, Admiral 115
Brooking, Admiral 48
Brunel, I.K. 110

Cater, Capt. 37
Clarence, Duke of 29, 48

INDEX

as 1st Lt. then Capt. HMS *Pegasus* 29
  became William III 29
  supporter of Harris 29
Clifton, Waller, private secretary to MPs 85, 86
Cockburn, Admiral Sir C. xii, 49
  fag of admiralty! 50
  First Sea Lord 49
  FRS 50
  Harris' supporter 50
  MP for Ripon 101
  ordered sea trials of lightning conductor 52
  organises Committees to destabilise Symonds 109
  reinstates School of Architecture 112
  tightens snare 114
  undermines authority of Surveyor 111
Codrington, Admiral 110
Collinson 11
  Kew Gardens 11
  Mill Hill School 11
  Ridgeway House 11
Combe, Capt. 37
Committee on Shipwreck by Lightning 87, 95
Condy N.M., artist xi
  Lt. in 43rd Foot 91
  meets Harris 91
  nephew of N. Condy 91
  sponsored to paint 143
Congo steam vessel 51
copper ore 35
Corn Laws 89
Croker, J. 69
  advises Barrow 81
  shared house with Barrow 87

Daniell, Prof. 63
Denyer, Mr 48
Dinwiddie, Dr 76

Earl of Derby 98, 161
Earl of Durham 98
Earl of St Germans 98
Eden, George, Earl of Auckland 60, 62, 98, 149, 150
Edgcumbe, Lord Mount 131
Edye, John 104
  assistant surveyor 118
  designed Agamemnon class 104
  FRS 120

lost sight of one eye 120
mentor was J. Tucker 120
objected to iron for ships 120
orders all ships to be fitted with wire rope 134
pilfered Harris' plans 119
suggested store increases 119
wire rope conductors 121
Ellenborough, Lord 98, 147
Elliot, Hon. George 56, 66, 83
  reply from Yards 57
  secretary to First Lord 56
Etoile, galley, 700 tons 28
  lightning conductor on 28
Ewart, engineer 83

Faraday, M. 47, 64
  advised American 47
  correspondence with Harris 93
  letter from Harris 140
  pension 64
  Royal Institution 47
Fincham 103
Fitzroy, Capt. Robert 99
Forbes, J.D., St Andrews University 93, 95
Franklin, Benjamin 1, 11, 12, 13, 20
  ally of the French 15
  American ambassador 15
  Copley medal in 1753 13
  ditty published 14
  French ships 14
  gilded lightning rod 10
  iron bars 1
  iron chains 1
  Le Roy 15
  letter from Winn, J.L. 12
  lightning rod 1, 20
  mistress 15
  security issues 13
  spied upon 15
  spindles on masts 11
  St Elmo's fire 10
  St Paul's Cathedral 13

George III 13, 14
Gilbert, 2nd Earl of Minto xii
  abrogates responsibility 130
  becomes First Lord 59
  dissembles in Lords 155
  doubts knowledge of lightning conductors 115

198

INDEX

draft for speeches 65
encouraged steam 51
lost papers 66, 71
Moore O'Ferrall's downfall 126
nepotism 59
obfuscation 65
prepares to answer critics 124
protector of Symonds 105, 117
revelations 126
scientist 63
scornful of Cockburn 144
Gilly, Canon 22
  collection of lightning incidents to ships 31
Golde, R.H. 2
  books on lightning 2, 4
Graham, Sir James 53, 162
  abolished Commissioners 54
  abolished Navy Board Victualling Board 54
  again First Lord 1852 60
  broken promises 60
  Crimean War 60
  discovered virement of budget 54
  duties for each Lord of Admiralty 55
  errors revisited 162
  First Lord Admiralty in 1830 53
  from Harris 98
  job losses 60
  orders own salary drop 58
  retrenchment and economania 53
  savings 54
  Whig MP for Carlisle 53
Great Exhibition 160
Great Western 150
Green, Pringle. Lt RN i, 61-62, 82, 140
  accuses Harris 37
  Admiralty Committee of 1839 44
  applications to Admiralty 40
  George St, Plymouth 39
  half pay 38
  heckles Harris at Plymouth Institution 42
  Henley, W. 37
  HMS *Victory* 39
  hostile critic 26, 37
  inventions, manuals 39-40
  large family 39
  lieutenant 1806 39
  master's mate 39
  opposed Harris 26, 37
  proposals invalid 44

  publications 40
  Trafalgar veteran xii
  Transport Service 39
Grey, Capt. William 67
  reports damage from lightning 141

Haddington, Lord 98, 110, 135
Harris W.S. xi
  Adam, Admiral 97
  attrition 124
  Bakerian lecture 95
  balls or points 46
  Beaufort scale 96
  born 1791 90
  Cockburn 97
  collected statistics 26, 27
  Committee of Royal Society 37
  Committee on Shipwreck endorses 95
  Copley medal 95
  copper conductor 2, 32, 35
  copper keel bolt 43
  copper milling 138
  copper pipe 35
  copper plates 35, 43
  correspondence 95
  Council medal 101
  criticism of fixed conductors 131
  demonstration 1822 33
  died 102
  dismisses wire rope conductors 152
  East India Co. 152
  failed to obtain trial result 62
  George St., Plymouth 35, 91
  good liaison 149
  grant 101
  heckled by Green 42
  his true feelings 158
  illustrations 100
  inventor 2, 26
  knighted 101,154
  lightning conductor 32, 33, 92
  marries 91
  meets Condy 91
  new book on thunderstorms, 1843 141
  order for first lightning conductor trial 52
  original letter 43
  pension 101
  plan rejected 45
  Plymouth Grammar 90
  Precept, House of Lords,1847 152

199

INDEX

publications 51
reports on *Scylla* 141
report for House of Commons, 1854 27
researches ii, 32
scientific referee 102
university 90
Henderson, Capt. 29
Henley, William in 1774 35
HMS *Acteon* 61, 67,151
HMS *Aigle* 134
HMS *Ajax* 31
HMS *Alarm* 11
HMS *Alligator* 52
HMS *Amphion* 31
HMS *Asia* 51
HMS *Avenger*147
HMS *Belleisle* 132
HMS *Bellona* 11
HMS *Bittern* 153
HMS *Blanche* 63
HMS *Caledonia* 33, 34, 148
HMS *Cleopatra* 41
HMS *Conqueror* 39
HMS *Coronation* 10
HMS *Decade* 42
HMS *Despatch* 41
HMS *Dido* 153
HMS *Dublin* 61
   Symonds orders; potential disaster 133
HMS *Electra* 68, 114
HMS *Elephant* 29
HMS *Endymion* 141
HMS *Eurydice* 105
HMS *Experiment* 10
HMS *Fisgard* 152
HMS *Fly* struck by lightning, masts broken 146
HMS *Forte* 63
HMS *Glatton* 76
HMS *Glory* 146
HMS *Gloucester* 51
HMS *Guerriere* damaged by lightning before fight with USS *Constitution* 146
HMS *Hazard*, wire rope conductors, damaged twice 153
HMS *Heron* unavailable after damage from lightning 46
HMS *Hindostan* 31
HMS *Impregnable* 132
HMS *Java* 35, 42
HMS *Kent* 38, 41

HMS *Leander* 170
HMS *Magpie* 31
HMS *Melville* 51
HMS *Minden* 35
   fitted under Harris' supervision 138
HMS *Nautilus* 31
HMS *Ocean* 30
HMS *Orestes* 140
HMS *Pegasus* 29
HMS *Perseverance* 41
HMS *Phaeton* 38
HMS *Pique* saved from lightning 105
HMS *Queen Charlotte* 31
HMS *Ramille* 11
HMS *Resistance* 1, 29
HMS *Resolute* 43
HMS *Retribution* 165
HMS *Royal James* 10
HMS *Russell* 67
HMS *Salvador* 41
HMS *Sceptre* lost by fire 31
HMS *Scylla* 68, 114
   Harris' report 141
HMS *Sir Francis Drake* 21
HMS *Southampton* 27
HMS *Spartan* 114
HMS *Sultan* 30
HMS *Surinam* 8
HMS *Sybille* 68
HMS *Terrible* 29
HMS *Thetis* 46
HMS *Topaze* 42
HMS *Tweed* 156
HMS *Vanguard*107
HMS *Vernon* 108, 109
HMS *Victory* 39
HMS *Warrior* 43, 166
HMS *Warspite* 46
HMS *Wellesley* 52
Hore 51
hulls, iron proposed in 1811 21, 22

Ingestre, Lord 128

Key, Capt. C. 67
Kriti Sun, total loss after lightning 170

Lambert, A. naval historian 75, 89, 116
Lambton, Lord 98
Lang 103
Lemon Sir C. 98, 129
Le Roy, J. B. 15

INDEX

Academie des Sciences 15
  brother 15
  fixed conductors on ships 15, 28
Lesley, Prof. J. 15
lightning
  contact strike 18
  direct strike 18
  side flash 19
lightning conductors
  Admiral Anson 11
  difficulties 1
  failure to trice up 21
  fixed conductor 2, 15
  Franklin's version 10
  French ships and 15
  Henley's invention 37
  hybrid types 133
  merchant ships and 28
  metal chain 11
  Nairne and Blunt 2
  portable chain type 1, 21, 22
  Purfleet powder magazine 12
  Watson's brass wire 11
  wire on hats 14
  wire rope 114, 121, 133, 152
Lightning ferry 51
lightning rod 12
  ball ended 13
  blunt or pointed 12
  Dr Nairne 12
  heretical rods 14
  riots 14
lightning strikes
  advice, general 174
  air breakdown strength 19
  amperage 18
  channel 7, 15
  dart leader 7
  Eddystone lighthouse 7
  flashes 7
  footballers 19
  frequency 3, 9
  humans, frequency, 17
  injuries from
    Admiral G Elliot, eye problems 5
    amnesia 21,22
    apparent death 17, 21
    burns 17, 21, 22-23
    deaths 17
    depression 22
    ear drums 21, 22, 25
    eye problems 22
    falls 24
    hair loss 25
    heart problems 17, 21
    keraunoparalysis 22, 24
    loss of consciousness 21
    mental problems 25
    mortality from 17
    multiple casualties 19
    neurological effects 22
    paralysis 21
    PTSD 22
    rhythm disturbances 21
  per year, UK 17
  resistance of the body 18
  sailors 23, 24, 25
  types of strike 18
Lloyds List and lightning 170
L'Orient 28

Martin, Byam Admiral xii, 36, 49, 75
  accuses Barrow 74, 87
  agrees to demonstration of lightning conductor 94
  asked for papers re York 57
  Comptroller 36, 94
  criticises Barrow in book 45
  criticises Graham and Whigs 58
  meets Minto 59
  reviews Barrow's book 75
  Symonds unsuitable 104
masts 30
  foremasts shivered 46
  height of mast 7
  iron in 1811 30
  mainmast shattered 30, 67
  main split 11
Melville, Lord, 49, 86
Milne, Capt. A 148, 163
Morriss, R., naval historian 110, 137-138

Nairne, Dr, experiments in 1779 12
Napier, Capt. Charles 53
  Admiral 113
  Whig MP for Marylebone 53
Napier, Prof. Macvey 75
Naval Chronicle 30
Nelson, Admiral Lord H. 29
New York Packet struck by lightning 46

O'Ferrall, Moore MP 85
  commits political suicide 128

INDEX

Osborne, R.B. MP 162-163

Parker, Admiral Sir William 31, 80, 131
Parry, Capt. 83
Peel, Sir John ii
Peel, Sir Robert 153
   quotes Fitzroy 129
Pepys, Samuel 10
   and lightning to ships 10
Pringle, Sir John 14
   committee of 36-37

Rice, M, Chatham Yard 108
Roberts 103
Rodger, Prof. N.A.M., naval historian 84
Royal Society 36-37
Russell, Lord John, Prime Minister 147

shipwrecks, losses of men 148
Smith, Andrew 153
Southern Queen 167
Sturgeon, William 152
Symonds, Capt. William 57, 103-122

Thompson, Prof. 166
thunder
   distance heard 3
   electrical charges 4
   frequency 3, 8
   heights of thunder cloud 4, 6
   isokeraunic lines 8
   length storms last 4
   movement 4
   radius of thunderstorm 4
   separation between storms 4
   storms 4
   variability 4

US Navy
   deaths in Norfolk, Virginia 168
   French accept Franklin's ideas for ships 15, 28
   gilded wire for US ships 10-11
   USN iron chain conductors for warships 2, 10, 28
   USS *Constitution* versus HMS *Guerriere* 146

Walker, Baldwin Capt. 124
warships
   effects of lightning on 173
   losses 144-145
   modern era 172-174
Watson, Dr 11
Wheatstone, Prof. 99
Whewell, Rev. 61, 93
Whigs i
   Boards 60
   cabal 47
   covert opposition to Harris 149
   economania 123
   French imperialism 13
   Mehmet Ali 123
   reactionary 83
   Syrian crisis 123
   vendetta 149
Wilbraham, Col. Hon. E.B. 161
Wilton, Earl of 155, 161
Winn, J.L. 12
Wood, Charles MP 66
   lost papers 71
   means of getting his way 127
   memoranda 85

yachts 170-172